General Editor's Introduction

Asbury Theological Seminary Series in World Christian Revitalization Movements

This volume is published in collaboration with the Center for the Study of World Christian Revitalization Movements, a cooperative initiative of Asbury Theological Seminary faculty. Building on the work of the previous Wesleyan/Holiness Studies Center at the Seminary, the Center provides a focus for research in the Wesleyan Holiness and other related Christian renewal movements, including Pietism and Pentecostal movements, which have had a world impact. The research seeks to develop analytical models of these movements, including their biblical and theological assessment. Using an interdisciplinary approach, the Center bridges relevant discourses in several areas in order to gain insights for effective Christian mission globally. It recognizes the need for conducting research that combines insights from the history of evangelical renewal and revival movements with anthropological and religious studies literature on revitalization movements. It also networks with similar or related research and study centers around the world, in addition to sponsoring its own research projects.

Yalin Xin's definitive study of the largest house church movement in China discloses the narrative and travail of one of our century's bold expressions of Christian witness amid often difficult political and social conditions. His is a courageous account of how the faithfulness of the people of God continues to beam hope in that land. He had access to invaluable primary sources to document his account and the research findings he shares bring into focus the contours of this distinctive witness to Christian revitalization in our day. As such, the volume will have interest for scholars as well as practitioners of revitalization in other places and times, and so finds its place appropriately as an entry in the Revitalization Studies Series. This study significantly enhances the research of the Center for the Study of World Christian Revitalization Movements.

J. Steven O'Malley, Director
Center for the Study of World Christian Revitalization Movements
Asbury Theological Seminary

Sub-Series Foreword

Intercultural Studies

The behavioral science approach to the study of revitalization movements has a long history that has developed several models. Anthropologists, among others, observed that people responded to colonialism and the expansion of the West in various ways including armed resistance, selective acceptance, and passive resistance. The problems of the colonial frontier led to a memorandum on acculturation written by Robert Redfield, Ralph Linton and Melville Herskovits in 1936. Elsewhere in the world, anthropologists observed "nativistic" or "cultural renewal" movements as well: cargo cults in Melanesia, messianic movements in South Africa, and political revolutions in Latin America.

Anthony F. C. Wallace brought some order to this area of study with his 1956 article where he named the stages and subsumed the movements under the name of "revitalization movements." Harold Turner contributed the notion of New Religious Movements to focus on the indigenous responses to mission work seen on every continent. This can be seen as part of a larger development, from the 1960s on, to develop Social Movement Theory where people are seen as agents intentionally acting to renew and reform society by organizing others to resist or dethrone the powers that be. Such movements develop a culture and social organization that give meaning and impetus to action on behalf of the movement's aims.

In this book, Yalin Xin examines the Word of Life house church movement in China from the perspective of revitalization movement theory. Xin surveys a number of approaches and produces a composite analysis that reveals significant attributes of the Word of Life churches. The study addresses an emerging concern of our times: how a changing church movement can adapt within a rapidly changing society. In this case, a rural church movement is faced with the increasing urbanization of not only society as a whole, but also its younger membership.

Michael A. Rynkiewich
Editor for the sub-series on Intercultural Studies

Inside China's House Church Network

The Word of Life Movement and Its Renewing Dynamic

The Asbury Theological Seminary Series in
World Christian Revitalization Movements in Intercultural Studies. No. 1

Yalin Xin

EMETH PRESS
www.emethpress.com

Inside China's House Church Network,
The Word of Life Movement and Its Renewing Dynamic

Copyright © 2009 Yalin Xin
Printed in the United States of America on acid-free paper

Library of Congress Cataloging-in-Publication Data

Xin, Yalin.
  Inside China's house church network : the Word of Life Movement and its renewing dynamic / Yalin Xin.
      p. cm. -- (The Asbury Theological Seminary series in world Christian revitalization movements in intercultural studies)
  Includes bibliographical references and index.
  ISBN 978-0-9819582-2-4 (alk. paper)
  1. House churches--China. 2. China--Church history. 3. Word of Life Movement. I. Title.
  BR1275.X56 2009
  280'.4095109045--dc22   2009034241

Dedication

To the Saints of the Word of Life movement

To: Ken Kong,

May the Spirit of God leads you, as he led the WOL Christians.

May 15, 2015

CONTENTS

List of Figures

List of Abbreviations

BTJ	Back to Jerusalem Movement
CCC	Chinese Christian Council
CCP	Chinese Communist Party
CIM	China Inland Mission
CMI	China Ministries International
GB	The Gospel Band
MG	Messenger of the Gospel (WOL Itinerant Evangelist)
TE	Theological Education (Underground Seminary)
TSPM	The Three-Self Patriotic Movement
WOL	The Word of Life Church (Movement)

Foreword

Most Christians in the West have heard about the house church movement in China and know of its remarkable growth in recent decades. Often that knowledge is so general, however, as to be misleading. Hence the significance of this timely book.

In fact there are numerous house-church networks and movements in China, as well as many other forms of the Christian church, and the story is complex. Not all house churches, or house-church networks, are the same.

The value of this book is threefold. First, it lays out in great detail the history and inner dynamics of the Word of Life movement, showing how the movement got started, how it is structured, and how it operates and grows. This is information previously unavailable outside China, at least in this depth.

Second, the book mines the considerable significant contemporary literature on renewal and revitalization movements. Theological, anthropological, and church-growth approaches to church vitality are creatively engaged, helping the reader understand the Word of Life movement in itself and in context. This novel theoretical approach adds depth of interpretation that is seldom found in studies of Christian movements in China.

Third, the author's perspective is unique. As a participant-observer and a researcher conversant with both Chinese and English sources, Dr. Xin brings a depth of insight and cultural sensitivity to the story that enriches and adds interest to the analysis.

The book not only informs readers about church growth and renewal in China; it provides insights that in fact have global relevance.

Howard A. Snyder
Distinguished Professor, Chair of Wesley Studies, Tyndale Seminary, Toronto
Formerly Professor of the History and Theology of Mission, E. Stanley Jones
School of World Mission and Evangelism, Asbury Theological Seminary,
Wilmore, Kentucky

Acknowledgements

I am eternally grateful for the opportunity that God has given me to have undertaken this research project. It has been an enriched learning experience for me, a journey indeed worthwhile.

I am deeply indebted to many who have aided me on this journey and made this book possible. First of all, I want to thank Dr. Howard Snyder, my mentor while I was pursuing my doctoral studies at E. Stanley Jones School of World Mission and Evangelism, who guided me through the whole research process, for his valuable advice, for his confidence in me and my project, and for his devotion to teaching and mentoring his students.

I also want to thank Terry Muck and Lalsangkima Pachuau for their valuable insights and support, and from whose expertise I have benefited tremendously. Darrell Whiteman, Michael A. Rynkiewich, and Eunice Irwin have all been instrumental in helping me think through the research and making it a workable project. Thank you all.

I owe my heartfelt appreciation to Christians of the WOL movement, whom I interviewed and fellowshipped with, and whose stories and experience constitute the core of this book. A special word of thanks is due to Peter Xu, founder and leader of the Word of Life Movement, for providing first-hand data concerning his personal story as well as the history and nature of the Word of Life Movement and its mission.

My deepest love and thanks go to my parents and siblings, God's most precious gift to me, for their selfless love, support, encouragement, and prayer wherever I am in my academic and spiritual journey.

Above all, I thank my Lord Jesus Christ, who faithfully sustains me through the entire project and enables me to fulfill my role as his servant.

Chapter 1

Introduction and Background

At 5:30 a.m. on a winter morning in 2005, some twenty students in their late teens and early twenties are already on their knees for their daily morning devotion in a three-bedroom apartment in T County, central China. After about two hours' prayer and Scripture reading, they walk out of their bedrooms quietly to the sitting room where corn flour porridge, steamed bread, and pickled vegetables are served as breakfast. Thus begins a new day in their six-month long biblical and theological training for ministry.[1]

This is one of the so-called "seminaries of the fields" in the Word of Life (生命之道) movement in China.[2] Seminaries like this gather devoted Christians together for intensive training in preparation for ministry. The Word of Life church considers it critical that those who serve the Lord in different areas of ministry of the church have a solid biblical and theological foundation. Theological education has been one of the three constituent parts of the Word of Life (hereafter WOL) movement, and a "military academy of the heavenly kingdom where God's soldiers are trained and dispatched into the world for the battle of winning souls".[3] The WOL house church network, which, through the devoted ministry of a small number of itinerant evangelists, began to establish and connect house churches in Henan province in the 1970s, experienced significant growth in the 1980s and 1990s when, through the guidance and empowerment of the Spirit of God, commitments and discernment of believers, and unique discipleship and training structures (such as the seminary mentioned above), its network stretched all over Henan province where the movement started and into the rest of the country. Today the WOL is generally recognized as the largest house church network in China.[4]

Historical Context

But God chose what is foolish in the world to shame the wise; God chose what is weak in the world to shame the strong. God chose what is low and despised in the world, things that are not, to reduce to nothing things that are, so that no one might boast in the presence of God. He is the source of your life in Christ Jesus, who became for us wisdom from God, and righteousness and sanctification and redemption, in order that, as it is written, "Let the one who boasts, boast in the Lord. (1 Corinthians 1:27–31)

Figure 1.1: Map of China

Henan (see Figure 1:1), which literally means "south of the (Yellow) River," is located in the eastern central part of the country. As one of the most populous provinces in China, Henan is also among the relatively poor provinces in the country. Even with today's urbanization process, 60 percent of its one hundred million inhabitants still earn their living by farming in a land as big as the state of Colorado. Beggars from Henan were often seen in the neighboring provinces and people from Henan in general are looked down upon.

It is from this humble land, nonetheless, that one of the most dynamic Christian movements was launched onto the China scene: the Word of Life (WOL) movement. It all started with the evangelistic zeal of a handful of faithful believers three decades ago and has now grown and spread all over Henan and into other provinces. Humble farmers were chosen by God as powerful leaders of the movement. Regarded as "one of the most powerful, sustained revivals in Church history," the WOL community is now recognized as the largest house church network in China, with approximately twenty million affiliated believers.[5]

Statistics tell us that, by 1949, about 150 years after Protestant Christianity was introduced into China, there were fewer than one million Protestant Christians.[6] This number gradually shrank for the next thirty years until there were rumors overseas during the height of the Cultural Revolution (1966–76) in China that the Christian Church was no more on Chinese soil.[7] However, three decades since the end of Cultural Revolution, Chinese Christianity has experienced phenomenal growth. A number of underground church movements came to be known in different regions of China, drawing in millions of believers. Huge house church networks came to form, stretching across provinces and regions. Statistical estimates indicate that, as of 2005, there were probably as many as fifty to eighty million Christians among the underground churches across China.[8]

Why are churches growing in China? Why has the Word of Life church in particular been growing with such remarkable speed and to such a size? With all the restrictions and opposition against its existence and development, Christianity has taken root in the Chinese soil and has been spreading like a wild fire, seemingly unstoppable. What is it that has sustained such growth? What are some of the common patterns that we can observe from the expansion of the house churches in China?

The Word of Life House Church as a Renewal Movement

The Word of Life house church movement was chosen for this study for several reasons: First, the Word of Life church is generally believed to be the largest house church group in China today, with approximately twenty million believers affiliated with it, and is one of the most influential house church groups. Secondly, there is no detailed study of the history and working dynamics of the Word of Life movement; thirdly, this movement seems to bear some of the significant characteristics of renewal movements, particularly those identified by Snyder (1997) in *Signs of the Spirit*. This study may serve usefully as a window of understanding on church growth and vitality in China.

This study examines the Word of Life movement in China during the past three decades from the perspective of renewal movements and identifies factors that appear to contribute to the vitality and growth of the Word of Life movement. It assesses the relevance of these factors for the vitality of the Chinese church in general. It answers questions such as: What factors have led to the vitality and growth of the Word of Life movement? What relevance might those factors have for the future growth of the church in China? Does the Word of Life movement exhibit all the marks of the "mediating model" articulated by Howard Snyder in *Signs of the Spirit*? Are there ways in which Snyder's model does not apply, which might open space for this study to clarify or add some nuance to the mediating model for church renewal? Are there important features of the Word of Life movement that might be culturally specific to the Chinese situation that are translatable to the future vitality of the church in China?

As such, this study (1) provides a historical description of the WOL movement in China for the past three decades, (2) analyzes the movement by critically employing Snyder's mediating model for church renewal, and (3) clarifies/amplifies the mediating model as well as proposes a model of renewal for the Chinese church.

In data collecting, attention was given particularly to the following areas:

1. What are the significant historical and cultural factors that have been relevant to the rise of the Word of Life movement?

2. How significant a role have the key leaders of the Word of Life movement played in the emergence and development of this movement, and how do they perceive the role of Word of Life movement?

3. What are the distinctive characteristics of the Word of Life movement, including ecclesiastical structure, community (*koinonia*),[9] forms of leadership, discipleship, ministry, worship, Christian education, social involvement, and mission emphasis?

A Brief History of Chinese Christianity

In order to fully understand the phenomenal growth of Christian churches in China in general, and the Word of Life church in particular, this book briefly surveys the history of Christianity in China, particularly in the twentieth century when the indigenous movement and revival movements started to grow in the 1920s, significantly shaping the church in China, and studies in more depth the emergence of the two main bodies of Protestant Christianity—the Three-Self Patriotic Movement (TSPM) church and the house churches.

Contact with a "Western" Christianity

Chinese Christianity can be traced back as early as the seventh century when Nestorian Christianity spread itself out along the "Silk Road"—the trade routes of Central Asia—and reached Chang-an, the capital city of the Tang dynasty (618–907 CE). According to the later-found "Nestorian monument" at Hsianfu, China, Nestorian Christianity was well received by the emperor who decreed for its dissemination.[10] Despite reactions from those influenced by Chinese religions, Nestorian Christianity was able to survive in China, primarily in monastic form, for more than two hundred years before it was disassembled by the Taoist Emperor Tang Wu Tsung in the mid-ninth century.[11]

In 1600 Roman Catholic Jesuit missionary Matteo Ricci entered China and was able to establish a church there and develop some Chinese Christian literature. At his death in 1610, it was believed that the Church had about two thousand members and the Jesuit mission was dynamic and influential.[12] Ricci's success in winning Chinese converts was due in part to his efforts in accommodating Christianity in China, a method that was opposed by many of the competing Catholic orders of the day, such as the Dominicans and Franciscans.[13] Ricci recognized the civil and social significance of the Chinese rites of veneration, particularly the rites performed by the gentry class in honor of Confucius.[14] To facilitate the lodging of the Christian faith among the Chinese population, Ricci made accommodations in such practices as ancestor veneration, Confucian veneration, and the use of the word *Tien* ("heaven") as a term for the deity.[15] This accommodation issue eventually heated up into the so-called Chinese Rites Controversy, which resulted in a papal pronouncement against the accommodationist approach.[16] The result in China was the opposite—the emperor decreed in 1692 to send away all the Catholic missionaries who did not accept "the rules laid down by Father Ricci."[17] When the Jesuit Order was disbanded in China in 1773, however, there were about two hundred thousand Chinese Christian believers in China.[18]

Protestant Missions to China in the 19th Century

Robert Morrison is forever remembered by Chinese Christians for his enormous contribution in producing the first translation of the entire Bible into Chinese.[19] He was also known as the first Protestant missionary to China.[20] He arrived at Canton (or, Guangdong, as it is preferred now), China on September 8, 1807, and spent twelve years there before he, with his Chinese helpers, completed the translation of the Bible in Chinese.[21] On September 19, 1853, Hudson Taylor, a young English missionary, went on board the Dumfries that was to leave Liverpool for Shanghai, beginning his life-long ministry there.[22] He wrote in his diary, "What peculiar feelings, arise at the prospect of soon landing in an unknown country, in the midst of strangers—a country now to be my home and sphere of labour. 'Lo, I am with you always.' 'I will never leave thee nor forsake thee.' Sweet promises! I have nothing to fear with Jesus on my side."[23]

Taylor's approach was much like that of the early Jesuits: "to become Chinese—to adopt Chinese dress and culture."[24] He was later to establish the China Inland Mission, one of most important mission agencies in rural China that was engaged in the business of saving souls.[25] Taylor's contribution to the church in China was much appreciated by the Chinese Christians.

Before the 1920s, Chinese Christianity was primarily Western in character: the churches were basically Western ecclesiastical models built on Chinese soil.[26] The Chinese pastors were dependent on the missionaries both for theology and ecclesiology. Furthermore, where money was involved, it almost always remained under the control of a Western administrator.[27] This fostered a sense of dependency and parasitism among Chinese pastors and church leaders, presenting a "constant reminder that their country was weak, poor, dependent, overrun by foreigners, and entirely lacking in self-respect."[28]

Mission societies from different Western countries started to send missionaries to China from about the time of Hudson Taylor. The London Mission Society had already started ministry in the central region of China, while the American Board of Commissioners for Foreign Missions, Northern Baptists, Presbyterian Church in the U.S.A (South), Southern Baptists, American Methodists, Lutheran Mission from northern Europe, etc., spread their ministries in various parts of China, establishing mission work in different regions.[29] By 1905, there were sixty-three Western mission societies in China, with 3,445 missionaries. Some 9,904 Chinese believers joined the Western mission societies as missionaries and teachers.[30] Churches started to grow in China, yet much in a denominational manner.

Chinese Indigenization Movement and the Spontaneous Revivalist Movements in the Early 20th Century

As early as in the second half of the nineteenth century, Rufus Anderson started to promote through his writings the establishment of indigenous churches that were to be characterized by "self-government, self-support, and self-propagation."[31] Anderson's "three-self" idea became commonly recognized among missionaries in Chinese Christian National Conference in 1922. And yet, how this Three-Self principle has played out in the China scene has proved itself to be a real issue at stake.[32] In the 1920s and 1930s, in response to the anti-Christian movement that swept across China,[33] many Chinese Christians broke away from the traditional denominations and formed their own independent groups. They were willing to "pay a price to achieve indigenization so that a church that was really Chinese could be established to counteract the accusations raised by the anti-Christian movement."[34] In the 1940s, these independent Chinese Protestant groups may have had as many as two hundred thousand Christians affiliated with them, about a quarter of the whole Protestant body in China at the time.[35] This autonomy was necessary for three fundamental reasons: First, to eliminate the Western ingredient in Christianity and clear the charge of being foreigners' slaves; second, to reconcile believers with their fellow Chinese; third, to conduct more productive evangelistic efforts among the Chinese population.[36] Among some of the bigger indigenous groups were the True Jesus Church (真耶穌教会), the Jesus Family (耶穌家庭), and the Little Flock (小群).[37]

The True Jesus Church was founded in Tianjin in 1917 by three Chinese believers: Paul Wei, Zhang Lingshen and Barnabas Zhang.[38] The church was Pentecostal in character, emphasizing faith healing, speaking in tongues, and communal living. The church grew very rapidly in Shandong, Hebei, Henan, and Zhejiang provinces in the first ten years of its formation. Despite the unstable years that followed, the church continued to grow. By 1949, statistical estimates indicated a membership of one hundred twenty thousand, with seven hundred churches all over China.[39]

In 1921, Jing Dianying founded the Jesus Family at Mazhuang, Shandong. Like the True Jesus Church, the Jesus Family was also Pentecostal in character, emphasizing healing and other spiritual gifts. However, one of the distinctive features of the Jesus Family was their communal style of living in which everything was shared.[40] Those who joined the Jesus Family had to renounce the world and all their properties. At a time when most parts of China were poverty-stricken, the Jesus Family provided "a love fellowship, a meeting-place for the weary, and a place of comfort for the broken-hearted."[41]

The Little Flock was founded by Watchman Nee (Ni Tuosheng 1903–72) in Shanghai in 1928. Even as a student at the Anglican Trinity College at Fuzhou, Watchman Nee was antagonistic toward the formalism and rituals of the Anglican tradition.[42] In the early 1920s, Nee joined the home meetings started by Leland Wang, a Chinese believer who had just resigned from his navy post, and whose group started to "break bread" together, a kind of lay communion without the ministry of a recognized pastor.[43] This group was involved in intense evangelistic work and very soon attracted large numbers of followers in Jiangsu, Zhejiang, and Fujian provinces. Within a year after the fellowship was formed, however, Nee was asked to leave the group because of differences on certain issues between Nee and the rest of the group. Leland Wang thought it necessary that they (members of the group) went through ordination by a pastor while Nee persisted that ordination was not necessary for Christian workers.[44] After the group split, Watchman Nee established his own central church in Shanghai and became the recognized leader of the Local Assemblies movement.[45]

Watchman Nee's preaching greatly inspired believers in the late 1940s when he often called upon his audience to follow the New Testament model of church as exemplified in Acts 4:32, and many in his congregation "obeyed and handed over their businesses, jewellery and ornaments to the church."[46] An "evangelism-by-migration" program was started in the Little Flock, in which whole families of believers were dispatched to different parts of the country to evangelize and establish new assemblies. "Nee had a vision of China being evangelized in this way within fifteen years."[47] His vision, however, was cut short when China experienced major political transitions in 1949 when the Communists defeated the Nationalists in the Civil War (1946–49). Nonetheless, the Little Flock had some seventy thousand members even by 1949.[48] Nee was arrested in the 1950s for opposing the TSPM, and died in prison in 1972. Today, the Little Flock is one of the largest underground church groups in China, numbering an estimated fourteen million.[49]

Nee was among the most prolific writers on theology and ministry in China. Among his many books, the three-volume *The Spiritual Man* targeted the instruction and the building up of the spiritual lives of Christians. Nee defined new birth as coming from accepting God's life through the quickening of the Holy Spirit on the part of the believer. "A life relationship is established with God in new birth. Receiving God's life in new birth is the starting point of a Christian walk, the minimum for a believer. Though the life received is perfect, it awaits to be matured."[50] Nee's theology influenced not only the Little Flock community, but also the Chinese Church in general. We will see marks of his influence in the WOL community this study is engaged in examining later on. Nee's theological language has been commonly embraced by Chinese Christians even to this day. His books have also had considerable influence in the English-speaking world and elsewhere.

In addition, the ministry of Wang Mingdao (1900–91), an independent evangelical preacher who built his own Christian Tabernacle Church in Beijing, was widely influential among Chinese Christians both before and after 1949. Wang was born in the midst of the siege on American missionaries and Chinese converts by the Boxer Rebels in Beijing in June 1900. He experienced conversion early in his life and determined to live a purposeful and meaningful life for God.[51] In his early twenties, Wang started to emerge as a powerful preacher who was frequently invited to speak in churches and evangelistic meetings. "A stern and rather dogmatic man, often critical of missionaries and vociferously opposed to 'liberal theology'," Wang's preaching powerfully impacted the evangelical and fundamentalist church in China.[52] He would tour the country for almost half of every year conducting revivals and evangelistic meetings, and was one of the leading figures in the revivalist movement in the early twentieth century in China. What's more, Wang Mingdao was also remembered by his fellow Christians for the simplicity of everything revolving around his life and ministerial style.[53] His teachings on Christian living still hang on the walls in many homes of house church Christians today.

In the wave of the search for indigenization of Christianity in China, Chinese churches experienced great revivals, and a generation of revivalists started to emerge, which greatly shaped the Chinese Church for the years to come. One such revivalist was Dr. John Sung (1901–44), the greatest revivalist and one of the most influential preachers in China in the first half of the 20th century, who inspired numerous young people to devote themselves to the work of the Kingdom.[54] Sung graduated with a Ph.D. in Chemistry in the U.S., but experienced spiritual awakening and decided to devote himself to full-time evangelistic ministry back in China.[55] In 1931, Sung joined the Bethel Worldwide Evangelistic Band, established and sent from the Bethel Church in Shanghai.[56] Andrew Gih was the leader of the band, who together with Sung, traveled to many parts of China, instrumental in bringing revivals in thirteen provinces in China. Sung became independent three years later, ministering powerfully for the next decade. He greatly impacted and molded the church in China.[57]

John Sung's theological legacy, the emphasis on the absolute necessity of 'rebirth" or being "born again," left clear marks on the Chinese churches in China and overseas. In his revival sermons, Sung repeatedly emphasized the absolute need for a Christian to be born again. He compares not being born again to being "blind," "deaf," "to come to a dead end," "to be shut outside the door," and "lame."[58] Sung specified a three-step rebirth procedure: rebirth of 'water', rebirth of the Spirit, obeying the Holy Spirit.[59] And the key in seeking the experience of rebirth was repentance—"a process of bitterness in the knowledge of my sins."[60] In other words, as Leung Kalun summarizes, in order to seek the rebirth experience, a Christian should come before God and confess, under the leading of the Holy Spirit, every single sin he/she had committed. Such repentance would enable the Christian to face the darkness of his/her inward being, feel utterly ashamed of the sinful conduct, weep, and become utterly broken before God.[61]

John Sung never defined rebirth in a succinct manner despite his repeated emphasis on the need to be born again, on the personal and corporate levels.[62] Sung saw the source of all kinds of problems existing in the Chinese churches was the missing of important element of rebirth.[63] We will see the influence of Sung's teaching played out in the WOL community half a century later.

Sung's father was a pastor in the American Methodist Episcopal Mission in China. From his childhood, John was often a witness and helper in the revival meetings his father led in his church. He wrote in his diary,

> Although the unforgettable revival meetings ended, their fires continued to
> burn and spread, to the point the old building (my father's church) seating 500–

600 could no longer accommodate the swelling number of new seekers. As a 12-year-old, I helped my father to group these believers according to their homes' distances from the church, so that each of them would have a chance to worship in one of the three services held each Sunday.[64]

Sung was also much imbued in John Wesley's spiritual tradition, particularly Wesley's Aldersgate experience, based on which Sung developed his teachings on rebirth, including seeking the filling of the Holy Spirit through thorough repentance of sins, the absolute necessity of experiencing rebirth, and the moral and ethical practice of rebirth.[65]

John Sung's evangelistic preaching brought revivals in many parts of China and Southeast Asia. His name is often mentioned in house church gatherings in China as well as in the overseas Chinese churches. His theological emphasis on the necessity of rebirth is also one of the distinct marks of the Word of Life movement that this study is focused on.

The indigenization and revival movements went hand in hand during almost the same period of time (1920s to 1930s). Many of the leaders and their indigenous movements were actually part of the revival movements. Both movements were significant in their influence in the formation of Chinese church and spirituality that was to last for a long time.

All the indigenous Christian groups as well as the revivalists demonstrated a "conservative, pietism based on evangelistic programme of saving souls, free of the 'contamination' of politics."[66] They stood in line with the "conservatives" or "fundamentalists."[67] The conservatives consisted of conservative evangelical Western missionaries and Chinese Christians who were in tension with the "liberals" or "modernists" who favored a social gospel approach during the same period of time. This tension was directly related to the fundamentalist-modernist controversy in North America in the early twentieth century when large numbers of missionaries from North America arrived in China, many of whom were "strongly influenced by the tenets of social Christianity," which naturally triggered the reaction from the conservative missionaries and Chinese believers who were thus engaged in theological debate with the modernists.[68] This fundamentalist movement among Protestant missionaries in China drew alliance from a broad spectrum of mission organizations and institutions including CIM, American Presbyterian missions, and North China Theological Seminary.[69] This fundamentalist movement had a "common theological core" which included such doctrinal tenets as

the truthfulness and infallible authority of the whole Bible as the inspired word of God, the deity of Christ, his virgin birth, his substitutionary atonement, his bodily resurrection from the dead, and the authenticity of the miracles both of the Old and New Testaments. Concerned with the spread of the social gospel and the explosion of social projects at the cost of evangelistic activities, the fundamentalists also reiterated their common belief in personal sin as the root of all social evils and the utmost importance of personal salvation. They insisted on the central place of preaching in mission work and the priority of evangelism over social service.[70]

Some mainline Chinese church leaders as well as leaders of organizations such as the YMCA and the YWCA were much influenced by the liberal trend of the time. A number of them went on to be leaders in the Chinese Christian Three-Self Patriotic Movement National Committee (TSPM) that was created after the Communist government came into being in 1949.[71] It is therefore not hard to recognize that the dispute between the liberals and the conservatives even as it first emerged almost a century ago has relevance to the understanding of the church in China today. Many of the arguments remain the same. The two camps remain separated, with the TSPM representing the liberals and the House Church representing the conservatives. The TSPM continues to advocate social involvement by participating, in accordance to the call of the government, in the social construction of the Chinese state. The majority of the House Church, on the other hand, continues to stress the repentance of sin and "pure" faith in Jesus Christ, and trusts the leading of the Spirit of God in bringing revival and renewing his church.

The Beginning of the TSPM and the House Church

For at least the past fifty years, there have been in China two primary bodies of Protestant churches. One is known as the Three-Self Church (三自教会), or the TSPM Church. TSPM stands for Three-Self Patriotic Movement,[72] a short form for China Christian Three Self Patriotic Movement National Committee. After the Communist Party won the Civil War in 1949, particularly in the next two years when China was involved in the Korean War, all institutional ties between the Chinese Protestant church and foreign missions were severed. The new government needed a mechanism through which churches could be "both monitored and directed towards behavior actively supportive of the new regime."[73] The TSPM was established in 1954 just to meet that purpose as the Chinese Communist Party (CCP) government-recognized institution governing the affairs of Christianity in China.[74]

The other main branch of the Protestant church is the House Church, also called "underground" or "unregistered" churches, which refers to all the Christian groups that do not associate themselves with the TSPM church. Officially, the "underground" churches are often referred to as "the unregistered churches" or "illegal meeting points," depending on who the speaker is.[75]

For the Catholic community in China, the situation has been parallel to that of the Protestant community. The registered Catholic churches are governed by the Chinese Catholic Patriotic Association (CCPA), formally founded in 1957, while others remain independent and exist in the form of house churches. The creation of the two main bodies of the Catholic Church looks very much like that of Protestant church. The underground Catholic house churches refused to recognize the leadership of the CCPA and continued to be loyal to the Holy See, for which they were opposed in no less severity compared to their Protestant counterparts.[76]

The emergence of the two Protestant church groups started at the beginning of the founding of the People's Republic of China in 1949, with a one-party rule—the Chinese Communist Party, which called on all citizens of China to be united in consolidating the newly-founded nation and fighting against Western imperialists. All foreign missionaries were asked to leave the country, and contact between the churches in China and the West was prohibited. Obviously, the church in China which was then regarded as the instrument of imperialism was restricted broadly by the new government.

Some Christian leaders such as Y. T. Wu and Liangmo Liu were convinced that the Chinese church as it was could not solve China's social problems unless it entered into "a broader social movement" and "responded to God's promise there."[77] They therefore advocated a reconciliation of national salvation with faith, which means a reconciliation of Communism with Christianity. A "Christian Manifesto" was drafted in 1952 recognizing the historical connections between the Chinese church and the "imperialists" as well as proclaiming the thorough support of the Chinese Church to the building of the new China.[78] TSPM was officially established in 1954.

As noted, the indigenous Christian leaders such as Wang Mingdao and Watchman Nee (John Sung had died earlier) who had always been suspicious of the motives of the liberals, saw the creation of TSPM as having compromised Christian belief for the sake of survival and having exchanged "the Kingdom of God for a lesser kingdom."[79] They therefore refused to associate themselves with the TSPM and continued their own church gatherings and activities. Of course, there were many other groups and individual believers who also deliberately distanced themselves from the TSPM and formed independent churches. They were to pay a heavy price for their stand in the years that followed. The subsequent arrest and imprisonment of indigenous leaders such as Wang Mingdao and Watchman Nee in the mid-1950s created further polarization and animosity between the TSPM leaders as representatives of the liberal camp and the independent church leaders as representatives of the conservative camp.[80]

Such was the beginning of the separation of the two churches. Both churches were broadly limited in their mobility and activity during the 1950s. Then came the Cultural Revolution, a movement called forth by the Chinese Communist Party in 1966 and officially ended in 1976 with the arrest of the "Gang of Four."[81] It stemmed out of factional struggle within the Chinese Communist Party that eventually "brought hundreds of thousands of students and other young people onto the streets in demonstrations and pitched battles and which toppled many of the old guard leadership."[82] During the Cultural Revolution, campaigns were launched against the old ideas, culture, customs and habits. Religion then became part of the old culture and custom and was under massive attack. All churches were closed down, Bibles were burnt, and church properties were destroyed. All religious personnel were either forced to change their profession or sent to "re-education" in the countryside. Christians, both of independent churches and TSPM churches, suffered the kind of persecution that "has very few parallels in the history of the Christian church."[83]

Many Christians were sent to the countryside or the remote western part of China for "reform through labor."[84] Independent church leaders suffered even more. Many of them were sentenced to long-term labor camps and some were not able to live through their terms.[85]

Strong political pressure did not root Christianity out of the Chinese soil, however. Lambert states,

> The Cultural Revolution was a severe trial to the Chinese Christians, but also, as they often themselves relate, used by God to create a church refined by fire and uniquely adapted to reach out to millions disillusioned with Maoism. It destroyed the last vestiges of the institutional church in China but, paradoxically, created conditions in Chinese society from which the church was to re-emerge invigorated in new, largely de-institutionalized forms when the fury of the storm had passed.[86]

Witnesses of the faithful Christian leaders and fellow believers served as encouragement to believers who continued to meet to worship and pray, even at the risk of their lives. With Bibles confiscated and burned, believers copied and spread pieces of Scripture from Christian radio broadcasts.[87] Suffering and opposition seemed to have stimulated Christian faith to grow and created an opportunity for the gospel to come home in the Chinese soil. Lambert observes,

> By sharing the sufferings of the nation at the deepest level Christians appear to have cast off the old suspicion of being somehow less Chinese through association with a "foreign" religion. This identification in suffering appears to have made the Christian faith much more acceptable to many other Chinese, especially the "lost generation of the Cultural Revolution who missed educational opportunities and, in many cases, became deeply disillusioned with Maoism.[88]

Lyall (1992) reports on the church life of a minority group in the south of China during the late 1970s and early 1980s:

> After long years of persecution many are hungry for the Word of God and think nothing of climbing up and down the steep valleys for miles to attend worship…An observer of Miao Christian communities reports that their life is their faith. The gospel has been integrated with their simple lifestyle to such an extent that there seems no sharp division between "sacred" and "secular". Their faith is expressed in gentleness of spirit and warmth of hospitality, qualities which have deeply impressed the few outsiders to visit their mountain villages in recent years.[89]

According to research done by members of the Chinese Church Research Center during the late 1970s and early 1980s, house churches continued to meet during the Cultural Revolution in various parts of the country including Shanghai, Ningbo, Wenzhou, Xiaoshan, Xiamen, Gutian, Shantou, Lanzhou, Tianjin, Shandong, and Henan.[90]

What is more, many Chinese Christians believe and even testify that the church was purified in the fires of persecution during that time.[91] Only those who were truly committed to Christ withstood the fierce opposition.[92] Some died for their faith, others were jailed, and many others suffered in various ways for the sake of Christ. Their examples presented powerful encouragement to fellow believers as well as bore witness to non-believers.

The Church in China from 1949 up to 1976, that is, from the establishment of the People's Republic of China with one party rule, the Chinese Communist Party, to the end of the Cultural Revolution, did not experience significant numerical growth. On the contrary, believers were forced to go underground during the ten years of Cultural Revolution in China (1966–76). Nonetheless, this period can be rightfully identified as what Donald McGavran calls "internal growth," because some Christians, after the "purification of the fire," were able to mature themselves in faith in the power of God through prayer, and "move from marginal to ardent belief."[93] Lambert observes that the Cultural Revolution (1966–76) was really the time when "the deep personal experience of the Christian faith enabled many Christians to reach out in love to their neighbors. Freed from Western forms and traditions, the Christian message took on new life and meaning, spread by the lives and words of ordinary Chinese believers."[94] The "underground form" in which the house churches had to exist undergirded the spiritual quality of the Chinese believers.[95]

Such is the context of the phenomenal growth of the church in China after the Cultural Revolution in 1976. The tension between the conservative and liberal camps that started almost a century ago had been an indispensable part of the story, and has also been present throughout the emergence and development of the Word of Life movement.

A few years after the Cultural Revolution the government restored the TSPM to its original function and relaxed religious policy in comparison to the outright pressure of the Cultural Revolution period. Christians enjoyed more freedom in practicing their religion although they were still supposed to conduct all religious activities within certain parameters laid down by the Chinese government. TSPM was officially recognized as having the only legal Protestant churches where, technically, all believers could worship freely. In many areas Christians gladly participated in services in the reopened TSPM churches, while in others, believers remained suspicious of TSPM, remembering the role of TSPM in the 1950s and 1960s. Tension between the house-churches and the TSPM was constant.[96]

House churches were particularly able to jump-start on the relaxed religious policy in China after the Cultural Revolution and spread themselves quickly all over the country, establishing churches through evangelism into the unreached areas. Before the first political campaign against the advance of the house church evangelistic activities,[97] many house church groups had already established thousands of house churches in various provinces of China with preliminary organizational structures, such as coworkers' meetings in the WOL church, to advance their ministry.

Paterson (1999) observes that about 80 percent of all Christians in China worship in house churches and they represented the most authentic voice of the

Church in China. "House churches have become the mainstream of Christianity in China today."[98]

The Word of Life Church

Against this background, the WOL church emerged onto the China scene. Starting with the evangelistic zeal of a handful of faithful Christians, in a matter of little more than thirty years, it grew into the largest house church network in China.

The church first got started in Henan in the 1970s. Peter Xu (1940–), the leader of the movement, was born into a Christian family that provided him with Christian upbringing. He started to engage in evangelistic activities when he was still in his teens, and became recognized as a leader in the early 1980s. Xu's theology bears marks of the conservative Christian camp in China, emphasizing the pursuit of spiritual life as the foundation of the Christian journey, the absolute importance of the repentance of sins before being "born again," holding on to "pure" faith in Jesus Christ in opposition to the union of faith and politics, church and state. Xu is also much appreciative of the foundational work done by such Western missionaries as Hudson Taylor, upon whose legacy the house churches in China continue to carry out the Great Commission.[99]

The WOL church has several characteristics. First, it is part of the larger house church movement in China that has been making a significant impact on the Chinese society for the past three decades. It is generally observed that the church in China has grown significantly since the Cultural Revolution with the number of Christians continuing to climb. Old indigenous or independent groups such as the Little Flock, the Jesus Family, and the True Jesus Church were renewed in their vitality and grew into significant large groups. Newer house church groups also sprang up, drawing millions of followers. In Henan Province alone are several of the largest house church networks in China, of which the WOL church has attracted the largest number of believers.

Second, the WOL church has within itself a huge network of house churches. Therefore, house churches are the essential structures of the movement. Most of the evangelistic work is done through the house churches, as are the teaching and edification of Christians. The Reformation recovery of the priesthood of all believers is commonly practiced within the movement. "Lay" leadership plays a key role in the general operation and continuous expansion of the movement.

Third, the WOL church stresses the Scripture as normative in the life and ministry of Christian believers (as also evidenced by the name they chose for themselves: the Word of Life) and constantly refers to the early church in Acts as the model of what the church should be. It sees the problem that inhibits much of the church in the world today from growing as residing in their failure to follow a biblical model of the church.[100]

Fourth, the WOL church exists for mission to others, not only for the Chinese population, but also the whole inhabited earth. It sees itself as being called to evangelize and fulfill the Great Commission. It sees evangelization as lying at the center of the existence of the church. In the process of evangelizing the Chinese population, the movement is already beginning to prepare and send missionaries toward the west of China with a vision of going "Back to Jerusalem" with the gospel.[101]

Definitions

This section offers definitions to some of the key terms and concepts that are used in this book, which provide technical concepts to this study and are sometimes used in non-conventional ways.

House church(es) and TSPM church(es)

In China, two terms are used interchangeably when referring to the unofficial Christian gatherings: *Di xia jiao hui* (the underground church), and *Jia ting jiao hui* (the house church). *Jia ting jiao hui* (the house church) is probably used more by believers themselves than *Di xia jiao hui* (the underground church). TSPM officials, however, refuse to openly recognize either of the two terms. For them, it is either the "registered churches" (those who register their churches with the TSPM so that their status becomes legally recognized) or the "unregistered" ones (those that refuse to register with the TSPM). The government, on the other hand, often uses "legal" and "illegal" to refer to the TSPM churches and the house churches.

"TSPM churches" refers to all the Protestant churches that are registered with the Three-Self Patriotic Movement, the government sanctioned organism supervising the Protestant churches in China. Colloquially, "Three-Self churches" is often used instead of "TSPM churches. They are, however, conterminous.

This study focuses on the Chinese Protestant house churches that are not registered with the TSPM. The term "house church(es)" as it is used in this book can refer to both the churches within the Word of Life movement and also all the Protestant Christian gatherings that are not registered with the TSPM. Such preference comes from the fact that, on the one hand, believers themselves prefer to use the term "house church(es)" more than "underground church(es)"; on the other hand, many house churches today are no longer in the underground state. They have been gradually emerging above the ground in an open or semi-open state. In the cities, it is often the case that everybody in the block knows that there is a house church in one of the apartment buildings and believers come to meet regularly. The local police also know about it, but often ignore it, unless the house church becomes too influential in terms of size and publicity of its activities. Special gatherings for leadership training are probably the kinds of gatherings that often incur interference from the local police, especially when overseas trainers are involved. Itinerant preachers can also be easily targeted. For most urban house church meetings with an attendance of twenty to thirty people, believers can meet fairly freely without pressure or fear. Rural house churches tend to be larger in size, as believers often meet in the courtyard of a house or even in an open area before the house.

The Word of Life Movement

The Word of Life movement is often referred to as the Born Again Family (Sect, or Community) because of its emphasis on the necessity of experiencing rebirth for its members. It was also called *Quan fang wei jiao hui* (the Full Scope or All Sphere Church) by the authorities because of its well-known trans-regional structural meetings (such as the WOL general conferences, regional and district coworkers' meetings, and system meetings) that extended all over China, a fact that was not normally tolerated by the state and local government. Leaders of WOL, however, prefer the Word of Life Movement or Church, a term adapted from 1 John 1:1.[102]

Liberal and Conservative

The terms *liberal* and *conservative* in this book refer primarily to the two Christian camps in China that emerged at the beginning of the twentieth century. They were better known as *modernist* and *fundamentalist* in their earlier stages, being related to the fundamentalist-modernist controversy in North America about the same time. In the Chinese context, the difference between the liberals and conservatives seems to lie in the relative importance of social service as compared to individual salvation.[103] This controversy has accompanied the church through the years. The locus of the argument also significantly shifted since the TSPM in the 1950s. How much one complies with the regulations of the state at the cost of the biblical authority appears to be the measure of orthodoxy. Generally, in China today, the TSPM leaders can be categorized as more on the liberal end of the spectrum, while the house church leaders tend toward the opposite end. The term liberal and conservative as they will be used in this dissertation are only intended to facilitate discussion over the relevant issues, not to draw a clear-cut distinction between the TSPM churches and the house churches.

Renewal Movements

According to Snyder, a renewal movement refers to "a sociologically and theologically definable religious resurgence which arises and remains within, or in continuity with, historic Christianity, and which has a significant (potentially measurable) impact on the larger church in terms of number of adherents, intensity of belief and commitment, and/or the creation or revitalization of institutional expressions of the church."[104] In comparison with revival movements, renewal movements can be "an ongoing process," that is, the "ongoing vitality of the church, a normal church life which can be continually renewed and renewing, but which may also benefit from occasional unusual, powerful movings of the Spirit."[105]

Delimitations

This study is limited to the Protestant house church community in China. Thus, it will not deal with issues concerning the Catholic community apart from necessary historical review of Catholic mission. Neither will this study discuss the TSPM churches in depth, except as relevant to the rise and development of the house churches in general and the Word of Life movement in particular.

Secondly, this study seeks to examine the Word of Life movement through Snyder's mediating model for church renewal for the purpose of understanding the inner dynamics of the movement. It will not comprehensively survey the history of discussion on renewal movements, but will focus on examining key concepts that Snyder deals with in *Signs of the Spirit*. Neither will this study go into any significant depth of categories such as church growth, anthropology, sociology, or comparative religion, etc. except in an auxiliary way. As this study primarily reflects historically and theologically on the growth of the house churches in China, based on the investigation of the Word of Life movement, it will not discuss the sensitive political issues in depth, either.

Nonetheless, in order to better understand the Word of Life movement, particularly at certain stages of its development, this study does not exclude referencing, at least to some extent, insights from relevant theories and models developed by commentators and scholars such as Charles G. Finney, J. Edwin Orr, and Richard Lovelace (on revivalism theories), William G. McLoughlin, Anthony F. C. Wallace, and others (on revitalization movements), Thomas P. Rausch (on renewal movements), Gregory P. Leffel (on social movements), and Donald A. McGavran and George G. Hunter (on evangelization and church growth).

Basic Assumptions

The Bible says that human beings are created in the image of God (Genesis 1:26, 27; 1 Cor. 11:7; James 3:9), and this image of God in which human beings were created included what Louis Berkhof called "natural endowments" such as "intellectual power, natural affections, and moral freedom" and "spiritual qualities" which include true knowledge, righteousness, holiness, spirituality, and immortality.[106] At the Fall, humans sinned against God by disobeying God's commandment, and thus marred the image of God, which means that human beings lost their "spiritual qualities" at the Fall.[107] As a result, humans broke the harmonious relationship with their creator and were sent out of the Garden of Eden (Genesis 3:23–24). In God's eternal love, however, God desired to reconcile his creation to himself, and he thus initiated the mission of reconciliation by calling out a people (Israel) as the agents of reconciliation. And yet God's people often failed him, backsliding into sins and becoming lifeless.

It is God's good purpose to revive his church so that it can continue the mission of reconciliation. God has been working all along in history seeking to renew the church especially at times when the church was not walking faithfully.[108] It is true that God is the ultimate source of the all genuine Christian growth, but God chooses to cooperate with his people rather than control them. Likewise, we assume that the Spirit of God empowers and enables believers in the Word of Life church to evangelize the population, to teach and disciple believers, to multiply house churches, to enlarge the house church networks, and to accomplish the seemingly impossible tasks that they have accomplished. Therefore, on the one hand, the phenomenal growth of this house church is ultimately the work of the Spirit of God, on the other hand, human wisdom and choice have played an inseparable part as well. Snyder contends, "renewal movements are neither direct, irresistable acts of God nor the mere outworking of inexorable sociological laws or constraints. Much depends on the wisdom, vision, sensitivity, foresight, and integrity of the characters in the drama."[109] After all, the Word of God promises that believers are being renewed in Christ "in knowledge in the image of its Creator" (Col 3:10) and "in true righteousness and holiness" (Eph. 4:24).

Although we cannot record all of God's activity because of the limitations of our physical being, we do witness the fruits of God's work. We see churches multiply, believers are revitalized with passions for mission, people become more receptive to the gospel message, Christian converts increase, fellowship become intensified, and the sick are healed. Therefore, this book seeks to study the human response to the empowerment of the Spirit of God through the use of convictions and testimonies, life and witnesses, worship styles, evangelistic strategies, house church networking, discipleship, and theologies, in an attempt to identify and understand the signs of God's work among the Word of Life house church movements.

As the Word of Life movement developed out of a particular historical and social context, this study assumes that the historical and social factors played a role in the birth and development of the movement. First, in the aftermath of the tremendous culture change in China in the late 1970s when the Cultural Revolution was over, Chinese people lost their faith in Marxism, Leninism, and Maoism, which created in their hearts and minds an "ideological vacuum" or a "vacuum of belief" that Christianity was able to lodge itself in and fill that vacuum.[110] Second, the Cultural Revolution not only did away with the visible church, but also pushed the Chinese folk religions off the ground, particularly in rural China. These folk religions used to present a significant social and psychological barrier against the spread of Christianity in China. With the forceful disappearance of the folk religious practices, the barrier was removed, thus allowing Christianity to take advantage of the opportunity, when it arose after the Cultural Revolution, to lodge itself in some of the rural areas of China with its simplistic form.[111] Third, as Bays (1991) observes that the rapid growth of Christianity in rural China in the 1980s was closely related to the folk religiosity of Christianity: "we might expect Chinese Christians today, especially in the rural areas, to behave somewhat like older semi-secretive sects, and perhaps even to show signs of syncretism with non-Chinese ideas and behaviors. This is precisely the case."[112]

While these assumptions may be true to a certain extent, the scale of the book does not allow detailed examination of the possibilities. Rather, this book will evaluate the WOL movement from the renewal perspective, seeking to identify signs of the Spirit of God at work through human response.

Sources Used in the Research

The data for this study were drawn primarily from:

1. Documents of Chinese Christianity, particularly since the second quarter of the 20th century when indigenous Christian communities started to emerge on the scene.

2. Documents/records of the theology, ecclesiology, and missiology of the indigenous Christian communities in comparison and contrast to other mainline denominations.

3. Documents recording the historical tension between the leaders of the indigenous denominations (largely conservative) and the leaders of the liberal camp.

4. Documents of the rise of the TSPM, its agenda, and the role it has been play-ing since its creation in the early 1950s.

5. Documents of the rise of the Word of Life church, its connection with the earlier independent Christian communities, its theology, ecclesiology, leadership, mission, and relationship with other house church groups and the TSPM.

6. Evidence documenting the vitality, dynamic, and influence of the Word of Life movement.

Research Methodology

This study was geared to understanding the Word of Life movement through the lens of Snyder's theory of renewal movements. It employed library research to collect data regarding pertinent theories and perspectives on renewal and revival movements from works of scholars such as Howard Snyder, Richard F. Lovelace, Thomas P. Rausch, J. Edwin Orr, Charles Kraft, Gregory P. Leffel, Donald F. Durnbaugh, and identified relevant models and theories that seemed to best translate the data concerning the Word of Life movement in China as a renewal movement. Regarding the history of the Chinese church, this dissertation also employed library research for relevant data from works of scholars such as Jonathan Chao, Kalun Leung, David H. Adeney, David Aikman, Tony Lambert, Philip Wickeri, Daniel Bays, Alan Hunter and Kim-Kwong Chan. Such history provided foundational information concerning why the church in China is what it is today, and was necessary for the understanding of the Word of Life house church movement.

In addition to library research, a variety of research methods were utilized to obtain the data needed to resolve the various questions related to the study. As there are few written documents available about the Word of Life movement, research was done primarily by means of interviews, and participant observation.

Interviews

Interviews were conducted primarily among the leaders and long-standing members of the movement who gave first-hand accounts of the movement concerning the origin and development of the Word of Life movement, theological and missiological emphasis, inner structures, leadership training and discipleship. Newer members and affiliates of the movement of different gender, age, and duration of membership were also interviewed. The following groups of people made up the interviewees of this research:

- three movement leaders, including the initial leaders of the Word of Life movement.
- five second level leaders within the Word of Life movement including former and present itinerant evangelists (locally termed "Messengers of the Gospel", hereafter, MGs).[113]
- six long-standing members of the movement.
- ten newer members of the movement, including students from "seminaries of the fields."

Participant-observation

This research also involved participant-observation within the Word of Life movement. This included Sunday worship services, Bible studies, prayer meetings, fellowship meetings, evangelistic events, coworkers' meeting, underground seminary training sessions, and other forms of house church gatherings. Each of these gatherings furnished first-hand data needed to solve the research problems.

Theoretical Framework

Many have studied the phenomenal church growth in China from different perspectives. Some focus more on political implications revolving around the church in China, i.e. Jonathan Chao; others view it from a sociological perspective, i.e. Hunter and Chan, and Kalun Leung; still others try to understand it from a revivalist perspective, i.e. Tony Lambert. This study chooses to look at one of the largest underground church movements through the lens of renewal movements because this movement seems to embody some of the significant characteristics of renewal movements. While social science and revivalism theories are important in helping explain some of the phenomena revolving around the Word of Life movement, this study focuses primarily on a theological model, seeking to understand the often neglected aspects by previous studies on the church in China: the normative life and structure of the local congregation, where, I believe, the dynamics are stored.

In this sense, by employing Snyder's mediating model for church renewal, it will

- give a more balanced and accurate view of the history of the church in China,
- help learn how the Spirit of God is working with those who sense and respond to his guidance,
- clarify the inner dynamics of the Word of Life movement that has been thriving in China,
- identify the translatable dynamics that can be applied to the church today.

The Word of Life movement has been going on for three decades and its dynamics continue to impact the population. What factors have sustained such renewal? What can we learn from this movement? This study hopes to look at the research data collected on the WOL movement through the lens of Snyder's mediating model for church renewal, in a critical manner, that is, one the one hand, this study uses Snyder's model to analyze the WOL movement and illuminate its dynamics, on the other hand, this study of the WOL movement, which is out of a very different historical and cultural context compared to the European context out of which the mediating model was developed, will further enrich the mediating model.

In *Signs of the Spirit*, Snyder (1997) proposes seven interpretive frameworks with which to explore the inner dynamics of the three post-Reformation renewal movements (Pietism, Moravianism and Methodism):

1. *Ecclesiola in Ecclesia*: a little church within the church. Both of these structures, in this view, are "normative" and "complementary" to each other "which together provide for a greater measure of spiritual health and vitality in the church."[114]

2. Sect/Church Typologies: "forms of Christian community which are mutually exclusive".

3. Believers' Church Theories: "a covenanted and disciplined community of those walking in the way of Jesus Christ. Where two or three such are gathered, willing also to be scattered in the work of their Lord, there is the believing people."[115]

4. Revivalism Theories: "that by more or less direct divine intervention, but with more or less human agency or cooperation, the church is periodically renewed by outbreaks of revival."[116] In contrast, renewal theories are concerned with the "ongoing vitality of the church, a normal church life which can be continuously renewed and renewing, but which may also benefit from occasional unusual, powerful movings of the Spirit."[117] J. Edwin Orr, Jonathan Edwards, Charles G. Finney and Richard Lovelace are among some of the advocates of the revivalism theories.

5. Revitalization Movements: Anthony F. C. Wallace is the primary initiator of the theory and he "defined a revitalization movement as 'a deliberate,

organized, conscious effort by members of a society to construct a satisfying culture'."[118]

6. Modality/Sodality Typology: a theory developed by Ralph D. Winter who identifies sodality as "a distinct subcommunity within the larger church (the modality), and is highly mission-oriented."[119]

7. Catholic Anabaptist Typology: exploration in the "parallels between Catholic renewal or monastic communities and the Believers' Churches, and the role or function of such groups in relation to the larger Roman Catholic or Protestant traditions, respectively."[120]

By employing these seven interpretative frameworks in his study of Pietism, Moravianism and Methodism, Snyder (1997) discovers some common characteristics existing in these movements and incorporates these elements in his mediating model for church renewal, which he believes can apply to the church today. This mediating model includes the following marks:

1. *The renewal movement "rediscovers" the Gospel.*[121] Initiators of the movement discover, both through experience and theory, "a new dynamic" in the Christian faith that leads them to forming/developing a new understanding of the nature of the Christian faith, from which a new "paradigm shift" takes place. Snyder considers this as a "distinctive factor in renewal movements" which should be "a key element of any mediating model."[122]

2. *The renewal movement exists as an ecclesiola.*[123] A renewal movement does not see itself as the only true church, but as a necessary part of the larger church.

3. *The renewal movement uses some form of small-group structure.*[124] Renewal movements make use of the small-group form within the local congregation.

4. *The renewal movement has some structural link with the institutional church.* Snyder contends that such a link is crucial for the renewal movement to "exercise a revitalizing impact without bringing division."[125]

5. *Because it sees itself not as the total church but as a necessary part of the church, the renewal structure is committed to the unity, vitality, and wholeness of the larger church.*[126] Such unity includes first of all the immediate denomination or theological or ecclesiastical tradition, and then expands to the universal church with a concern for united witness.

6. *The renewal structure is mission-oriented.* The renewal movement has a strong sense of its "specific purpose and mission," such as renewing the church, evangelization, church unity, or social reform.[127] The renewal movement will often have more dynamic social transforming power when its perceived mission goes beyond merely spiritual renewal.

7. *The renewal movement is especially conscious of being a distinct, covenant based community.* "It sees itself as a restricted community of people voluntarily committed to each other."[128] It stresses the scriptural concept of *koinonia*, mutual encouragement, and admonition within the body.

8. *The renewal movement provides the context for the rise, training, and exercise of new forms of ministry and leadership.*[129] Out of its experience of

community comes a practical stress on the gifts of the Spirit and the priesthood of believers.

9. *Members of the renewal movement remain in close daily contact with society, and especially with the poor.* Snyder concludes on this point that "movements which appeal to and spread among the poor are both more radical and more socially transforming than those which do not."[130]

10. *Finally, the renewal structure maintains an emphasis on the Spirit and the Word as the basis of authority.*[131]

This mediating model for church renewal, according to Snyder, is useful not only in comparing and evaluating renewal movements that remain within the institutional church but also groups that become independent sects. As "all those who confess Jesus Christ as Savior and Lord" can be considered as part of the "church," independent churches and sects "may still be seen as *ecclesiolae* within the church of Christ, even though they are independent of any particular ecclesiastical structure larger than themselves."[132] This, I believe, is relevant to the situation in China, where, to this day, house churches remain detached from the institutional TSPM church, refusing to recognize its authority.

Apart from the mediating model, Snyder also proposes five dimensions of renewal: personal, corporate, conceptual, structural, and missiological renewal. According to Snyder, renewal may often start in any one or more of these five dimensions. However, in order that renewal continues in faithful obedience to Scripture, and the church becomes an agent of God's mission of reconciliation, all five of these dimensions need be integrated into the renewal of the church.[133]

Snyder's mediating model, which is interdisciplinary, draws from several related fields of inquiry including revivalism, revitalization theory, believers' church, church growth and social movement. It is one among various tools that provides a comprehensive and most relevant framework for the study of the WOL movement.

Significance of the Study

The significance of the study is, first, a historical description of the Word of Life house church movement; second, an analysis of the movement from the perspective of renewal movements, and identifying features that are culturally specific to the Chinese situation, verifying whether these feature are translatable to the continuous vitality of the church in China; third, an evaluation of Snyder's mediating model for church renewal based on the result of the study of the Word of Life movement; fourth, a clarification of the dynamics of the Word of Life movement as a renewal movement for the future development of the Chinese church.

Notes

1. Cf. Yalin Xin, "Inner Dynamics of the Chinese House Church," *Mission Studies* 25 no. 2 (2008): 157–84.

2. The term "seminaries of the fields" was first used in reports on the underground seminaries by Chinese Church Research Center published in its journal *Zhongguo yu Jiao hui* (China and the Church). The term was chosen in particular consideration of the illegal status of the seminaries among the house churches in China. For details of the reports, see *Zhongguo yu jiao hui* (Sept.–Oct., 1986). In the WOL community, though, the underground seminaries are simply referred to as theological education (TE).

3. Peter Xu, taped interview with author, Dec. 2004.

4. Cf. Patrick Jonestone, et al, *Operation World* (Cumbria, UK: Paternoster Lifestyle, 2001), 160; Paul Hattaway, *Back to Jerusalem* (Carlisle, UK: Piquant, 2003), 63. David Aikman, *Jesus in Beijing* (Washington, DC: Regnery Publishing, Inc., 2003), 86.

5. Paul Hattaway and Joy Hattaway, "From the Front Lines with Paul & Joy Hattaway," *Asia Harvest* 2 (March 2002): 2–11. Cf. Jonestone, 160. Tony Lambert, "Counting Christians in China," *International Bulletin of Missionary Research* 27 (Jan. 2003): 6–10.

6. Wu, Yao Ting. "The First Eight Months of the Three-Self Reform Movement," in *Documents of the Three-Self Movement: Source Materials for the Study of the Protestant Church in Communist China*, edited by Wallace C. Merwin & Francis P. Jones (New York, New York: Far Eastern Office, National Council of the Churches of Christ in the U.S.A., 1951), 34–40. Cf. Jonathan Chao and Wanfang Zhuang, *Dang dai zhongguo ji du jiao fa zhan shi, 1949–1997* (A History of Christianity in Socialist China, 1949–1997) (Taipei: CMI Press, 1997), 16. Alan Hunter and Kim Kwong Chan, *Protestantism in Contemporary China* (Cambridge, UK: Cambridge University Press, 1993), 67.

7. See pp. 29–30 for discussion on the Cultural Revolution.

8. The statistical numbers given by these authors are for reference purpose only. It is indeed difficult for researchers on Christianity in China to get an accurate count of number of Christian believers, simply for the fact that unregistered churches (house churches, or underground churches) are not in legal status in China. Figures given by leaders and evangelists of various house church networks were rough estimates and often overlapped with one another. Cf. Tony Lambert, "Counting Christians in China," 6–10; Jonestone, 160; Hattaway, *Back to Jerusalem*, 2; Ross Paterson, *The Continuing Heartcry for China* (Tonbridge, England: Sovereign World Ltd., 1999), 216.

9. The Greek term *koinonia* conveys the basic meaning of "participation" and "mutuality." It is also translated as "fellowship," "communion," "sharing and self-sacrifice," and "community" (Acts 2:42; Romans 12:13, 15:26; 1 Corinthians 10:16; 2 Corinthians 8:4, 9:13, 13:14; Galatians 6:6; Philippines 4:15; Hebrews 13:16; 2 Peter 1:4). Howard Snyder (1983) defines *koinonia* as "a group of people bound together by what they share. As sharers in God's grace, the [New Testament] believers devoted themselves to being and becoming the community of God's people" (1983:79).

10. Stephen Neil, *A History of Christian Missions* (New York, New York: Penguin Books, 1986), 81–82. Cf. Samuel Moffet, *A History of Christianity in Asia, Vol. I: Beginnings to 1500* (Maryknoll, NY: Orbis Books, 1998), 291.

11. Michael Dillon, ed., *China: A Cultural and Historical Dictionary* (Richmond, Surrey: Curzon Press, 1998), 263. Cf. Neill, 82.

12. Neill, 141.

13. Ruth Tucker, *From Jerusalem to Irian Jaya,* revised. ed. (Grand Rapids, Michigan: Zondervan, 2004), 68–69.

14. George Minamiki, S.J., *The Chinese Rites Controversy from Its Beginnings to Modern Times* (Chicago, Illinois: Loyola Universtiy Press, 1985), 20.

15. George Hunsberger, *Evangelical Dictionary of World Missions*, edited by A. Scott Moreau (Grand Rapids, Michigan: Baker Books, 2000), 32.

16. Tucker, 69.

17. Neill, 165.

18. Dillon, 159.

19. Tony Lambert, *China's Christian Millions* (London, UK: Monarch Books, 1999), 11.

20. Kenneth Latourette, *A History of Christian Missions in China* (New York: The Macmillan Company, 1929), 211. Cf. Tucker, 178.

21. William Townsend, *Robert Morrison: The Pioneer of Chinese Missions*, reprint. Originally published in New York: Fleming H. Revell, 1888. (Salem, Ohio: Allegheny Publications, 2004), 80.

22. Dr. and Mrs. Howard Taylor, *Hudson Taylor in Early Years: The Growth of a Soul*, reprint. Originally published in London: China Inland Mission, 1911. (Littleton, CO: OMF International, 1997), 187.

23. Ibid., 201.

24. Tucker, 188–89.

25. Hunter and Chan, *Protestantism in Contemporary China*, 136.

26. Ibid., 114.

27. Thomas Harvey, *Acquainted with Grief* (Grand Rapids, Michigan: Brazos Press, 2002), 33.

28. Ibid., 33.

29. Cf. Ching Tang, *Zhongguo ji du jiao bai nian shi* (The First Hundred Years of Protestant Mission in China) (Hong Kong: Daosheng Press, 1987), 167–525; Muffet, 472.

30. Tang, 550.

31. Pierce Beaver, "Rufus Anderson 1796–1880: To Evangelize, Not Civilize," in *Mission Legacies: Biographical Studies of Leaders of the Modern Missionary Movement*, edited by Gerald H. Anderson et al (Maryknoll, New York: Orbis Books, 1994), 550.

32. Philip Wickeri, *Seeking the Common Ground* (Maryknoll, New York: Orbis Books, 1988), 40.

33. The anti-Christian movement (1922–27) was preceded by the May Fourth movement in 1919 student demonstration triggered by the unequal treaties of the Paris Peace Conference that resulted in the transfer of the rights of Germany in Tsingtao to Japan. At the time, a deep anti-Western feeling was aroused among the Chinese who staged a series of demonstrations, strikes and boycotts. Following the May Fourth movement, a New Culture movement was started by the Chinese intellectuals who spoke out on issues relating to nation-rebuilding. This movement gave rise to two different responders to the China problem: one turned to Marxism for revolutionary answers; the other, in reaction to western materialism, turned to Chinese spiritualism for answer (cf. Lee 1988:82–84). One of the common grounds shared in the movement was the need to replace the old culture with a new one, which led to debates on whether or not contemporary China still needed religion, including Christianity. Returning students from studying in the West, influenced by the western rationalism, conducted lectures and discussions that further fueled the anti-religion feeling among the Chinese population, giving rise to the anti-Christian movement (cf. Chao 1997:xiii). On March 9, 1922, an Anti-Christian Student Federation was set up in Shanghai in protest against the eleventh World's Student Christian Federation convention to be held in Qinhua University in Beijing. This symbolized the first organized attack on Christianity in China since the founding of the republic in 1911, and followed by a series of other anti-Christian

organizations set up in different cities of China. In this movement, Christianity was targeted as imperialistic influence in China.

34. Chun Kwan Lee, "The Theology of Revival in the Chinese Christian Church, 1900–1949: Its Emergence and Impact," Ph.D Dissertation (Westminster Theological Seminary, Philadelphia, Pennsylvania, 1988), 101.

35. Cf. Daniel Bays, ed., *Christianity in China: From the Eighteenth Century to the Present* (Stanford, California: Stanford University Press, 1996), 310.

36. Hunter and Chan, *Protestantism in Contemporary China*, 119.

37. The Little Flock was also known as The Assembly Hall (聚会所) or, more recently, Local Assemblies (地方教会).

38. Christian Study Center on Chinese Religion and Culture (CSCCRC), "The True Jesus Church Yesterday and Today, Part 1," *Bridge* 62 (Dec. 1993): 5.

39. Hunter and Chan, 121. Cf. CSCCRC, 5.

40. Tony Lambert, *China's Christian Millions,* 50.

41. Guang, "My Visit to 'The Jesus Family'," *Bridge* 34 (1989): 17.

42. Siu Kwan Tung, "The Wave of the 'Local Church'," *Bridge* 56 (1992), 3–4.

43. Angus Kinnear. *Against the Tide: The Story of Watchman Nee,* (Wheaton, Illinois: Tyndale House Publishers, 1973), 66.

44. Norman Cliff, *Fierce the Conflict: The Moving Stories of How Eight Chinese Christians Suffered for Jesus Christ and Remained Faithful,* (Dundas, Ontario: Joshua Press, 2001), 65–66.

45. Tung, 6.

46. Cliff, 74.

47. Ibid.

48. Norman Cliff, "Watchman Nee—Church Planter and Preacher of Holiness," *Evangelical Review of Theology* 8 no.2 (1984), 290. Cf. Leslie Lyall, *China's Three Mighty Men* (London: OMF Books, 1973), 64.

49. Johnstone et al, 160.

50. Watchman Nee, *The Spiritual Man,* vol. 1 (New York: Christian Fellowship Publishers, Inc., 1968), 66–67.

51. Lyall, 99–103.

52. Bays, *Christianity in China,* 314.

53. Harvey, 41.

54. Kalun Leung, "Fen xing bu dao jia dui hua ren jiao hui de su zao," (The Influence of Revivalist Preachers on the Chinese Church) *Jian Dao* 41 (1999), 114.

55. Leslie Lyall, *Urgent Harvest* (Chicago: Moody Press, 1964), 34–41.

56. Bethel Church was established by Jeannie V. Hughes (1874–1951) and Meiyu Shi (1873–1954) in Shanghai in 1920. Jeannie's father was a superintendent of the Methodist Episcopal Church, while Meiyu's father was a MEM pastor. Meiyu received her medical degree from the University of Michigan and returned to China as a medical missionary. Bethel Church was instrumental in bringing revivals locally in Shanghai and beyond through organizing revivals meetings and sending out evangelistic bands.

57. Leung, "The Influence," 110–11.

58. John Sung, *Forty John Sung Revival Sermons,* vol 1, translated by Timothy Tow (Singapore: Christian Life Book Centre, 1978), 59.

59. Ibid., 53–54.

60. Ibid., 59.

61. Kalun Leung, "Song shang jie de chong sheng jiao dao," (John Sung's Teaching on Rebirth) *Jian Dao* 4 (1995): 8–9.

62. Cf. Leung, "Rebirth," 6.

63. Ibid.

64. Stephen Sheng, *The Diaries of John Sung: An Autobiography*, translated by Stephen Sheng (Brighten, Michigan: Luke H. Sheng & Stephen L. Sheng, 1995), 3.

65. Leung, "The Influence," 111.

66. Hunter and Chan, *Protestantism in Contemporary China*, 136.

67. While the fundamentalists and the conservatives in China were basically alike in their theological stand, the fundamentalists were prone to acting more aggressively in their confrontation with the modernists. Cf. Kevin Xiyi Yao, *The Fundamentalist Movement among Protestant Missionaries in China, 1920–1937* (Lanham, Maryland: University Press of America, Inc., 2003), 14; Chao and Zhuang, xv–xvi.

68. Yao, 41–42.

69. Ibid., 281.

70. Ibid.

71. Cf. Wickeri, *Seeking the Common Ground*, 125.

72. The Three-Self is a short form for self-governing, self-supporting, and self-propagating, an idea originated with two 19th century missionary administrators, Henry Venn (1796–1873), Church Mission Society secretary in England and Rufus Anderson (1796–1880) of the American Board of Commissioners for Foreign Missions. TSPM is a more formal name used in publications in English, while colloquially as well as in publications in Chinese, Three-Self movement is more often used.

73. Daniel Bays, "Chinese Popular Religion and Christianity Before and After the 1949 Revolution: A Retrospective View," *Fides et Historia* XXIII:1 (1991), 74.

74. Chao and Zhuang, 80.

75. Any religious gatherings not registered with the local religious bureaus are considered illegal. In the case of Protestant Christianity in China, any gatherings not registered with the TSPM are regarded as illegal gatherings. As the majority of house churches are not registered with the TSPM, they, therefore, are illegal meeting points. At a meeting in New York during their recent visit to North America, the president of the TSPM insisted that the only distinction in Chinese church was on the one hand the registered churches (TSPM churches), and on the other hand the unregistered ones (underground churches).

76. John Peale, *The Love of God in China* (Lincoln, NE: iUniverse, Inc., 2005), 21-31.

77. Wickeri, *Seeking the Common Ground*, 124. Y. T. Wu was the chief editor of China YMCA publications in Shanghai, and Liangmo Liu was the director of the students section of China YMCA. Both of them became leaders of the TSPM movement.

78. Ibid., 130.

79. Harvey, 39.

80. Tony Lambert, *The Resurrection of the Chinese Church* (Wheaton, Illinois: OMF IHQ, Ltd., 1994), 15.

81. The Gang of Four is a name designated to the chief members of the radical faction that played a key role in directing the Cultural Revolution and tried to seize power after the death of Chairman Mao in 1976. The group includes Jiang Qing (first lady, Mao's wife), Wang Hongwen (vice Chairman), Zhang Chunqiao, Yao Wenyuan, who were arrested and imprisoned for treason.

82. Dillon, 65.

83. Tony Lambert, *The Resurrection of the Chinese Church*, 11.

84. "Reform through labor" is the kind of sentence that is often applied to criminals, including political criminals, in which prisoners are enforced to engage in manual labor as means of reform from their crimes. For detailed definition of the term, see Lawrence R. Sullivan, *Dictionary of the People's Republic of China, 1949–97* (Lanham, Maryland: Scarecrow Press, Inc.), 179.

85. Wang Mingdao was jailed for twenty-three years; Watchman Nee died at the end of his prison term of seventeen years; Samuel Lamb served more than twenty years; Moses Xie was also imprisoned for more than twenty years.

86. Lambert, *The Resurrection of the Chinese Church*, 10.

87. Chao, *A History of Protestant Christianity in China*, 201.

88. Lambert, *The Resurrection of the Chinese Church*, 12.

89. Leslie Lyall, *The Phoenix Rises* (Singapore: Overseas Missionary Fellowship Ltd., 1992), 84.

90. The Chinese Church Research Centre is an evangelical organization that monitors the religious situation in China. It is based in Hong Kong. Jonathan Chao was the director of this Centre. Among its publications are a bi-monthly journal *Zhongguo yu jiao hui* (*China and the Church*), *China News and Church Report*.

91. Jonathan Chao, *Ling huo cui lian* (Purified by Fire) (Taipei: CMI Press, 1993), 29–41.

92. The author's interview with leaders of WOL produced fairly consistent responses regarding suffering and spirituality: the Cultural Revolution served as a test to Christians—only those who went through the test of fire and yet were able to stand to their faith were truly born again and committed to the Lord's work.

93. Donald McGavran, *Understanding Church Growth*, revised ed. (Grand Rapids, Michigan: Eerdmans Publishing Company, 1980), 100.

94. Lambert, *The Resurrection of the Chinese Church*, 19.

95. Kalun Leung, *Gai ge kai fang yi lai de zhongguo nong cun jiao hui* (The Rural Churches of Mainland China since 1978) (Hong Kong: Alliance Bible Seminary, 1999), 88.

96. Cf. Lambert, *The Resurrection of the Chinese Church*, 80.

97. Beginning with the 1983 "anti-spiritual pollution campaign" called on by the government when house churches experienced their first blow since the end of the Cultural Revolution. This campaign was followed by a series of others such as the "anti-bourgeois liberalization campaign" in 1987, in which house churches often became the target.

98. Ross Paterson, *The Continuing Heartcry for China* (Tonbridge, England: Sovereign World Ltd., 1999), 220.

99. Hattaway, *Back to Jerusalem*, 6, 63–64.

100. Ibid., 66-67.

101. Back to Jerusalem (BTJ) refers to a rekindled vision from the early twentieth century when some Chinese Christians felt called of God to go westward from China and preach the gospel and establish Christian communities along the way until Jerusalem. This vision has been enthusiastically shared by the house church groups since the 1990s. See also Chapter 4 for discussion on BTJ movement.

102. Cf. Chao and Zhuang, 521–25; "Han Wenzhao Slanders House Church Leader," *China Prayer Letter and Ministry Report* 112 (1997), 1; Aikman, 86, 238; Hattaway, *Back to Jerusalem*, 63; Leung, *The Rural Churches of Mainland China*, 177–78.

103. Hunter and Chan, *Protestantism in Contemporary China*, 123.

104. Howard Snyder, *Signs of the Spirit* (Eugene, Oregon: Wipf and Stock, 1997), 34.

105. Howard Snyder, "Survey of Renewal Movements," syllabus (Wilmore, Kentucky: Asbury Theological Seminary, 2003).

106. Louis Berkhof, *Systematic Theology* (Grand Rapids, Michigan: Eerdmans Publishing Co., 1996), 202–10.

107. Ibid., 202–05.

108. Snyder, *Signs of the Spirit*, 9.

109. Ibd., 251.

110. Cf. Lambert, *The Resurrection of the Chinese Church*, 102; Bays, "Chinese Popular Religions and Christianity," 76.

111. Leung, *The Rural Churches of Mainland China*, 224.

112. Bays, "Chinese Popular Religion and Christianity," 76.

113. Messengers of the Gospel (MGs) is a designated name for those devoted Christians (usually young adults) who are separated for the work of evangelism in the Word of Life Church. These MGs form the Gospel Band that is responsible for the work of theological education in the WOL, sending evangelists (MGs) to frontier evangelism, and establishing house churches.

114. Snyder, *Signs of the Spirit*, 35.

115. Donald Durnbaugh, *The Believers' Church*, (New York, New York: The Macmillan Company, 1968), 33. As cited in Snyder, *Signs of the Spirit*, 40.

116. Snyder, *Signs of the Spirit*, 42.

117. Snyder, "Survey of Renewal Movements."

118. As cited in Snyder, *Signs of the Spirit*, 48.

119. Snyder, *Signs of the Spirit*, 52.

120. Ibid., 55.

121. Ibid., 276.

122. Ibid., 277.

123. Ibid.

124. Ibid.

125. Ibid.

126. Ibid., 278.

127. Ibid.

128. Ibid., 278–79.

129. Ibid., 279.

130. Ibid., 279–30.

131. Ibid.

132. Ibid., 281.

133. Cf. Snyder, *Signs of the Spirit*, 285–93.

Chapter 2

Review of Relevant Literature

This chapter is devoted to the review of literature that is relevant to the discussion on the WOL house church as a movement of renewal. It reviews, first of all, literature concerning renewal movement, revivalism, revitalization movements, believers' church, church growth and social movement, all of which are relevant to the study of renewal movements; secondly, it surveys writings on Christianity in China in general, which provides background information for our understanding of the WOL movement and puts it in context; thirdly, it focuses on research done on the WOL house church community, which informs, supports, and supplements the research on the WOL movement. As such, this chapter is an inseparable part of the whole project on the WOL house church as a movement of renewal in China.

Part One: Renewal Movements

Part One reviews literature concerning renewal movement, revivalism, revitalization movements, believers' church, church growth and social movement. These disciplines interrelate with one another to certain extent and are relevant to the study of renewal movements. It is not an exhaustive survey of literature in these disciplines, but only focuses on some of the primary writings as they are more closely related to the study of renewal movements.

Thomas P. Rausch

Rev. Thomas P. Rausch, S.J. is the T. Marie Chilton Professor of Catholic theology at Loyola Marymount University in Los Angeles. He has written thirteen books and over a hundred articles in the areas of his expertise: ecclesiology, ecumenism, and the theology of the priesthood.

Through eight case studies in his book, *Radical Christian Communities* (1990), Rausch demonstrates to readers the common characteristics of these radical Christian communities in their emergence—commonly recognized as an individual or individuals who found a fresh vision or conviction as to the nature of the gospel and shared it among others who followed him or them, their life and ministry—mostly covenant communities with guidelines and disciplines drawn up by the founder(s). According to Rausch, it has been a historical pattern that at every age of the church there have been those who responded to the gospel in a radical way: "to discipleship with Jesus and community with one another."[1] These radical Christian communities were initially countercultural communities, standing at some critical distance from the culture around them, rooting their life and ministry in the example of Jesus. As such communities flourished and became established, however, "their success has time and again been the cause of their undoing," and they often compromised their original vision and conviction to "a lifestyle which had emerged or to support a work undertaken."[2] Then men and women emerged with yet again a new vision of renewal and formed new communities, and committed themselves to living out "more perfectly the call to discipleship in light of new circumstances and new times."[3]

Rausch particularly highlights the positive and negative effects of the institutionalization of the religious communities. On the positive side, "ecclesial recognition brought many communities the guidance which kept them in communion with the church," as well as provided the stability for these communities to survive.[4] On the negative side, institutionalization tended to discourage other Christians not considered canonically as "religious" from forming radical Christian communities.[5]

Rausch also recognizes some common characteristics that associate with the contemporary Christian communities: first, they combine a contemplative spirituality with a commitment to solidarity with the poor; second, they rediscover monasticism in the Protestant tradition; third, they challenge the contemporary social order in the name of the gospel. Future challenges, according to Rausch, will be gradually presented before the radical Christian communities: remaining countercultural in a secularized society, tension between movement and institutionalization, how to attract new members, issues revolving around ministry and ordination, living out the call to be examples of holiness for the entire church.

Howard A. Snyder

Distinguished professor, Chair of Wesley Studies at Tyndale Seminary in Toronto, Howard A Snyder has written several books in the area of church renewal including *The Problems of Wineskins* (1975), *The Community of the King* (2004), *The Radical Wesley and Patterns for Church Renewal*(1980), and *Signs of the Spirit: How God Reshapes the Church* (1997).

Snyder (1997) carefully studies renewal movements in the history of the church in order to find common themes and trends that run through them. Based on his conviction that "God works by his Spirit to create Christian community and to renew his people when they fall into unfaithfulness," Snyder's study primarily focuses on the inner dynamics of renewal movements through which to identify the work of the Spirit of God. Four movements have been chosen to "illuminate the issues in renewal" and offer insights for the church today: the New Prophecy movement, Pietism, Moravianism, and Methodism.[6]

Out of detailed description of Pietism, Moravianism, and Methodism and analysis of the movement dynamics, Snyder finds these three movements were interrelated in a number of ways such as, 1) all of the three movements were part of a larger current of renewal during the seventeenth and eighteenth century, 2) there was a significant network of relationship involving key leaders of these movements, 3) all three movements made use of small cell groups in the form of *collegia*, bands, classes, etc. 4) education played a key role in these movements, 5) books and tracts produced a significant impact in promoting the movements, 6) all three movements stressed the normative role of the Scripture in the life and experience of believers and held the early church as model, and 7) lay leadership was a key to the vitality of these movements.[7]

The comparative study of the three renewal movements not only produces significant common characteristics in renewal movements but also opens the readers to the importance of human wisdom and choice in the emergence and continuous development of renewal movements:

> ...renewal movements are neither direct, irresistible acts of God nor the mere outworking of inexorable sociological laws or constraints. Much depends on human wisdom and choice. Spener, Francke, Zinzendorf, and Wesley all intended to see renewal come to the church and worked self-consciously to achieve it. The impact of the movements they led was due in large measure to the quality of the leadership they provided. If the essential dynamic in movements of spiritual renewal is a fresh personal sense of the reality of God, then the direction a movement takes, and its continuing influence over an extended period of time, depend largely on the human leadership under which the movement develops.[8]

Toward the end of the book, Snyder proposes a model for church renewal today—a mediating model between the typical institutional and charismatic perspectives on church renewal. All the marks of this mediating model are identifiable in different capacities in Pietism, Moravianism, and Methodism that Snyder examines in *Signs of the Spirit*, and are relevant to other renewal movements. Snyder's mediating model for church renewal will be the primary theoretical framework guiding the interpretation of the research data on the Word of Life movement.

Richard F. Lovelace

An emeritus professor of Church History at Gordon Conwell Theological Seminary, Richard F. Lovelace draws from biblical models and church history in presenting a comprehensive approach to spiritual renewal in his book, *Dynamics of Spiritual Life—An Evangelical Theology of Renewal* (1979). He provides exhaustive analysis of the elements of revival which include conviction of sin, deep understanding of justification, movement of the Spirit, prayer, community, mission and social compassion.

Lovelace identifies the substitutional atonement as "the heart of the gospel," because "it gives the answer to the problem of guilt, bondage and alienation from God."[9]

> People come to Christ initially for a variety of reasons, some of which are eccentric to their principle need for redemption: loneliness, a sense of meaninglessness in the godless life, suffering, fear and so on. Only those lastingly converted, however, whose eventual motivation is to turn from their sin to God and receive the answer to sin in the work of Jesus Christ: "For everyone who does evil hates the light, and does not come to the light, lest his deeds should be exposed. But he who does what is true comes to the light, that it may be clearly seen that his deeds have been wrought in God" (John 3:20–21).[10]

Lovelace distinguishes between the primary and secondary elements of renewal and identifies the following elements as the primary elements of continuous renewal: justification, sanctification, the indwelling Holy Spirit, and authority in spiritual conflict.

> The primary factors are those involved in traditional theories of the atonement, which answers most immediately the urgent hunger and thirst for righteousness awakened in the individual who has come into the light concerning the nature of the true God and his or her own sinful condition. They are the heart of the gospel, the good news of the reconciliation Christ accomplished through his death and resurrection."[11]

To Lovelace, the primary elements of renewal are foundational to "a pure and lasting work of spiritual renewal" that takes place within the church. Only on this foundation the secondary elements of continuous renewal naturally extend. "The secondary conditions of renewal are also closely connected with our union with Christ, and they flow out of the primary elements secured in the atonement."[12] In other words, some elements are sequential to others because they provide solid basis in order to sustain a continuous renewal. Lovelace identifies these secondary elements as mission, prayer, community, and theological integration. "Primary responses of faith are centered in individual Christians, as they appropriate the fruits of his redemptive work. Secondary responses of faith move beyond individual growth to encompass the world, the church and the whole of life and thought."[13]

Charles G. Finney

The name Charles Grandison Finney was among the several mentioned western church leaders and missionaries who were looked up to within the WOL leadership circle, and his "new measures" in revivals seem to have inspired the WOL community in its ministry.

Finney basically identifies revivals as the way God works to lead people into an obedient relationship with him.[14] He contends that it is necessary that the "excitement" be raised among men who are "sluggish," so that they will break over the "counteracting influences" of the world, and obey God. The history of Israel, according to Finney, reflects exactly how "God used to maintain religion among them by special occasions, when there would be a great excitement."[15] And the result of revival would be a short time obedience before Israel once again would backslide, until God acted again to revive them. Therefore, Finney observes that periodical excitements are the only way to "bring the church to act steadily for God,' although it would be desirable that the church should live in obedience to God without these excitements, and to be able to counteract the excitements of the world that are drawing believers' attention.[16]

According to Finney, three agents are involved in revivals: God, men, and sinner. God's involvement is two-fold: first, by his Providence, that God provides the possibility for a revival to take place; second, by his Spirit, that God converts the sinner by pouring in "a blaze of convincing light upon their souls, which they cannot withstand, and they yield to it, and obey God, and are saved." The role of men in revivals is to be an active instrument of God, "promoting the conversion of sinner," through preaching and witnessing, which present such a reproach to the sinner that he is convicted and converted.[17] Finney argues that, although God superintends and controls the universe, we are not exempt from employing means for promoting a revival of religion, for "every event in nature has been brought about by means."[18]

Finney contends that "a revival is not a miracle," but "a purely philosophical result of the right use of the constituted means."[19] He sees the problem of the churches as primarily setting down into "a form of doing things," that "they soon get to rely upon the outward doing of it, and so retain the form of religion while they lose the substance."[20] Therefore, the solution to the problem is to bring about new measures, which is how God has always chosen to work with the church. In reasoning how present measures all derive from new measures in succession, from dress code for ministers to the using of hymns, Finney recommends some present useful innovations or new measures such as Anxious Meetings, Protracted Meetings, and the Anxious Seat, and contends that "without new measures it is impossible that the church should succeed in gaining the attention of the world to religion."[21]

Richard M. Riss

Richard Riss is the author of six books including *A Survey of 20th Century Revival Movements in North America*, in which he offers us a concise overview of spiritual awakenings of the 20th century in the United States and Canada. Riss identifies "three major reawakenings" of Christian faith in North America: the Azusa Street revival in Los Angeles of 1906, the Healing and Latter Rain movements in 1947 and 1948, and the Charismatic renewal in the late 1960s and early 1970s.[22] These revival movements occurred against the background of the century that God was no longer regarded as taking an active role in history, and thus miracles no longer took place. Yet, Riss asserts, miracles as recorded in the Bible did take place during times of revival. Riss generalizes some of the common characteristics of revivals based on his study of revival movements in history: 1) During times of revival, people cultivate a strong desire for God and enthusiasm for Christianity; 2) people's hearts are open to the Word of God; 3) theologically during a time of revival, the emphasis is on suffering, cross, blood, death, and resurrection of Jesus Christ; 4) people become deeply conscious of their sins and wickedness and recognize the need to have God's forgiveness; 5) a revival typically results in sins and bad conduct being dealt with, and freedom and joy come to reside instead; 6) miracles, such as physical healings, and spiritual gifts often accompany revivals and people have a great sense of the presence of God; 7) revivals usually emerge against a backdrop of very serious spiritual and moral decline or during a time of intense spiritual dryness; 8) important awakenings seem to emerge simultaneously in many different locations; 9) a spirit of sacrifice is often prevalent during an awakening.[23]

Riss offers a good phenomenological study of revival movements, dealing with such details as factors contributing to the emergence of revivals, key figures of the revival movements, their ministry and worship styles, spiritual gifts that accompany revivals, and dynamic and influence of revivals. His identification of the common characteristics of revivals can be a useful tool in analyzing Christian renewal and revival movements.

J. Edwin Orr

As a proliferate writer on revivals and awakenings J. Edwin Orr basically observes the phenomenon of evangelical awakenings throughout the world from the perspective of revivalism.[24] Orr identifies evangelical awakenings as movements of "the Holy Spirit bringing about a revival of New Testament Christianity in the Church of Christ and in its related community," with significant impact touching both "an individual" and "a larger group of believers." "The outpouring of the Spirit effects the reviving of the Church, the awakening of the masses, and the movement of uninstructed peoples towards the Christian faith; the revived Church, by many or by few, is moved to engage in evangelism, in teaching, and in social action."[25]

Primarily among some of the common characteristics of Evangelical Awakenings are "some repetition of the phenomena of the Acts of the Apostles," such as "extraordinary praying among the disciples," "self-judgment and confession and reconciliation," the preaching of the "death and resurrection of Jesus Christ," followed by the revitalizing of nominal Christians and by bringing outsiders into vital touch with the Divine Dynamic causing all such Awakenings—the Spirit of God."[26]

Orr, from a revivalist point of view, finds it normal that revivals take place periodically, and identifies some of the common patterns in revivals. He does not, however, particularly emphasize the human active participation in revivals compared with Charles Finney who, while recognizing God's providential role in revivals, stresses human active role as God's instrument.

William G. McLoughlin

The late William G. McLoughlin was professor emeritus of history and religion at Brown University. He was author of numerous books, including *Revivals, Awakenings, and Reform* (1978), and *Modern Revivalism: Charles Grandison Finney to Billy Graham* (1959).

In *Revivals, Awakenings, and Reform*, McLoughlin proposes that "Great awakenings (and the revivals that are part of them) are the results, not of depressions, wars, or epidemics, but of critical disjunctions in our self-understanding. They are not brief outbursts of mass emotionalism by one group or another but profound cultural transformations affecting all Americans and extending over a generation or more." McLoughlin identifies revivals and awakenings as only "folk movements," taking place universally, through which a people or a nation revitalizes itself and "sustains a healthy relationship with environmental and social change."[27] He is primarily concerned with "social function of religious systems and with achieving a historical perspective on their periodic transformations," and therefore views religious conversion in great numbers as "natural and necessary aspect of social change."[28] McLoughlin treats awakenings as "periods when the cultural system has had to be revitalized in order to overcome jarring disjunctions between norms and experience, old beliefs and new realities, dying patterns and emerging patterns of behavior."[29]

Charles H. Kraft

In *Christianity in Culture: A Study in Dynamic Biblical Theologizing in Cross-Cultural Perspective*, Kraft contends that "cultural transformation" goes through "a series of preparatory developments" over a period of time. When tension within these developments becomes intolerable, a paradigm shift occurs, which "in turn sparks a series of rapid socio-cultural readjustments."[30] People concerned with the change then mount a "movement with the specific aim of bringing about the changes recommended." Kraft (1979) sees a movement as "culturally revitalizational, providing the necessary reintegration to give a dying culture a new lease on life."[31] Kraft recognizes the contributions of Gerlach and Hine (1970) in their research on movements in relation to social transformation, particularly the five key "operationally significant" factors. He proposes some useful points concerning "the place of movements in cultural transformation":

1. A movement is "the type of social change that can be caused by a dedicated minority willing to call out the repressive force of the majority."
2. "Real or perceived opposition from the society at large" is necessary.
3. Without a movement, the "advocacy of any paradigm shift...is doomed to substantial failure."
4. Basic distinctions exist between "the way participants in a movement seek solutions and the way the "establishment" seeks solutions.
5. Movements start as "demands for change in the existing system, not specific blueprints for social institutions of the future."

6. "Movements involve major changes in the self-image of the participants."
7. Long-term social changes often result from the fact that movements, whether or not they succeed, initiate experimental new approaches to the solution of needs that are more widely recognized throughout the society."[32]

Anthony F. C. Wallace

Wallace defines a revitalization movement as "a deliberate, organized, conscious effort by members of a society to construct a more satisfying culture."[33] When a society and its members are under stress, and find the cultural system incapable of reducing the level of stress, it is necessary to "make changes in the 'real' system in order to bring mazeway and 'reality' into congruence." Such effort to reduce stress is identified as the effort at revitalization, and "the collaboration of a number of persons in such an effort is called a revitalization movement."[34] Such movement develops in the five stages:

The first stage—"Steady State." This is the stage when "chronic stress within the system varies within tolerable limits."

The second stage—"The Period of Increased individual stress." Gradually individuals in a society "experience increasingly severe stress as a result of the decreasing efficiency of certain stress-reduction techniques," and feel the need of seeking some alternative way out.

The third stage—"the Period of Cultural Distortion." At this stage, "the culture is internally distorted; the elements are not harmoniously related but are mutually inconsistent and interfering."

The fourth stage—"The Period of Revitalization." In face of a deteriorating social system, no longer able to cope with the stress laid on the society, a revitalization movement rises, often "religious in character," and functions in at least six capacities: 1) restructuring of elements and subsystems which have already attained currency in the society; 2) communicating the vision of change; 3) organizing followers; 4) adapting to resistance; 5) revitalization taking place; 6) new norms being established.

The fifth stage—"The New Steady State." "Once the movement organization has solved its problems of routinization, a new steady state comes into being.

Wallace contends that revitalization movement is a cultural phenomenon, recurrent in human history. "Both Christianity and Mohammedanism, and possibly Buddhism as well, originated in revitalization movements...In fact, it can be argued that all organized religions are relics of old revitalization movements, surviving in routinized form in stabilized cultures."[35]

Donald F. Durnbaugh

A noted historian of Anabaptist and Pietist religions, Donald F. Durnbaugh has published a number of books, including *The Believer's Church: The History and Character of Radical Protestantism* (1968), *Fruit of the Vine: A History of the Brethren* (1997), and more than 200 articles, reviews and essays on the history of the Brethren Church as well as other Anabaptist religious movements.

In *The Believers' Church*, Durnbaugh (1968) defines the Believers' Church as "the covenanted and disciplined community of those walking in the way of Jesus Christ. Where two or three such are gathered, willing also to be scattered in the work of their Lord, there is the believing people."[36] The following characteristics are identifiable in a Believers' Church:

First, the Church consists of the voluntary membership of those confessing Jesus Christ as Lord.

Second, the covenant is made between God and themselves and with each other to live faithfully as disciples of Christ.

Third, as regenerated Christians, they will be expected to maintain a higher level of life than the common man.

Fourth, they accept the necessity of being "reproved, corrected, cast out, or excommunicated," according to the principle of Matthew 18:15–20.

Fifth, they urge "benevolent gifts to be willingly given and distributed to the poor."

Sixth, there was to be neither complete formalism nor complete spontaneity; forms evolve from the group, and can be changed if need be.

Seventh, they "center everything on the Word, prayer, and love."[37]

Discipleship is at the heart of the Believers' Church. Durnbaugh quotes Harold S. Bender on this point: "the first and fundamental…was the conception of the essence of Christianity as discipleship. It was a concept which meant the transformation of the entire way of life of the individual believer and of society so that it should be fashioned after the teaching and example of Christ."[38] For the Believers' Church, it has been their conviction that the fundamental nature of discipleship was lacking within Christendom" and Christianity had lost the "first zeal of the apostles."[39] The solution seems to lie in the "restitution of the beliefs and practices of the early church" exemplified in the New Testament, through a "disciplined community". [40]

Believers' Church also has a strong sense of mission. "The Anabaptists were the first to make the Great Commission the responsibility of every church member. There is indeed impressive evidence that most members felt the call to convince and convert others, relatives, neighbors, strangers."[41] Count Zinzendorf and his Moravian Brethren "was responsible for the most extensive missionary activity of the eighteenth century."[42]

The Believers' Church manifests some similarities with the perspective of renewal movement. For example, it offers us the authentic expression of a covenanted community, stressing the Word of God, faith in Jesus Christ, good works as regenerated Christians, discipline, and charity.

Gregory P. Leffel

As co-founder of Community and president of One Horizon Foundation, Gregory Leffel implores the issues revolving around the role of the church in society as a social movement in *Faith Seeking Action: Mission, Social Movements, and the Church in Motion* (2007). He proposes an interpretive framework consisting of six variables, based on which the movement case studies are interpreted. These six variables include: (1) the opportunity structure, (2) rhetorical framing, (3) protest strategy, (4) mobilizing structures, (5) movement culture, and (6) participant biography.

Opportunity Structure

Leffel identifies this element as the context variable, which implicating the "social, political, and cultural environment within in which a movement is embedded and from which it emerges." Leffel argues that the context sets "the limits of the range of strategies available to activists and determining the potentional intensity of social conflict." The social, political, cultural, and economic context "defines the nature of the opportunity." According to Leffel, the context "conditions what is likely to occur and the possibility that potential recruits, and the general public will find resonance with a movement's claims and goals .[43]

Rhetorical Framing

In Leffel's terminology, Rhetoric Framing is basically the "conceptual architecture." "Movements seek to redefine reality as much as they seek in disrupt or change political and social structures. The ways in which their grievances are named, and a positive vision for the future is put forward, play an essential role in motivating and sustaining movement activism."[44] The basic argument for Leffel is that movement visions and ideas have to be "framed" in such a way that they "articulate dissatisfaction with existing social life" and "define the terms of engagement with the opposition." There must be continuity between the existing cultural themes and the movement's rhetorical frames in order that "the movement is rooted deeply within an existing social history." A new language has to be created that "unites the movement" within its own environment. Leffel finds it essential to the success of the movement how the movement participants craft "a powerful thought world," and "promoting and defending its message in public."[45]

Protest Strategy

Protest strategy "involves raising public awareness, public support, and attracting growing numbers of participants." To do this, movement entrepreneurs often have to make choices such as "framing protest campaigns, selecting protest tactics, deploying groups, making public demands, long-term maintenance of public support, and sustaining conflict with elites in order to force a crisis of decision in favor of the movement's demands." Leffel contends that "the strategic performance of movement organizers is crucial to a movement's success no matter how popular the movement may be in its own right."[46]

Mobilizing Structures

Mobilizing structures are concerned with the patterns of organization, formal and informal, large and small, that are needed to structure and direct the movement. These include the structures required to advance social protest, to support working relationships and friendship among the activities, to support communication both inside and outside of the movement's ranks, to recruit others to the movement, and to procure the financial, technical and material resources needed to meet the movement's objectives." "Networks" or "convergences" are often formed, which both incorporate existing organizations and create new ones. "An efficient and well supported leadership structure" is crucially important in this variable.[47]

Movement Culture

According to Leffel, a movement provides a context where "a new way of life" is experimented and experienced, and "where the movement's ideals, values and common vision are put to the test." A movement's culture draws the limitation of one's identification distinguishable from the larger world.

> Thus the movement's cultural markers—its music dress styles, graphic arts, street performances, activist nick-names, and its moral ethos—provide both a clear sense of belonging and a set of screens to help determine who is part of the movement and who is not. A rich and well-developed movement culture is a powerful tool for attracting, socializing and supporting activists; its ability to nurture a high quality of life is a measure of the maturity and value of the movement itself."[48]

Participant Biography

"The life histories, personalities, motivation, and abilities of movement actors play important roles in the emergence and progress of movements." How movement activists "come to discover grievances and become motivated to do something" about their life experiences "that open one to become involved in a movement" furnishes "clues to why certain movements arises at particular times." Leffel finds it also important to understand "how involvement leads to personal transformation and a long-term movement lifestyle."[49]

Leffel's theoretical framework provides a new way of looking at social movements. He demonstrates the usefulness of the six-variables in the interpretation of the social movement case studies and the clarification of the movement dynamics throughout his book.

Luther P. Gerlach and Virginia H. Hine

Gerlach and Hine (1970) deal with the fundamental issue of the relationship of movements and social transformation through their research into two movements—"the Pentecostal Movement and the Black Power Movement." At the start of the book titled *People, Power, Change: Movements of Social Transformation,* the authors define a movement as a "group of people who are organized for, ideologically motivated by, and committed to a purpose which implements some form of personal or social change; who are actively engaged in the recruitment of others; and whose influence is spreading in opposition to the established order within which it originated.[50]

Protestant Christian movements, the authors contend, have produced such social change. For example, the Methodist denomination, which started as a "revival movement" among a small group who were "incompatible with the established order of the Anglican church," and who formed "cell-like organizations linked by the activities of charismatic leaders," grew to be a significant Christian community from which Pentecostalism as a new religious revival emerged.[51] Both the Pentecostal Movement and the Black Power Movment, from the authors' point of view, have religious influence as well as social influence, as each has incurred significant social changes whether it is their initial purpose or not.[52]

Gerlach and Hine's research on the "internal dynamics" of the two movements led them to identifying five characteristics accompanying a "social, political, or religious movement":

> (a) segmented organizational units linked together into a reticulate network by various personal, organizational, and ideological ties; (b) face-to-face recruitment along lines of pre-existing significant social relationships of positive affect; (c) personal commitment on the part of most, if not all, participants resulting from an identity-altering experience, a bridge-burning act or both; (d) an ideology which provides the basis for overall unity as well as segmentary diversity, which exploits the motive power of an ideal-real gap, and which constitutes a comprehensive conceptual framework by means of which events are interpreted and the opposition defined; (e) the perception of opposition from the established order within which the movement is spreading."[53]

The authors further observe that, "when all five of these key factors are present and interacting, the movement becomes an autonomous social institution and can grow independently of the original generating conditions." At this time, "opposition from the established order" will only serve to "provide optimal conditions for its growth."[54] For those who are committed to a movement, the authors contends, it involves

- personal commitment on the part of individuals who believe they have the power to initiate changes within their own sphere of influence;
- enthusiastic persuasion of friends, relatives, and neighbors to join in the small-scale effort;
- articulation of beliefs and ideals appropriate to this particular period in national and world history and to this particular stage of technological development;
- flexible, non-bureaucratic cell-group organizations which can be created, altered, or dissolved at the desire of participants; and

■ expectation of and willingness to face opposition from those dedicated to the maintenance of the status quo in spite of its present deficiencies, weaknesses, and flaws. Opposition may come in the form of physical force, or various types of pressure exerted through institutional channels. Or it may come in the form of ridicule from those who are still secure in the notion that power is based only on position within and ability to manipulate the existing power structure.[55]

Donald A. McGavran

A Missionary to India for more than thirty years and a specialist in strategic church growth, Donald McGavran wrote extensively on the topic of church growth. *The Bridges of God* challenges the widespread missionary policy, which so much focuses itself on institutions and mission stations, of its validity at the time, especially in light of the revolutionary changes in the world situation, and presents his strategic observation of how the social network within people groups can be bridges through which the gospel spreads.

Defining the term "People Movement" as large numbers of people, who receive much instruction in the Christian faith, achieved only by the conversion of a series of small groups over a period of years. McGavran (1955) examines the New Testament narratives for reference to his theory, and contends that "peoples become Christian fastest when least change of race or clan is involved. When it is felt that 'we are moving with our people and those who have not come now will come later,' then the Church grows most vigorously."[56]. McGavran also offers examples of the "People Movement" at work throughout the ages in the expansion of the church from the first century through the time of Reformation, which affirms his observation of the social nature of religious development.

McGavran is convinced that the stimulation and support of the People Movement churches will produce great development, and should be the primary concern of Christian mission today. He lists five great advantages of the People Movement:

1. People Movement produce permanent grassroots churches.

2. These churches are naturally indigenous, with Christians immersed in their own cultures without the supervision of the missionary.

3. There is a spontaneous expansion of the Church with the People Movement, which "involves a full trust in the Holy Spirit and a recognition that the ecclesiastical traditions of the order churches are not necessarily useful to the younger churches arising out of the mission from the West."

4. These movements have enormous possibilities of growth, both due to external and internal reasons.

5. These movements provide a sound pattern of becoming Christian. People do not come to Christianity for change of standard of living, but seek "change in inner character made possible by the power of God."[57]

One of prominent points that runs through McGavran's argument for the People Movement against the Mission Station Approach is the issue of individual/group conversion. While Mission Station Approach disconnects the individual convert from his community and social environment, People Movement Approach leads to the discipleship of families and groups. In many societies group decision means shared decision, with the understanding that "every member has had a share in the final decision."[58] McGavran asserts, "We believe, then, that in the initial discipling of a people participation in a group decision is a sufficient following of the light to confer salvation on each person participating in the decision. It is not 'membership in the group' but 'participation in following Christ' which is the vital factor."[59]

Part Two: Christianity in China in General

This part surveys literature concerning the Christianity in China in general. As noted in the section on delimitation of the study, the literature surveyed here primarily focuses on Protestant Christianity as it closely relates to the study of the WOL as a Protestant Christian movement, and it provides valuable background information for the understanding of the WOL movement.

Jonathan Chao

Jonathan Chao was one of the most proliferate writers on the church in China. He followed the development of Christianity in China for more than 30 years and offered insightful observations from theological, historical and missiological perspectives. He was also an expert in dealing with the political implications on the Church in China. In his writings Chao would often treat the history of the church in China by means of phases or epochs before 1949, i.e., Western mission in the 19th century; Chinese Church in time of the Republic; the Unification of the Chinese Church and the Indigenous Movement; the influence of liberal theology,[60] and, after 1949, according to the political development and its implications in the church in China, i.e. 1950–58; 1958–66; 1966–76; 1976–82.[61]

In *Lead Me to Go Forward*, Dr. Jonathan Chao (1993) introduces to readers the process of the formation and the development of his vision: the evangelization of China, the kingdomization of the Church, and the Christianization of culture. This vision has become the shared vision of the Chinese Ministries International. First, the evangelization of China means to share the gospel to 95 percent Chinese unbelievers, including the mainland Chinese unbelievers. Second, the kingdomizaiton of the Church: God's salvation scheme through Jesus Christ meant to reconciled the world to Himself. This should be the guiding principle of ministry of the local church. Understanding this principle, the local church is able to participate in God's salvation work in history. This is geared toward renewing and releasing the church from the bondage of denominationalism and culture so that it can enter into God's whole salvation history. Third, the Christianization of Chinese culture: To transform the Chinese culture with the Christian faith, and furnish the realms of culture, ideology, education, politics and society with contributions from the Christian faith. This is geared to encourage Christians to influence the society, and even to transform the worldly culture and social system by means of participating in politics and education.[62]

This vision is significant also because the WOL movement seems also to have incorporated this vision into their ministry goal, though whether or not this vision has been carried out is another question. We, however, can see the influence of Chao and the Chinese Church Research Center had for at least the leaders of the WOL movement.

In "The Process of Indigenization of Christianity in Contemporary China," Chao (2005) observes the indigenization of Christianity in China from a historical and theological perspective. He traces the origin of the Chinese indigenous movement to the beginning of the 20th century when the idea of indigenous churches built on the foundation of self-support, self-governing, and self-propagating (Three-Self) first raised by missologists Rufus Anderson and Henry Venn was introduced to the China scene and tried out in what Chao categorized as five different models in the 1920s: The model of external Chinese expression, the model of Christianization, the model of sinocization, the model of ethical common ground, and the model of syncretism.[63] Chao distinguishes these initial indigenization efforts from the indigenous movement among the Fundamentalist churches from the end of 1920s to 1949. Famous evangelists and revivalists such as Watchman Nee and Liland Wang, Wang Mingdao, Jing Dianying, Ye Zhiwen and John Sung, were forerunners of this indigenization trend. They emphasized the authority of the Bible, being born again, and training lay Christian leaders, which left clear marks on the church in China today.[64]

With the open policy in China after the Cultural Revolution, religious policies were relaxed, and house churches experienced great revivals in the 1980s and developed their indigenous organizational systems for evangelism, training, and establishing churches.[65] Despite the rapid growth of house churches, Chao (2005) points out the limitations of the indigenous effort among the house church community: First, the negative influence (from the indigenous movement within the Fundamentalist camp from 1928 to 1949) of anti-denominationalism, anti-rationalism, and anti-theological reflection; second, comparatively low educational level among the house church leaders. These limitations have become gradually prominent as the house churches continue to grow, the Chinese society continues to experience rapid change, questions in ministry continue to surface.[66]

Chao (1993) observes that out of the many secrets of phenomenal growth of the church in China, walking the way of the Cross has been the one most important secret. By walking the way of the Cross it means that Christians in China were willing to sacrifice all for the sake of the Lord, and they have been through the worst of all trials, especially during the Cultural Revolution. The way of the Cross is the way of suffering and opposition, and yet in the end the way of triumph for the Chinese Christians. "Suffering purified and strengthened the Chinese Church, and enabled Chinese believers today to be bolder and wiser. Suffering contributed to the continuous growth of the Church in China."[67]

Tony Lambert

As a former British diplomat to China Tony Lambert (1994) provides his readers with information and insights into various spheres revolving around the Christian church in China after the Cultural Revolution in 1976: political situation, social environment, religious policy, revival and renewal in house church community, TSPM churches and Roman Catholics, revival and renewal, etc. The resurrection of the Chinese Church, according to the Lambert, had much to do with the suffering just previous to it, namely the period dating back from the beginning of the Communist rule to the end of Cultural Revolution in 1976. This period of suffering endured by the church in China, according to Lambert was allowed by God for the purpose of refining believers through the test of fire. Despite the fact the visible church in China was totally destructed during the Cultural Revolution, the church in China came out stronger than ever.[68] Lambert is certain that the suffering of Christian believers as they shared the sufferings of the whole nation during the Cultural Revolution actually helped to remove the blockade against accepting Christianity in the minds of the Chinese people.[69]

In one of his later books, *China's Christian Millions: The Costly Revival*, Lambert (1999) identifies the contributions of many conservative evangelical missions and churches in laying a firm foundation for the Church in China. In many ways the conservative heritage has provided solid "theological underpinnings" for the house church movement. In other words, the house church movement remains firmly evangelical and conservative in theology to this day. On the part of the TSPM, a mixture of liberal and evangelical theology is taught at its seminaries. The liberal influence, according to Lambert, does not touch down significantly at the grass-roots.[70]

Lambert (1994) also notes in his study the situation among the house church community in central China: how house church Christians in these areas have been active in participating and operating extensive theological and biblical training courses. He is confident that this kind of training or theological education is decisive for the "future growth and maturity" of the Chinese Church.[71] For Lambert, the quality of theological training seems to hold the key to a more promising future of Christianity in China.

Kalun Leung

Leung's excellent study on the rural churches in China is reflected in his book *The Rural Churches in China since 1978*, in which he offers insightful observation on phenomenon of the growth of rural churches (including both the registered churches and the unregistered ones) in China since 1978. Rural churches, according to Leung, represent the mainstream of Chinese Christianity today.[72] To Leung, sinicization of Christianity among the rural believers who developed a Christianity with folk religious forms based on their own religious emotions and needs was the key to the acceptance of the Christian religion by the grass-root population. Leung is critical of historians on Chinese Church such as Tony Lambert and Jonathan Chao who attributed the phenomenal rural church growth in China since the 1980s to the foundation laid by the non-conformists of the 1950s such as Wang Mingdao, Allan Yuan, and others, who chose to persevere in faith and suffer for the Lord instead of compromising to the government and the TSPM.[73] Leung contends,

> Rural churches that started to emerge in the late 1960s had no direct relationship with these urban confessors and were not established by these church leaders who were still serving their prison terms; from the 1980s, rural churches as the "principle part" of the House Church have had little indirect influence from those confessors who are well-known overseas. Therefore, their suffering for the sake of the Lord had only minor relationship with the continuation of the Chinese Church.[74]

Leung was confident that the phenonmenal growth of the rural churches in the 1980s was basically a new faith movement, representing a brand new stage of the spread and development of Christianity in China.[75]

Out of many possible elements that contributed to the phenonmenal growth of the rural churches in China in the 1980s, Leung examines two important areas: the relationship between Christianity and Chinese folk religions, and the special environment of the rural society. First, Leung contends that since the establishment of the Communist regime, the government has been sparing great efforts to rid folk religions out of the Chinese soil, thus removed the biggest obstacle inhibiting the spread of Christianity among the grass-root rural population and provided space for Christianity to grow.[76] The failure of significant expansion of Christianity in China historically lies not in the doctrines and rituals of Christianity, but in the exclusiveness of Christianity, i.e. to accept Christianity meant to reject traditional ancestor worship and other folk religions. When folk religions were extinguished in rural China, people turned to Christianity as a substitute of their previous religion. Leung argues that Christianity in its simple form, such as rituals of worship, location of worship, etc., attracted rural folks who adopted the house church form of gathering without complicated religious systems and professional religious personnel so that all believers could participate.[77]

Second, Leung identifies several special advantages in the rural society that contributed to the growth of rural church in China in the 1980s: family influence, and ethical concern. On the one hand, Chinese rural society belongs to the homogeneous community that the sense of family and clan is strong among the rural folks, while in comparison, the concept of individuality is weak. And this provides opportunity for what Donald McGavran calls "group conversion." According to a certain statistics, "in the rural area, 57.7 percent of converts came to faith primarily because of family influence."[78] On the other hand, ethical concerns of Christianity occupy a significant position. Christians believe that by complying with the ethics one fulfills God's will in his/her life. Thus, rural churches lay much emphasis on the Ten Commandments and require believers to recite and comply.

From a sociological perspective, Leung probes deep into the phenomenal growth of rural churches in China since the 1980s. He is suspicious of the astronomic figures on the estimate of numbers of Christians in China, and discourages any romantic expectations on the house church movement that has been exaggerated and wishful. Leung is concerned with how Christianity continues to exist in the Chinese society, participating in and influencing public life such as culture and society.

David Aikman

Aikman's book, *Jesus in Beijing*, offers us very good overview of history and present situation of the church in China. His interviews cover a wide spectrum of Christian communities in China that lead his reader to an eye-opening experience of the life and ministry of the faithful in China. Aikman (2003) states at the beginning of his book, "From the grassroots of the peasantry to high within China's establishment, the country was being seeded with believing Christians...perhaps 7 to 8 percent of the country's 1.2 billion population."[80] Aikman's research covers Christian believers among government officials, entrepreneurs, actors, singers, Communist Party members, those serving in the army, students and scholars, workers and peasants, and political dissidents. Why has Christianity been growing in China? Aikman speculates that, first of all, the open-door policy and the economic growth since 1978 "combine to create an opportune atmosphere for the growth of Christianity in China both as a movement and as an ideology"; secondly, Christianity was able to fill in the "ideological vacuum left in society by the nationwide collapse of belief in Marxism-Leninism."[82]

Aikman also provides brief background information as to how some of the significant large house church networks got started as well as their leaders to whom Aikman shows much appreciation. He seems to be confident of the future of the Chinese Christianity and the role it is going to play in the Christendom worldwide, particularly how the Chinese Christians are to bring the gospel back to Jerusalem, which means to evangelize the Muslim world to the west of China.[82]

Paul Hattaway

As director of Asia Harvest, a ministry devoted to planting churches among unreached people groups throughout Asia, Paul Hattaway had intimate relationship with the house church community in China. In *Back to Jerusalem*, Paul Hattaway basically interviewed three of the influential house church leaders in China on the vision of bring the gospel back to Jerusalem. The book covers historical background as well as present progress in how to execute the vision. By interviewing these Christian leaders, Hattaway clarifies an issue that could be easily misunderstood. Back to Jerusalem "refers to a call from God for the Chinese church to preach the gospel and establish fellowships of believers in all the countries, cities, towns, and ethnic groups between China and Jerusalem."[83] And it represents "the present and future vision of the twenty-first-century Chinese church" (1). This vision both has its historical root in the 1940s when a small group of Christians at the Northwest Bible Institute felt called of God to carry the gospel "beyond their evangelistic outreach to Muslims, Buddhists, and scattered Chinese living in Gansu, Qinghai, and Ningxia provinces and to consecrate themselves to the vision of carry the Gospel outside China's borders into the Islamic world, all the way back to Jerusalem."[84] This vision was rekindled in the mid-1990s by house church Christians and has become a significant part of the ministry task for the house church community in China.

Peter Xu, leader of the WOL movement, was one of the interviewees of Hattaway's book, who now lives in the U.S., fully committed to mobilizing and strategizing for the Back to Jerusalem (BTJ) movement, a vision Xu felt God has put on his heart.[85]

Alan Hunter & Kim-Kwong Chan

The focus of Hunter and Chan in their co-authored book, *Protestantism in Contemporary China,* seems to be on the historical and socio-political implications in the development of the Protestant Christianity in China. They recognize the continuities in Chinese Christianity between the beginning and the end of the 20th century, and the "historical legacy" plays an important role in what the Christian church in China has become today.[86] "The current church is the outcome of a historical process, with roots in the missionary enterprise and the response of Chinese to that period of evangelism."[87] First, "the religious policies of the communist government followed on from those of its predecessors," which means the "absolute right to control religious organizations" on the part of the state. The response of the Christians in China was to retreat underground with a "conservative pietism" in their theological position, "consistent with ideas imported from pietist elements in western Christianity," but "accord well with the mainstream tradition of Chinese religiosity, whereby religion is firmly rooted in family worship and localized, well away from political concerns." Second, "the continuity in the location of Christian communities" is well manifested in the revivals in the 1980s, whereby many of the areas with concentrated missionary activities in the beginning of the 20th century such as Jiangsu, Zhejing and Fujian, are exactly where revivals took place. Third, Hunter and Chan also identify the influence of the early revivalists such as John Sung, Wang Mingdao, and Watchman Nee had on the present house church communities. For example, the emphasis on "spiritual matters" against "intellectual pursuits or social welfare," special emphasis on the "deadly power of personal sin," public confession of sins, more female participation in revivals, which provided them with "an outlet for their energies often denied by Chinese conventions," the tendency toward "sectarian, dogmatic and separatist," etc., are some of the continuities that are evident in the Chinese Christianity today.[88]

Hunter and Chan find that "revival meetings, a Pentecostal style of worship, healing and emotional forms of religious expression," which were marks of Chinese Christianity in the 1930s when there were much conversions and growth, continue to be responsible for the revivals in the 1980s. "People were attracted to this new religion which preached good conduct, promised fellowship with divinity, afforded healing and exorcism and offered forms of worship that could be corporate or individual according to circumstances," all of which are still "deep needs" of the Chinese people. House churches, the authors believe, are in a better position to fulfill such needs.[89]

In terms of indigenization, throughout the Chinese Church history there have been those who are more enthusiastic about it than others. As early as the 1920s some indigenous denominations started to emerge in reaction to the anti-Christian movement that swept the major cities of China. According to Hunter and Chan, this indigenization movement was necessary at this particular moment of Chinese history when the anti-Western feeling was high in China, and enabled Christian believers to reconcile with their fellow Chinese, which in turn led to more productive evangelistic efforts among the Chinese population. Among some of the largest indigenous groups of the time were the True Jesus Church, the Jesus Family, and the Little Flock.

Equally significant was the ministry of Wang Mingdao, one of the most powerful preachers and evangelists in the history of the Christianity in China. As early as the 1920s, Wang Mingdao voiced the need of an indigenous Christianity, recognizing that Western missionaries had become a liability to Christianity in China, and dependency and parasitism among Chinese pastors and church leaders were common. Wang's evangelistic preaching, together with the evangelistic work of other indigenous leaders such as John Sung, and Watchman Nee, brought important revivals in China since the 1920s.[90]

Hunter and Chan examine the socio-political context (from 1949 to 1993) that implicated the development of the Chinese Christianity. For the revivals of Christianity during the 1980s, social change played a significant role:

> The 1980s was a period of radical transition in the countryside, seeing the rebirth of family farming and a market economy, and at the same time a liberalization of political controls. The economic changes brought great prosperity to many, but also more uncertainty. Traditional rural isolation was increasingly broken as people traveled and traded far more, and there was greater contact with the outside world. There was perhaps a sense of loss of identity...At the same time there was far less rigid social control after the abolition of the People's Communes in 1979/80 and less pressure to display political conformity. In short, most families had more cash, more freedom to participate in religious activities, and also perhaps more anxieties which they needed to assuage.[91]

The relaxation and tightening of the CCP religious policies over the years, the authors observe, also significantly affected the Christian community in China. As a result, the majority part of the house church community today, the authors contend, in terms of its structure, "diffuse, spread through cities but more particularly through the countryside…with "local leadership structures and informal networks that seem to rise, fall and be replaced." [92]

Part Three: The Word of Life House Church Movement

As scarce as the writings on the WOL movement are, this part seeks to survey research done on the WOL community over the years. Although there has not been a comprehensive study of the WOL movement, the following survey covers authors who have written on different aspects of the WOL movement. Jonathan Chao and his Chinese Church Research Center (now China Ministries International) are among the chief contributors of research on the WOL community.

Jonathan Chao

In one of the chapters in his book *Purified by Fire: The Secrets of House Church Revivals in China*, Chao discusses the development of the house churches in central China.[93] Four articles (previously published in journals) are collected in this chapter, categorized under three headings: (1) The model of development of the house churches in central China (2) Understanding the "seminaries of the fields," and (3) Observation and analysis of the "Life Meeting" among churches in Mainland China.

In "model of development," Chao briefly introduces to the readers how the church in China experienced the stages of control, opposition, and destruction from 1949 to 1976, and how the house church network in central China (WOL) as a movement got started during the Cultural Revolution. The network started with a few itinerant evangelists who preached the gospel and established house churches in Henan, Shandong, and Anhui provinces. During the few years (1977–82) after the Cultural Revolution, the WOL experienced great revivals and grew rapidly into a significantly large network stretching out to several provinces. In order to prevent confusion and heresy, the WOL developed a "theology of the Cross," laid out in seven principles as the guiding principles of ministry.[94] In order to better facilitate ministry, the WOL also formed the basic structures to coordinate the work in different regions. The basic model of development for the WOL was a cycle of "four units": itinerant evangelism (the Gospel Band) → establishing churches → discipleship training → theological training.

One of the controversial aspects of the WOL has been its organized "Life Meetings," in which weeping was much emphasized as marks of rebirth. Some labeled the WOL as the "Weeping Sect" or "Born Again Sect." For this reason, Chao went into China for investigation, and came back with the analysis that was published in *China and the Gospel*.[95] Chao interviewed some thirty evangelists and believers of WOL on the issues involved in the "Life Meetings," and found that the so-called "Life Meetings" are actually revival meetings prepared for those seekers of Christian faith as well as those who came from Christian families and yet had not experienced being born again.[96] Weeping was common in such meetings because many who attended the meetings, under the illuminating of the Holy Spirit, realized the deprivation of sin as they engaged themselves in the four steps of repentance: counting sins, confessing sins, repentance of sins, and hating sins, all of which were elements of revivals led by John Sung in the 1930s. The teaching and preaching during those few days covered all the important elements in salvation theology including God's creation, human fall, sin and redemption, repentance, righteousness through faith, sanctification, Christ's second coming in glory. Chao affirms, in conclusion, that the "Life Meetings" in WOL were unique kind of evangelistic and revival meetings producing great result, imbuing new hope and life to rural China.[97]

China Ministries International (CMI)

In the mid-1980s Chinese Church Research Center (later renamed as China Ministries International) revealed to the outside world, for the first time, the theological, biblical, and evangelistic training that was going on among the house churches in central China, including the WOL church, the first of such organized training among the house church community in China. A team was sent to the underground training center, which was named Theological Education by the WOL, and reported by editors of Chinese Church Research Center (CCRC) as the "Seminaries of the Fields."[98]

According to the report, the "Seminaries of the Fields" emerged on the horizon of the China soil as a significant milestone of the Chinese church construction, which incorporated training, sending out evangelists, and establishing churches.[99] One seminary started in the middle of 1985, enlisting about 30 students for a three-month intensive training program and sending them out as evangelists when they graduated, which means, in one year up to the time of the report, this seminary had produced 120 evangelists who were then sent out. The report (1986 & 1987) covers such information as the entrance requirements for the students, the curriculum, timetables, process of training, the sending out of graduates, coworkers' (evangelists') manual, disciplines, evangelism, as well as the basic structure of the WOL.

In 1997, Peter Xu was arrested and sentenced to three years imprisonment. He was accused as the leader of a cult by the authorities and certain leader of the TSPM. China Ministries International convened a seminar titled "Orthodox, heresy, and religious policies of the CCP," to confront the issue. Papers presented in the seminar were then published in the journals *China and the Gospel* (in Chinese) and *China Prayer Letter and Ministry Report*.[100]

From the perspective of the religious policy of the Chinese government since the 1980s, Chao (1997) explains how the "cult" was defined according to the Chinese religious law and why Xu was regarded by the Chinese government as a cultic leader. According to "Document No. 19" issued by the government in 1982, any religious activities outside patriotic religious organizations such as the TSPM would be regarded as illegal. In this sense, it is only natural that Xu's church was condemned by the Religious Affairs Bureau as a "cultic organization and Peter Xu himself a "cultic leader." The arrest of Xu was only the execution of the religious policy of the Chinese government against the house churches.[101]

Ruizhen Wang

In a comparative study on the soteriology of the Word of Life church and that of the Westminster Confession of faith, Ruizhen Wang (1997) examines the content of one of the WOL manuals *Salvation through the Cross* in a systematic manner. According to Wang, *Salvation through the Cross* was the product of the WOL Christians in ministry. Wang identifies that the manual starts with God's creation, moves on to the Fall of human beings, and lays out God's salvation scheme which is treated in three parts: (1) the preparation of salvation, (2) the fulfillment of salvation, and (3) the execution of salvation.[102] In comparison, *Salvation through the Cross* does not cover as much ground as the Westminster Confession of Faith, but there is nothing heretical in it. Wang identifies the strength of the WOL manual as being "evangelical," "evangelistic," "systematic," and "practical" despite of some of the weaknesses such as "emotional," functional," and "fundamental."[103]

Gonghe Zhou

Zhou (1997) defends the WOL by analyzing Life Meeting and the training of the Messengers of the Gospel among the WOL. He contends that, as far as the content of preaching is concerned, WOL is not heretical as accused by some. However, problem arose from their practice when some MGs did insist on a standard of being born again, which depended on the extent one wept in the meeting.[104] In terms of training the MGs, Zhou (1997) critiques it as "too narrow" and "not encouraging self-reflection." The discipline revolving the training of MGs is also strict, to the extent that the freedom of marriage is strictly restrained. Many MGs did not have any chance to support or even visit their parents for years because of the fact that they had been sent to evangelize and establish churches far away from home.

Summary

The review of the relevant literature has helped in laying some foundational work in the description and analysis of the Word of Life movement from the perspective of renewal movements. First, through the survey of literature closely related to studies on renewal movements, it underscores the different aspects and disciplines involved in the study of renewal movement. While we can engage in the study of the life of the church from any of these angles, they seem to mutually complement one another when a renewal movement is evaluated as a living, organic, and dynamic Christian entity. Some of the models and theories, therefore, will be employed, in an auxiliary way, in addition to Snyder's mediating model for church renewal as the primary theoretical framework, in the analysis of the movement dynamics and in constructing a theology of renewal for the Chinese Church. Second, the review of the literature concerning Christianity in China in general as well as the WOL in particular provides relevant background information and support with regard to the interpretation and understanding of the research data on the WOL movement. The WOL movement is not an isolated phenomenon, but grew out of a context when the general health of the church in China was on the decline and in need of renewal. All of these are essential before we turn to the amazing story of the emergence, growth, dynamic, and impact of the WOL house church movement.

Notes

1. Thomas Rausch, *Radical Christian Communities* (Collegeville, MN: Liturgical Press, 1990), 12.

2. Ibid., 13.

3. Ibid.

4. Ibid., 188.

5. Ibid.

6. Snyder, *Signs of the Spirit* (Eugene, Oregon: Wipf and Stock, 1997), 10.

7. Ibid., 245–53.

8. Ibid., 251–52.

9. Richard Lovelace, *Dynamics of Spiritual Life* (Downers Grove, Illinois: Inter-Varsity Press, 1979), 97.

10. Ibid.

11. Ibid., 95.

12. Ibid., 145.

13. Ibid., 161–63.

14. Charles Grandison Finney, *Lectures on Revivals of Religion*, edited by William G Mcloughlin (Cambridge, Massachusetts: The Belknap Press of Harvard University Press, 1960), 9.

15. Ibid., 9–10.

16. Ibid., 16.

17. Ibid., 18.

18. Ibid., 21.

19. Ibid., 12–13.

20. Ibid., 269.

21. Ibid., 272.

22. Richard Riss, *A Survey of 20th Century Revival Movements in North America* (Peabody, Mass: Hendrickson Publishers, 1988).

23. Ibid., 3–7.

24. Cf. Snyder, *Signs of the Spirit*, 43.

25. J. Edwin Orr, *Evangelical Awakening in Africa* (Minneapolis, Minnesota: Bethany Fellowship, Inc., 1975), vii.

26. Ibid., vii–viii.

27. William McLoughlin, *Revivals, Awakenings, and Reform: An Essay on Religion and Social Change in America, 1607–1977* (Chicago, Illinois: The University of Chicago Press, 1978), 2.

28. Ibid., 8.

29. Ibid., 10.

30. Charles Kraft, *Christianity in Culture* (Maryknoll, New York: Orbis Books, 1979), 371.

31. Ibid.

32. Ibid., 373–75.

33. Anthony Wallace, "Revitalization Movements," *American Anthropologist* 58 (April 1956): 265.

34. Ibid., 267.

35. Ibid., 267–68.

36. Donald Durnbaugh, *The Believers' Church* (New York, New York: The Macmillan Company, 1968), 33.

37. Ibid., 32–33.

38. As quoted in Durnbaugh, *The Believers' Church*, 210.

39. Durnbaugh, *The Believers' Church*, 212.

40. Ibid., 218–20.

41. Ibid., 233.

42. Ibid., 235.

43. Gregory Leffel, *Faith Seeking Action* (Lanham, Maryland: Scarecrow Press, Inc., 2007), 59.

44. Ibid.

45. Ibid., 59–60.

46. Ibid., 60.

47. Ibid.

48. Ibid., 61.

49. Ibid.

50. Luther Gerlach and Virginia Hine, *People, Power, Change* (Indianapolis: Bobbs-Merrill, 1970), xvi.

51. Ibid., xv.

52. Ibid., xviii–xix.

53. Ibid., 199.

54. Ibid.

55. Ibid., 217.

56. Donald McGovran, *The Bridges of God* (London: World Dominion Press, 1955), 23.

57. Ibid., 87–92.

58. Ibid., 96.

59. Ibid., 97.

60. Cf. Jonathan Chao and Wanfang Zhuang, *Dang dai zhongguo ji du jiao fa zhan shi, 1949–1997* (A History of Christianity in Socialist China, 1949–1997) (Taipei: CMI Press, 1997), vii–xvii.

61. Jonathan Chao, *Ling huo cui lian* (Purified by Fire) (Taipei: CMI Press, 1993), 29–32.

62. Jonathan Chao, *Fu wo qian xing* (Lead Me to Go Forward) (Taipei: CMI Press, 1993), 9–70.

63. Jonathan Chao, *Xin jin huo chuan* (The Undying Fire of the Burning Branches) (Taipei: CMI Press, 2005), 44–47.

64. Ibid., 48–49.

65. Ibid., 56–57.

66. Ibid., 64.

67. Chao, *Purified by Fire*, 4, translated from Chinese by author.

68. Tony Lambert, *The Resurrection of the Chinese Church* (Wheaton, Illinois: OMF IHQ, Ltd., 1994), 11–12.

69. Ibid.

70. Tony Lambert, *China's Christian Millions* (London, UK: Monarch Books, 1999), 48.

71. Ibid., 138.

72. Kalun Leung, *Gai ge kai fang yi lai de zhongguo nong cun jiao hui* (The Rural Churches of Mainland China since 1978) (Hong Kong: Alliance Bible Seminary, 1999), 20.

73. Ibid., 25–26.

74. Ibid., 28.

75. Ibid., 30.

76. Ibid., 216.

77. Ibid., 223–25.

78. As quoted in Leung, *The Rural Churches of Mainland China Since 1978*, 229.

79. Leung, *The Rural Churches of Mainland China Since 1978*, 233–34.

80. David Aikman, *Jesus in Beijing* (Washington, D.C.:Regnery Publishing, Inc., 2003), 8.

81. Ibid., 13–17.

82. Ibid., 12.

83. Paul Hattaway, *Back to Jerusalem* (Carlisle, UK: Piquant, 2003), x.

84. Ibid., 23.

85. Cf. Hattaway, *Back to Jerusalem*, 69.

86. Alan Hunter and Kim Kwong Chan, *Protestantism in Contemporary China* (Cambridge, UK: Cambridge University Press, 1993), 135.

87. Ibid., 19.

88. Ibid., 126–37.

89. Ibid., 140.

90. Ibid., 129.

91. Ibid., 5–6.

92. Ibid., 64–65.

93. Although there are several significantly large house church groups or networks in central China, they were one 'family' in the 1970s and early 1980s, and then split into several groups because of denominational influence that came into China at the time. These house church groups, however, continue to share some of their basic structures and training systems. Chao's research may not be limited to the WOL church itself, but this chapter weighs heavily toward observations on the WOL.

94. Chao, *Purified by Fire*, 62–65.

95. For details analysis of the "Life Meetings" in the WOL community, see *China and the Gospel* 92 (1992):11–15.

96. Chao, *Purified by Fire*, 115–16.

97. Ibid., 116–26.

98. For a detailed account of the operation of the "Seminaries of the Fields," refer to *China and the Gospel* 57 (1986): 13.

99. CCRC, "Seminaries of the Fields," *China and the Gospel* 57 (1986): 13.

100 . Details of the seminar report can be found in *China and the Gospel* 21–22 (1997–1998).

101. Chao, "Cong dang qian de zhong gong zong jiao zhengce ji fa zhi kan xu yong ze shi jian" (The Arrest of Yongze Xu from the Perspective of Contemporary Religious

Policy and Legal System of the Chinese government), *China and the Gospel* 21–22 (1997–98): 11.

102. Ruizhen Wang, "Chong sheng pai de jiu en lun" (The Soteriology of the Born Again Community in China), *China and the Gospel* 21–22 (1997–98): 18.

103. Ibid., 20.

104. Gonghe Zhou, "Chong sheng pai shi fao yi duan?" (Is Born-again Group Cult?) *China and the Gospel* 21–22 (1997–98): 25.

Chapter 3°

A History of the Word of Life Movement

Peter Xu has been with the Word of Life movement since the beginning and has been the recognized leader of WOL over the years. In order to trace back into the history of the Word of Life movement, it is helpful to follow the storyline of its leader, from whose experience of walking with Jesus we enter into the story of how the Spirit of God has led the Word of Life church and how Christians of the Word of Life church have responded to the guidance of the Spirit of God during the past three decades.

Preparatory Stage

This section examines the earlier stage of Peter Xu's life and ministry before he became the recognized leader of the WOL house church movement. Family influence is an integral part of what made Peter to be who he is. Therefore this section first of all provides a picture of how Peter was brought up in the family and how the experience of his childhood has had great impact for his life. As the story unfolds, the hand of God in the life of Peter becomes clearly visible. Through the prayers of Peter's family, the opposition of the hostile environment, and willingness of Peter to follow him, God led Peter onto a journey with him—a journey of an evangelist, in this earlier stage of his ministry, who established and connected house churches.

Family Influence

Peter Xu was born in a Christian family in Henan in 1940. His grandparents and parents were all Christians. Lacking male descendents in the family at the time when Peter's parents were married, Peter's grandmother prayed to God for a grandson. Her prayer was answered and Peter was born into the family as his parents' first-born. Wrapping Peter in white cloth, Peter's grandmother dedicated him to God: "I dedicate this baby to the Lord Jesus, and through Jesus as the mediator to the LORD. This baby is the baby of the LORD." Peter Xu stated with gratitude, "God listened to my grandmother's prayer and has kept me for the past 64 years. I have never left the LORD."[1]

In sharing memories about the influence of his grandmother, Peter Xu was full of respect,

> She was the Abraham of our family, living as a witness for God. She was well respected in the world around her. Every night she would lead the whole family to kneel down and pray to God. Sometimes I prayed until I fell asleep. And my grandmother would always end our prayers with the following hymn: "I now lie down to sleep peacefully. Pray that our heavenly Father will sustain me until morning. If I am called to leave this world tonight, please save me to return to your paradise." Every morning when she woke up, she would begin the day with prayer. And prayer accompanied her throughout the day: when she was walking, she prayed that "my feet will walk in the truth of your word"; when she washed her face, "water cleanses the face, and blood cleanses the heart. Worshipping the true God, I am cleansed inside out"; when she swept the floor, "cleanse my heart of all filth"; when cooking, "fuel my spiritual fire." All day long I heard her call on the name of the Lord. And she did so all her life.[2]

According to Peter's grandmother, it was Norwegian Lutheran missionaries who brought the gospel to the inland area where her family was. Some of her family members became Christians through the evangelism of the Norwegian missionaries including Peter's grandmother and her brother who later became a missionary with the Norwegian Lutheran Mission.

Having grown up in such a Christian family, Peter's whole being was immersed in the Word of God, prayer, and worship. Every evening there was family worship in his home. Peter recalled how he would stand by the door and watched his mother read the Bible, his uncle and his family sing hymns, and his grandmother's brother preached from the Word of God. Peter thus cultivated a heart of trusting and fearing God from an early age.

One day in 1945 when Peter was only five, he saw a vision as he stood in the shallow river. In the vision he saw the sky opened and God in three persons appeared with books like the Bible. Peter did not understand the meaning of the vision then, but was in awe: "I felt like a light shining down from heaven all over me like a cascade." Later when he read from Ezekiel, he was convinced that the vision was from God and for a purpose in his life.[3]

From then on Peter developed in his heart a desire to preach the gospel. He said,

> Even when I was only six years old, God put this burden into my heart—to share the gospel to the kids in the neighborhood and school. I was, however, the introvert kind in nature and timid and did not have the courage to do so. Many times I had desire to share the gospel with one of my classmates, and yet courage betrayed me. Later, this classmate of mine became sick, and I never saw him again. Until this day, I felt deeply indebted toward him, owing him the debt of the gospel.[4]

As the leader of the WOL church that was often referred to by others as the Born Again Family, Peter's experience of being born again cannot be separated with the way that he was brought up in his family through family worship, Bible stories, and hymn singing. As one of the hymns says:

There is only one true God who is the Lord of heavens and earth.
He provides me with food to eat, clothes to wear, and blessings.
There is only one Savior who can forgive my sins.
So I rely on him and follow his words until the end of the time.

There is only one Holy Spirit who convicts me of my sins.
He helps me, comforts me, and reminds me of my guilt.
With the Holy Spirit in my heart, I am full of the love of the Lord.
And the Spirit encourages me to live for the Lord until he comes again.[5]

Hymns like this narrate succinctly and clearly the triune God, salvation through Jesus Christ, sanctification, and other theological tenants. Being imbued in such environment for such a long time, Peter came to the understanding of the love of God, the sinful nature of human beings and his own sins, and necessity of salvation through Jesus Christ. He was born again.

In 1949 the Communist Party defeated the Nationalist Party after a three-year Civil War, establishing the People's Republic of China with a one-party rule, the Chinese Communist Party. Under the new regime, all religious beliefs were regarded as counter-revolutionary, backward, and superstitious, and therefore needed to be restrained, and eventually displaced. The formation of the TSPM in the early 1950s served exactly that purpose in the perspective of the new government. All Christians were called upon to join the TSPM. Those who refused to join became in opposition to both the TSPM and the Chinese government, and therefore were subject to persecution.

Then, from 1958, when the government initiated the "Great Leap Forward" campaign,[6] to 1964, when the "Four Cleansing" campaign was in full swing throughout the country,[7] Christian churches, both urban and rural, were gradually forced to close. In 1966, the Cultural Revolution was launched that threw the whole country in turmoil.

With one political movement after another, each incurring more damage to the Christian church, the opposition became so violent that few dared to openly confess that Jesus was Lord and Savior. As a young man at the time, Peter had to face his own internal struggle over what was happening. Discouraged and bewildered, he would often recall the vision he saw when he was only five, and weep before God: "If all the people in the whole wide world do not believe in you, I ask that you forgive them. If I deny you, then my sins will not be forgiven, because you yourself appeared to me and let me have the opportunity to witness your holy Trinity. You are so real."[8]

Onto the Route of a Missionary

In 1960, at the age of 20, Peter was accepted to study at a vocational school in D City, Shanxi province. In D City, he went to the local TSPM church for fellowship and worship. He also influenced fellow students to join him for discussions about the Bible and Christianity. Because of these involvements, Peter became a target in a series of political movements later on. In the "Four Cleansing" campaign in 1963, he was restrained of his freedom for forty days and refuted daily at meetings. During this time of detention, Peter prayed earnestly and confirmed God's calling to him, that is, to leave everything behind and follow Jesus. He was released just before Christmas and returned home.

In 1967, Peter and his wife left D City where they had lived for eight years and started "a life in exile" following the will of God. This was the beginning of Peter's missionary journey.[9]

At that time, the government was very strict in managing and controlling the so-called "floating population."[10] When Peter left his work in D City, he actually "joined" the "floating population" becoming a person without proper legal identification, registration, and no right to get access to allocated food.[11] Worst of all, Peter's previous work unit reported him as a counter-revolutionary, and he literally became a criminal wanted by law all over the country!

During that same period of time, Peter's father was also forced to leave where he had been working at the Agricultural Department, and, together with the rest of the family, moved about to find jobs such as making bricks in order to make a living. But wherever they went, there was the church. They started house church gatherings and led people to Christ. Among the floating population there were also Christians, who heard and found the house church gathering at Peter's parents' temporary dwelling place. In 1968 Peter was able to join with his parents briefly with his wife and two daughters in Hubei, only to find that his parents' place had already become a regular meeting point for Christians, entertaining a sizable floating population. During that brief period of time Peter and his two sisters started to go out and share the gospel.

However, in May 1968, the local government started to arrest the "floating population" because of social unrest caused by them. Therefore, all the floating population started to scatter around, and became what was called by the police "criminals at large." Peter's family was also forced to leave where they were to find a safer place to stay, and they moved around for about two months before they could find another opportunity to work—to blow up the hills for stones for the local agricultural bureau. So they settled down again. When fellow Christians heard about it, they came to join them. The work started there, and the house church meetings continued.

Later, personnel from the Special Crime Department of the revolutionary committee came to arrest Peter. Luckily he was informed about it earlier, and so he got away and stayed at Y County about thirty miles away. From that time on, for twenty-three years from 1968 to 1991, Peter had not been able to see his family.

Later Peter learned that all his family members had been taken and sent back to Henan to be restricted. Peter was in exile again. He had to run from police constantly and sometimes he had to hide in mountains and caves for weeks. How he longed for somebody to greet him with some comforting words such as "the peace of the Lord be with you," and welcome him into his home even to be able sleep on the straws in the kitchen for a night! "God was my only support. When I totally depended on him, miraculous things happened. In situations such as when I was chased by the police and there was no way out, God opened a safe passage for me. I witnessed the faithfulness and wondrous acts of God, his love, and his concern even for me."[12]

Establishing House Churches

In 1971, the Lord led Peter to N County, Hunan Province. As he was strolling on the hill one evening, he came across a tombstone with a Christian inscription on it. His heart was stirred for he knew that God had comforted him through this tombstone, knowing that he was lonely, and had led him here for a purpose. "If the remains of Christian believers were buried here, Christian descendants should still be in the area."[13]

Peter eventually got in touch with the owner of the tomb, a senior Christian, Brother D. On a Christmas day, Peter and Brother D met and celebrated together as they recalled God's grace to them, and they repented to God for their weaknesses and sins. "With the Spirit working mightily that night, we wept heartedly together." Brother D confessed: "I was a born again believer and God's servant. But now, I dare not even mention God's name." After that night, his life changed completely. He would start every morning with hymn singing.[14]

Brother D had hidden some Christian literature and Bibles in the wall of the pigsty. He and Peter decided to dig them out. So now they had a Chinese Bible, an English Bible, a hymnal, and a concordance Bible! That was the first time in a long time that Peter was able to read from the Bible.

Brother D introduced Peter to the local believers and some former leaders and coworkers of the local church. In fellowship with these Christians Peter learned that the church was established through the evangelistic ministry of some American Methodist missionaries. Brother D was converted and were later sent to study at a seminary in Hunan, and became the minister of the church upon completion of his seminary studies.

Peter praised God for leading him into the midst of such people. He was able to enjoy close fellowship with ministers and coworkers in X county and N county. House churches were established there and, for the next few months, Peter and the local Christians met frequently for worship, communion, and fellowship.[15]

At the end of 1971, Peter was picked up by police and put into prison. He trusted that God had a good purpose in putting him to the test yet once again and affirmed to God in prayer that he would follow God to the end even though he had to go through all these trials. In prison, Peter was able to witness to other detainees by sharing with them his portion of food and water, and he made use every opportunity to share the gospel among those detainees.[16]

Peter learned many spiritual lessons through this experience of imprisonment. On one occasion he prayed to God for release, trusting that the God who was able to miraculously release Paul, Silas, and Peter from imprisonment could also release him as well. When the opportune moment came (that the chains locking the jail gates became loose), Peter was so taken back that he was not able to gather himself together to action. To Peter this was God's miraculous provision which he failed to embrace in faith. He was eventually able to escape in a foggy morning when an opportunity arose. Peter's faith grew significantly after this experience in prison, and he trusted that God had already had him in his divine plan and was with him all the time.[17]

Revival Stage

The revival stage covers roughly from the early 1970s to the beginning of the 1980s. During this period, the Cultural Revolution was to gradually fade out from the China scene, which means less opposition on religious activities, and revivals broke out in many rural areas of Henan. Peter Xu was able to make more frequent itinerant visit to the house churches established and became instrumental in the revivals. He was also respected and loved by believers for his diligent work in the Lord. At the end of this stage, Peter's leadership position became naturally established among his fellowship coworkers.[18]

God's Furnaces of Revival

The rest of Peter's family (his wife, three children, parents and siblings) after being sent back to their hometown in the south of Henan settled down and continued to be a witness for God. In China in the early 1970s, although the worst of the Cultural Revolution was almost over, life was still anything but better. The economy was in total chaos, education was devalued, and rural people lived on the margins of the chaotic Chinese society. And yet in their midst people saw a family like Peter's, a family full of joy and goodness. Especially the example of Peter's younger sister Deborah Xu, who willingly took over the burden of supporting the family, including her nieces and nephews, attracted many ladies in the neighborhood, who often came to her for advice. Deborah took the opportunity, helping them in whatever way available and sharing the gospel with them.[19]

Soon, house church meetings became regular in Peter's house. Both Deborah and Peter's mother were involved in teaching these sisters about the Bible and leading them to live a life of faith in the Lord. Together they studied the Bible and prayed to God in unity. Because most coming to the meetings were young women, the house church did not produce suspicion. Very soon, the gospel was shared among the young people in the neighborhood and the house could no longer accommodate the influx of young people. Some of the believing neighbors opened their houses as "hospitality family"—a term commonly used among the house churches in central China referring to devoted Christian family that opens their house or other properties for the purpose of holding various house church meetings, trainings, and receiving coworkers, etc.

By the mid-1970s, Chairman Mao had died, members of the "Gang of Four" were arrested, and the Cultural Revolution was pronounced over. There was suddenly relaxation in the restrained atmosphere over the Chinese society. House church meetings in southern Henan area turned from clandestine to open. People could gather together to worship and praise God without much interference from the neighborhood and the local government. Peter's house and its surroundings were like a "revival furnace,"[20] drawing people to gather around "fire." Within months, the whole neighborhood became Christian and became a spiritual center. Without notice, the "revival furnace" spread outward and more "furnaces" were created. God worked wondrously. The gospel spread from family to family, neighborhood to neighborhood, region to region. Every Sunday, even the students in primary schools came to join the worship meeting, singing hymns and praying together.

When asked about his role in the revivals during this period in the early 70s, Peter stated,

> The Spirit of God inspired his followers to form such a 'revival furnace' in different areas of China. My family was one of them. Those who withstood the trials became the lights in the darkness, and stars at night. When people had lost all hopes with the country, society, family, individual, and life itself, the witness of the Christians, who suffered no less and endured no less pressure than others and yet appeared so joyful and full of life, made them pause and turn their heads.[21]

Witnessing the Spirit of God working so mightily in China, Peter went from one "revival furnace" to another. These "revival furnaces" were separate from one another and there were no connections between them except through Peter's visits. "At times when it was extremely difficult to connect with fellow Christians, "revival furnaces" did not have "horizontal" relationships with each other. Their relationship was "vertical," with God, and independent. Peter says, "Because I was a 'wanderer' who had no home to return to, I became a connector and a seeker." Peter believed it was God who released him from the worldly restraint by means of opposition from the authorities, so that, as a "criminal wanted by law," he totally devoted himself to the work evangelism wherever he had to go. And this was exactly what he had hoped for, waited for, and sought after. "I therefore went from one 'revival furnace' to another, connecting the individual 'furnaces' into lines, forming small areas of house churches, and eventually into big areas of house churches. This was how I see God used me during the 1970s."[22] This experience also helped Peter understand the importance of interlink and fellowship within the body—one of the principles of in the WOL theology that was to be formulated later in the 80s.

Emergence of a Leader

Because of Peter's Christian background and experience in ministry, he was well received and respected wherever he went. Also because of the suffering and loneliness that Peter and other believers had experienced, they would often weep in love and spirit when parts of the same body were reconnected, a feature that is still recognizable in the WOL community today. And so he went, continuously, from one "furnace" to another. The preaching and teaching of this period of time focused on salvation through the cross, how to reject evil and live a new life in Christ, willing to suffer and witness for the Lord, and some basic doctrinal truth.[23] Other times the gatherings were simply prayers and testimonies of God's miraculous deliverance and power in the life of these Christians. Over time, some young believers would follow Peter wherever he went. So, some twenty to thirty people walked together from meeting to meeting. "It was like a fire burning wherever we went," one coworker recalled.[24]

Once, Peter and his coworkers arrived at a place where a small-scale meeting was already going on. When brothers and sisters heard that Peter had just arrived, they quickly spread the news and people started to come in hundreds. "This was the work of the Holy Spirit who pressed on believers the eagerness to meet brothers and sisters in the Lord, to have fellowship, to listen to the Word of God read, and to gather together. Like gathering wood around a fire, the more the people gathered around, the bigger the fire, and the more heat it produced."[25]

That gathering was in the mountain area in the west of Henan. People came from all directions, with some even from more than ten miles away. Some people hurried toward the meeting place after work and only got there at midnight. It was in an open outdoor space outside a hospitality family's house. Peter preached for five straight days and nights until his lips and tongue started to bleed. When in the middle of the meeting there started a sudden shower of rain, Peter had hoped that they would call off the meeting for a while because he was totally exhausted. People, however, went to cut branches from trees to make a temporary tent. Then the rain stopped, and Peter saw lights in the distance, which meant more people were coming to the meeting! How could he stop and rest? Peter continued preaching throughout the night, totally submitting himself to the Lord, who gave fresh strength and sustained him. Peter rendered all glory to God:

> The Holy Spirit worked mightily, imprinting His own word on the hearts of the people, who, when understanding the love of God in Jesus and seeing the sins of their own, wept heartily, confessing their sins, and repented. When they wept, we leaders went to kneel beside them and see how the Holy Spirit was moving them, for example, when they felt the love of God and their own sinful nature, we reminded them the work of Christ on the Cross and declared to them God's forgiveness of sin. When they received the confirmation of their sins being forgiven in the Word of God through our declaration, they were comforted in the heart through the work of the Holy Spirit. Together we witnessed the work

and power of the Holy Spirit, delivering many and giving them peace, joy and comfort.[26]

On another occasion in the beginning of 1980s, Peter and his coworkers preached for thirteen consecutive days and nights without sleep. Brother Yun was also with Peter Xu at the time.[27] Why didn't they sleep for thirteen days and nights? This is what happened: they went to a meeting place in the morning. After breakfast, during which people started to gather, they began to preach; after preaching, they ministered to the people according to needs. Through the work of the Holy Spirit, some were saved (others were already saved), and were baptized in the river or pond at dark (for sake of safety). This was followed by the breaking of the bread and sharing of the cup (communion) deep into the night. And before daybreak, Peter's team had to move to another location to continue another revival meeting. And the procedure was about the same as above. Every day there were at least several scores to over a hundred people being baptized, and this continued for thirteen days and nights.[28]

Sometimes, Peter would send some of his coworkers on itinerant visitation and evangelism. These workers engaged themselves in teaching, encouraging, comforting, and evangelizing. In the process, devoted Christians among house churches in various areas were selected as either elders (and teachers) of the local house churches, or as itinerant evangelists. Other times, Peter would take his coworkers along in his itinerary visitation. This form of evangelism and establishing house churches was not limited to WOL in Henan, though. It was a fairly common practice among other house church groups in Shandong, Hebei and Anhui.[29]

Organizational Stage

It was only natural that, when revivals after revivals brought so many new house churches into being, leaders of the WOL church started to think about how to administer the word of God to the new believers. How the church could effectively train and equip workers needed for the task was no doubt a big challenge. We should not forget that the unfavorable environment in which the WOL church was operating its ministries.

This section delineates how the WOL community identified the need for theological training, how the WOL theology was formed, and how the underground seminaries were established.

Need for Spiritual Food

Throughout the 1970s, Peter was led by the Holy Spirit to various places to preach the gospel. He was instrumental in bringing many revivals in central China regions, particularly in Henan Province. Hundreds of 'furnaces of revival" were connected and many more were established. The number of people at each "revival furnace" grew rapidly over a short period of time. Often when after some time Peter had made a circle in his itinerary and come back to the ones he visited or established, the number of people had already doubled or tripled.

Toward the beginning of 1980s, however, while "furnaces of revival" continued to multiply, Peter was startled by a phenomenon, which he phrased as, "one group rose up, another fell down." The fact was that house churches were constantly filled with new faces that did not stay. At coworkers' meetings there was a common saying describing the problem: "The sick were healed, and demons were driven out, and that was the end of it." This had to do with the lack of solid follow-up and discipleship among the established house churches. Many new believers' faith stayed at the level of healing the sick and driving out the demons. This kind of problem existed in many places for some time.[30]

Peter and his coworkers wept and prayed before God, and found comfort in the Word of God: "Can a woman forget her sucking child, that she should not have compassion on the son of her womb? yea, they may forget, yet will not I forget thee."[31] They felt also reminded of their responsibilities as leaders of the church. Peter reflected,

> The church did not allocate food to her family in time. As a result, her family were not supplied and the children became weak with hunger. And yet they were hungry not because of lack of bread, thirsty not because of lack of water, but because of the lack of the words of the Lord. If a woman could only give birth to sons and daughters and was not able to feed them, she failed to fulfill her responsibilities. In the same way, if the church could not supply sufficient spiritual food to its members, it also failed to fulfill its role. Who was the church? We were! So the responsibility lay on our shoulders. This helped us to understand the importance of the ministry of training workers for the Kingdom.[32]

Then in 1982 the first house church general conference was convened by Peter and his coworkers in S.Z., Henan Province.[33] Peter presided over the conference, with leaders and co-workers from various parts of Henan and neighboring provinces present in this special meeting that, they believed, was convened by the Holy Spirit. In this conference, coworkers reflected as a community on the phenomenon of seemingly shallow faith foundations in the house churches and realized training of workers was badly needed.

This first conference was followed by the second one the next year in S.C., Henan. At the end of the second house church conference, a memorandum titled "General Guidelines of the House Church" was drafted, in which leaders particularly filled the blanks in the area of training workers and providing spiritual nourishment to members of the church. However, the issue at stake was: Who was qualified to shoulder the task of training workers?

The house churches in Henan up to the mid-1980s were one big family. There was no name given to this house church family. They were simply referred to as house churches, or, sometimes, by locations, such as the house churches in Fangcheng. Peter was the recognized senior leader, together with other regional elders and coworkers forming the inner leadership circle where general direction and coordination of ministry was dissipated. Although in the mid 1980s several regional elders and coworkers localized some of the house churches under their supervision when they embraced some denominational emphasis brought in by certain overseas evangelists, thus causing a split in the Henan-centered house church family, the WOL church was coming to form in the beginning of 1980s.

In 1982, the WOL church selected seventeen evangelists, who were then designated as "Messengers of the Gospel (MGs), and sent them out for trans-provincial mission to Sichuan province, home to Deng Xiaoping, leader of the CCP.[34] This may have been the first trans-provincial mission team sent from the house churches in China. In less than a month, sixteen churches were established.[35] The mission, however, ended in the arrest of all seventeen MGs who were sent back to detention in Henan. Peter was arrested in the same incident and was jailed for 100 days, while others served terms of different lengths. Before the Chinese New Year in 1983, however, they were all somehow released. Upon release, they came together for fellowship and reflection, and felt God was teaching them the spiritual value and significance of service and ministry in the Lord by means of chains and imprisonment. "Our faith increased because the mark of the cross, which we saw as a reward, was added onto our physical bodies. And the Macedonian call became louder to our ears."[36] Since then evangelistic teams were dispatched back to Sichuan on many occasions.

Leadership Issues

Peter's leadership position was recognized and supported quite naturally over the years of his faithful ministry in Henan and other provinces. In the late 1970s and beginning of 1980s, however, his leadership was more distinctly recognized among his group and others. Peter himself humbly explained,

> When in 1983 I was released from prison after the Sichuan mission trip, all the released MGs had become full-time workers of the Gospel. I myself was a full-time servant of God and was a constant target of the police and therefore stayed in places not known to many. Wherever I was, I was like a centre sustained by God. The seventeen MGs became the inner circle where decisions were made on various aspects of ministry through prayer and fellowship.[37]

Brother Yun regards Peter as the most respected leader of the house churches in China and was willingly abiding whatever ministry Peter assigned him in the Lord.

> When, in fasting and prayer, I received calling from God to take the gospel to the southwest part of China and be a witness for the name of the Lord, I went to see Peter and other coworkers for confirmation and blessing. Peter led the reading of the Word of God in Acts 6 and prayed for me, confirming that it was the will of God that I went to the west of China to start evangelistic and training work because house churches in Shaanxi (west of China) had just sent requests to Peter for help.[38]

In decision making, however, leaders of WOL tried to follow the model of the Jerusalem conference recorded in Acts 15, with consideration given to Chinese cultural traditions. Although, as Brother Yun recalls, Peter was very solid on principles, he always respected and was ready to accept better suggestions from his coworkers.[39] Peter explains,

> We engaged in prayer, fellowship, self-examination, and seeking together. It was not one man's words that decided. We sought to be one in intention, one in love, one in will, and one in the Spirit and spoke the same words, so that we shared visions as one body. And we recognized that we were all saved saints, kings, priests, and prophets. With each standing in the proper position given from God, respecting one another, ministering in order and in the order of the Spirit. Of course, the young needed to respect the old, juniors respect seniors. This, however, should not prevent the young from speaking the truth which all believers should respect.[40]

Influence of First Generation Church Leaders

Leaders of WOL were very appreciative of the rich Christian heritage they received from the first generation Christian leaders such as Wang Mingdao, Watchman Nee, Jia Yuming, and John Sung, primarily in forms of the books and articles first generation Christian leaders left or testimonies and witnesses of their ministry.

> History did not create the best opportunity for us to interact with the first generation leaders directly and inherit from them. We, however, learned from John Sung's emphasis on confession of sins, repentance, born again, salvation, transformation of life, and manifestation of the power of the new life. Wang Mingdao also emphasized the experience of being born again and living a vitorious life style. Then there was Jia Yuming whose Systematic Theology from which we benefited.[41]

Not only the Chinese Christian leaders, but also revivalists such as Charles Finney were also regarded as forerunners of revivals in China. There among Christian believers were a few of Finney's books after 1949 which they copied with their hands and transmitted the copies among themselves. Since the beginning of 1980s, Deng Xiaoping, new leader of China at the time, introduced an open-door policy, encouraging overseas investors and tourists to visit China, and promoted economic reform. Suddenly there was a lot of international traffic through China, which made it possible for some Christian literature to get into the hands of Chinese believers. One former MG said,

> We learned from Finney the way he handled revival meetings, when through vigorous preaching of sin, he held seekers from letting out their emotions until they all reached home and prayed before God. In this way Finney's revivals touched many cities in the U.S. Likewise, the work of the Holy Spirit in China resembled of that in the U.S. during Finney's time. We inherited from the legacy of Marie Monsen, the Norwegian missionary sister, who led revival

meetings and preached with great emotion and compassion the devastation of sin and emphasized the need for repentance of sin and being born again.[42]

Marie Monsen was often mentioned whenever WOL coworkers talked about the influence from their forerunners. She was based in Nanyang district for a significant period of time of her mission, leading revival meetings, teaching at Bible studies and discipling believers. Stories about her ministry and life testimonies, especially how she was miraculously delivered countless times from dangerous situations of brigandage and war, continued to be an encouragement to Christians in WOL and Henan in general. One of her favorite scriptural verses was Psalm 46:1: God is our refuge and strength, a very present help in trouble.[43]

Formation of the WOL Theology—*The Seven Principles*

In 1983 leaders of WOL had their first retreat for seven consecutive days. During the retreat, they meditated on the Word of God together and discussed issues that surfaced from ministry. There had been cases that some of the WOL preachers' teaching were faulty and biased which caused a lot of problems in ministry and criticism from other Christian groups. Leaders of WOL felt that a training manual was needed that integrated theological education with spiritual practice in ministry. Therefore, according to the spiritual needs as they perceived from practice in ministry, leaders of WOL decided on the following seven principles to be taught and focused in theological education:

1. *Salvation through the cross.* This is foundational in establishing a solid Christian faith when one starts with the issues revolving the fall of man, and God's eternal salvation plan through faith in Jesus Christ. Based on the Bible, this principle explores such areas as creation by God, the fall of humans, and the redemption of Jesus Christ on the cross. The emphasis is on the birth, ministry, death, burial, resurrection, ascension and second coming of Jesus Christ.

2. *The way of the cross.* When a person is born again, he is to deny himself and follow the Lord on the way of the cross. As a disciple of the Lord, he is to be willing to suffer with the Lord, taking suffering as a shield and overcoming it by the Lord, so that the salvation of the Lord will be preached.

3. *Discerning the adulteress.* All coworkers and evangelists are to clearly discern that the TSPM does not represent the true church. In fact, it is an adulterous political organism serving for the benefit of atheism. Believers are not to be fooled by the TSPM. As members of the Body of Christ, believers are to live a life of purity, loyal to the Christ, the Bride.

The above three points are the life, way, and quality that every believer should possess.

4. *Building the church.* We are to build the church according to biblical teachings, gathering those who are born again, serving the Lord and one another according to the spiritual gifts given to believers. Unless believers are in the Body, they would be like bed of sand. With Christ as the chief cornerstone, "In

him the whole building is joined together and rises to become a holy temple" (Eph. 2:21).

5. *Providing for life*. In order that the churches may grow healthily, the Word of God as spiritual food must be provided to believers through preaching and teaching in various forms of meetings. Otherwise, a new church will soon become deserted.

6. *Interlink and fellowship*. Established churches should commit themselves to fellowship and partnership with churches in other localities so that they will supply, build, and grow together. This is done through establishing and developing coworkers' meetings and conferences extensively in counties and provinces for the sake of fellowship in the Lord and coordination of ministry.

7. *Frontier evangelism*. This is the Great Commission of Christ to the Church for the fulfillment of God's eternal salvation scheme. As Chinese Christians, we are burdened with the one hundred million souls that need salvation. In order that the gospel be preached to all the peoples in China, frontier evangelistic teams should be organized and sent to the unreached areas.

After the retreat, a team of eight experienced coworkers formed a committee to undertake the work of WOL training manual. The committee then engaged itself in studying the Bible in a systematic manner, recording and summarizing the ministry experience of WOL, and compiling the WOL training manual. According to Brother Yun, this work was led by Peter Xu because of his rich knowledge in both the history of the Christian church and the Chinese church.[45] In the spring of 1984, the committee was able to produce parts of the training manual which, because of the need of the time, was immediately put to use in training.

In 1987, three years after the initial parts of the manual were produced and used in training, the committee was able to complete the whole training manual of WOL in two volumes, which covered the *Seven Principles* mentioned above (hereafter WOL Manual I & II).

Leaders of WOL recognized that the *Seven Principles* were not an all-inclusive biblical theology, but fruits of the whole WOL community in their suffering with Christ in ministry. "They could be seen as principles of ministry, methods of Bible study, or theological reflection." Whatever they were called, WOL leaders thought these *Seven Principles* were like "a dagger, easy to carry and effective in battle."[46]

The creation of the manual indeed reflected the suffering experience of the WOL evangelists and their theological reflection in history. Peter and some of his coworkers went through the political movements in the '50s and '60s and the Cultural Revolution (1966–76), having suffered physically and witnessed with their own eyes the destruction of the visible church. In Peter's own words,

> God permitted the atheists to test His own construction through the wind, rain, and flood of the numerous political movements, so that the church in China experienced the baptism of the fire. During the trials, however, some died for their faith, some were imprisoned for their faith, some went in exile abroad, some became timid, and some even betrayed the Lord and friends.[47]

For WOL leaders, those who fell from grace during the trials were in striking contrast to those who persisted even in face of persecution and imprisonment, or even death. And it was exactly the "new life" in Christ that made the difference. "Those who did not own "life" (new life in Christ through the Cross) could not be expected to walk the way of the Cross. It is only natural that they failed before the trials." Therefore, the focal point of entrance fell on the first two principles: *Salvation through the Cross* and *the Way of the Cross*, from which all other principles developed.

This was the crucial stage of development for the WOL, distinguishing it from others. They saw the absolute necessity of being born again by the Spirit through the Word of God in Jesus Christ before one could truly walk the way of the cross as exemplified by Jesus Christ. Some "Christians," even "Christian leaders" from before 1949 who had utterly failed the trials in the wave of persecution and opposition served as foils to them. The first two principles in their manual served to restore the missing "life" among believers and strict requirement for new members.

Theological Education ("Seminary of the Field")

In 1983 the government launched a nation-wide counter-crime campaign and there were immediate rumors that the police would arrest the seventeen MGs (evangelists) again. All of them left home and went into hiding. And the police indeed came after them and they could not return home any more. God separated these young people for full-time ministry by means of opposition and persecution—the beginning of the Gospel Band! As Peter's younger sister Deborah was the team leader in the mission trip to Sichuan and was the teacher of the Gospel Band because of her age and experience in walking with the Lord, she and several other coworkers took the responsibility of leading the first training classes.[48]

In the preparatory period leading to the establishment of the theological training schools in 1985, leaders of the WOL busied themselves in training those committed to full-time ministry. They would often organize five to seven day intensive training sessions to equip those committed believers for effective evangelism and church ministry. Those students would then return to their home churches to involve themselves in evangelism as well as discipling new converts.[49] This went on until time was ripe for establishing the more formal theological training schools. Toward the end of 1985, the first house church seminary, locally termed Theological Education (TE),[50] was established in S County, Henan Province. It was a three-month intensive training program and was named "Seminary of the Field" by overseas observers of the Chinese Church.[51]

Therefore, the first TE was established in S County, Henan and later moved to B County, Henan because of lack of support from the local house churches. Later on the house churches in S County realized they had neglected their responsibilities in supporting the TE, and they then pledged support for a TE. A third TE was then instituted in S County. The fourth one was established in O

County, near Hubei province. The fifth TE was established in C County, Henan, the sixth in Anhui Province, and the seventh in S County in Shaanxi Province.[52]

These TEs started with three-month sessions, with thirty students in each session each school, which meant there was a turnover of 210 graduates every three months, who were immediately sent out to the fields. Within a few years, thousands of workers were trained for the Kingdom work. In 1986, Rev. Jonathan Chao of the Chinese Church Research Center in Hong Kong sent his student Rev. Yu, the now vice president of the China Evangelical Seminary, to visit the first TE in B.M. County. Hearing the report from Yu about various aspects of the TE in B.M. County including training materials, curriculum, administration, teaching, student response, Rev. Chao was quite surprised to recognize that the three-month training session actually equaled one and a half years' coursework in overseas seminaries.[53] The Chinese Church Research Center then reported their learning about the TEs in China on their journal *zhongguo yu jiao hui* (China and the Church), titled "the Seminary of the Field."[54]

Entrance requirements

All prospective students should be born again and clear of their calling of God into preparation for ministry. They should be recommended by the local house church. Based on the qualifications above, students came from two different channels: first, they went through "Truth meeting" ("*Zhen li hui*"),[55] and were recommended by the coworkers leading the training; second, they went through the local church training class and were recommended by the elders of the local church. A Bible content exam was required when prospective students came to the training location, followed by interviews with the professors before final selection was made.[56]

Curriculum

At the establishment of the first TEs among the WOL, there was just one curriculum, which was simply an intensive study of the *Seven Principles*. Chao categorized the curriculum into two basic parts: Part 1: Establishing the foundation of new life, which included systematic study of relevant passages and verses in the Bible concerning Christ, his salvation, faith in Christ, the necessity of confession of sins and repentance. This part served for the purpose of facilitating students to establish pure faith in Jesus Christ. Part 2 included salvation history, salvation theology, life and ministry of Jesus, church history, mission history, and theology of evangelization. Scripture reading, apologetics, discerning cults and heretics, prayer and fellowship were a constant part of whole session of training.[57] Later on when the second and third grade TE were established, appropriate curriculums were developed for each grade of TE.

Daily schedule

Because of the nature of the intensive training in a closed location, where students actually stayed within or close by the compound for the whole three months, scheduled was designed in a way that may look quite different from a seminary schedule:

Personal devotional time:	6:30 - 7:00 a.m.
Prayer in small groups:	7:00 - 9:00 a.m.
1st Meal:	9:00 - 9:30 a.m.
Bible reading/recitation:	9:30 - 10:00 a.m.
1st Class:	10:00 - 12 noon
Noon Break:	12:00 - 12:30 p.m.
2nd Class:	12:30 - 2:50 p.m.
Break:	2:50 - 3:00 p.m.
3rd Class:	3:00 - 5:00 p.m.
Bible Recitation:	5:00 - 5:30 p.m.
2nd Meal:	5:30 - 6:00 p.m.
News Time:	6:00 - 6:30 p.m.
4th Class:	6:30 - 8:30 p.m.
Break:	8:30 - 8:40 p.m.
Music/Hymn Lesson:	8:40 - 9:40 p.m.
Writing Bible Verses:	9:40 - 10:00 p.m.
Lesson Recorded on Tape:	10:00 - 11:00 p.m.
Rest:	11:00 p.m. - 6:00 a.m.[58]

Repercussions of the Publication

The publication of the reports on the TEs ("Seminaries of the Fields") received great attention both in and outside China. From 1987, the authorities started to investigate the operation of the TEs all over the country. Some teachers of TEs were arrested and put in jail. And one of the TEs was rounded up by the police, after being informed of the activities on top of a hill where the TE was operating. The students were eventually released because there was hardly a place to accommodate so many young people in the local police detention center.[59]

Nonetheless, the police never stopped searching for these TEs in various parts of the country, which was also why, up to 1987, no new TE was added to the seven. Yet the influence of the TEs was tremendous. After producing so many graduates and sending them out to various parts of the country, many established churches witnessed the result of theological education and therefore imitated the TE model by starting some smaller scale local training classes. On the basis of the already established seven TEs, there arose fifteen local training classes toward the end of 1980s.[60] In the wave of suppression and opposition on TEs, more theological training arose among the WOL spontaneously.

In face of the new situation of the growing desire for more theological/biblical equipment among house churches, and in order to prevent confusion and disorder, leaders of WOL movement reconstructed the fifteen local training classes into fifteen classes of first grade TE (hereafter called TE-1). These TE-1 classes were directly local house church supported and the students also came from the local house churches.

System of Training

Since the 1980s, in face of the governmental restrictions on any unsanctioned organized activities, a system of training gradually took shape in the WOL community, enabling Christians in WOL to serve God in clandestine and yet orderly way in the given circumstance. First, the church in various areas conducted evangelistic meetings, to which believers invited families and friends and in which the good news of Jesus Christ was shared to those attending the meeting. A typical evangelistic meeting usually lasted three to five days, in which the preacher would address questions concerning the meaning of life, i.e. (in their own words) "Where did humans come from and where were they going in death? What state were they in right now, and what can they do about it? Through the speaking of the Biblical truth, we helped the people realize the reality about themselves. When they realized their situation and how dangerous their positions were, they started to seek a way of salvation, and there was one available."[61]

Seekers from evangelistic meetings were then led to the "Life meeting." The content teaching and preaching in the "Life meeting" included: God's creation, human fall, the judgment of sin, the consequence of judgment, the love of God, salvation through Christ (birth, ministry, death, burial, resurrection, ascension, second coming of Jesus Christ, with focus on the Cross), the work of the Holy Spirit, repentance, belief, being born again, righteousness, salvation. A typical "Life meeting" lasted about seven days, with intensive teaching on the above aspects.

> When seekers, under the illumination of the Holy Spirit, understood in their heart and mind the reality of human sin, the love of God in Jesus Christ, the salvation through Jesus Christ, they accepted Jesus Christ as their Lord and savior and received salvation, just as those Israelites who looked up to the bronze snake in faith and were healed. When they were clear about their salvation, their whole being were renewed and they were totally different! And a desire of seeking God was developed in their hearts because the Spirit of God was in them pressing them forward.[62]

The next level of training was the "Truth meeting" that normally lasted between seven to fifteen days. In this training the participants were devoted to the study of the key content of the *Seven Principles* and relevant scriptural teachings, engaged in personal and group devotions, and participating in other needed area of the temporary communal life. Typically, these trainees were those who responded to God's calling in faith, preparing for Christian service.

Why were the *Seven Principles* preached and emphasized in the "Truth meeting?" Peter stated, "We thought that, once one was saved in Christ, he/she should spread the message of salvation to others. And these seven points would enable him/her to do the job properly. In learning the seven points believers understood their responsibilities, and some even became clear of their calling from above."[63]

At the end of the "Truth meeting," some with affirmed conviction for service would be recommended, after sessions of counseling with the leaders of the training and regional/area elders, to the short-term training classes, which were later called pre-TE, in which, for about forty days, the theme of salvation through the cross was dealt in a systematic manner. "When these believers graduated, they knew how to share the gospel to others. And often they were able to, with the support of experienced co-workers, lead evangelistic meetings and 'Life meetings.' Some even participated in leading the 'Truth meetings.'"[64]

After about six months of ministry exercise, these new workers were called back from the fields to start TE-1 (three to four months in length), where the *Seven Principles* were dealt in a more systematic and detailed manner. On graduation from TE-1 they were sent out to the fields to lead evangelistic meetings, "Life meetings," "Truth meetings" and short-term training classes. These ministerial practices (almost like internships) usually went on for about a year before these TE-1 graduates were once again called back to TE-2 for another six months, where they would study the whole Bible one book after another. Students, after completing TE-2, were able to grasp fairly well the content of the Bible, background, authors, themes and outlines of each of the books, Christology in each of the books, church history, and basic apologetics. Students graduating from TE-2 were also qualified as MGs.[65]

For teachers involving in TE-2 they attended twice annual retreat organized by the WOL Church, where, under the leadership of seniors and leaders, they studied the Scripture together, analyzing the issues that appeared and might appear in teaching. So, there was a conscious communal efforts involved in the TE trainings, that, as teachers, they were bearers of the responsibility of equipping believers for ministry, by the power of the Spirit of God, through the support of the WOL community. It was a group project.

Toward the beginning of 1990s, increased interaction with overseas missionaries prompted leaders of the WOL movement to the need to study Western theological tradition as an effort to broaden their own theological reflection for the best benefit of ministry. As an actual measure to meet this need, TE-3 was established. "TE-3 was based on our Chinese indigenous theological training, which was brought into being under the guidance of the Spirit of God, while absorbing and inheriting from the rich historical legacy and foundation of western traditional theology," one of the leaders said. The WOL community was much enriched at this time, being able to dialogue with the parts of the same body vertically and horizontally. They were also able to send some students overseas to study in degree programs in formal seminaries.[66] This was called special TE (hereafter called TE-Sp). In this way, theological education among

WOL was connected with international theological education for mutual enrichment.

The success of the system of training was obvious. According to the Chinese Church Research Center, the majority of students at various levels of training (which were conducted in a number of regions and provinces) came from the same region or province where training was operated. After a year's training, house churches in the regions and provinces experienced great revivals and the number of Christians and churches more than doubled. Through TE training, there were not only increased numbers of workers in the churches, but also the quality of the whole congregation increased as well. Therefore, TE training was the primary reason behind the revivals of the house churches.[67]

This system became gradually stabilized toward the beginning of 1990s and was able to function tremendously in the continual development of WOL. Devoted believers constantly joined the cycle of training, as the system continues its spinning, yielding workers for the kingdom in hundreds, thousands, and tens of thousands.

Several written materials/books were also produced in WOL in the process: *Truth Practical Curriculum, Part 1: Salvation through the Cross, Truth Practical Curriculum, Part 2, Sermons of Life, The Gospel from Heaven: Selected Sermons from Revival Meetings, Marriage and Celibacy*, etc.

Mission-oriented Stage

As much as the WOL community of believers had accomplished so far, in terms of significant expansion and impact, it was from this stage onward, that the WOL church started to stretch its network more extensively and rapidly through the work of the MGs, who were sent to all provinces of China by the WOL church to do frontier evangelism and establish house churches, sustained by the unique WOL structure, and guided by the biblical principle.

Structure of the WOL

The growth of the WOL was phenomenal toward the end of the 1980s. According to statistical investigation from the Chinese Church Research Center based in Hong Kong, by 1988, WOL had established more than three thousand house churches in central and northern part of China with five to six hundred thousand Christians scattered in twenty provinces of China.[68] The MGs were continuously sent to different regions of China to evangelize and establish house churches. Because of its growth and influence, WOL had been targeted by the authorities in a series of campaigns. Some MGs as well as coworkers were arrested. Then in 1988, Billy Graham came to China on an official visit. Arrangement was made for Peter Xu to meet with Graham in Beijing. Peter Xu arrived in Beijing, only to be arrested just a day before the meeting was ever to take place. According to the Press Release from Chinese Church Research Center on April 25, 1988, Peter Xu "went to Beijing intending to share this phenomenon of church growth, revival, and persecution with fellow-evangelist Billy Graham, but unfortunately Xu was arrested before he had a chance…. Xu was arrested in Beijing on April 16th 1988."[69] He was sentenced to three years in labor camps.[70]

Peter's imprisonment did not hinder the continuous growth of the WOL. In fact, after Peter's arrest, his coworkers continued to develop the evangelistic ministries of the WOL. Peter's sister, Deborah Xu, as a respected senior coworker of the WOL was much involved in the decision-making of the overall operation of the WOL network. Regional elders were able to coordinate ministry accordingly. Common vision was continuously being shared through the coworkers' meetings, as well as fellowship meetings.[71] Their TE training continued, so were their evangelistic meetings, "Life meetings," and "Truth meetings." In accordance with the situation of the time, leaders of the WOL stretched their evangelistic Gospel Band to the border areas of China such as Heilongjiang, Jilin, Inner Mongolia, Nixia, Xinjiang, Qinhai, Yunnan, Guizhou, Hainan, and Tibet, etc.[72]

By 1991 when Peter was released after serving the three-year labor camp term, the WOL church had sent MGs all over China, evangelizing and establishing churches. During retreats when MGs came back from different regions and provinces for fellowship, a common question was raised: With the fact that the effective evangelistic ministry of the WOL in different regions had resulted in establishing many more house churches, naturally creating a much larger community. How was this enlarged community of house churches to be properly coordinated in terms of discipleship and ministry? A common need was identified for proper structural organization, to coordinate ministry across the WOL community of house churches, which had extended to every province of the country, and to prevent disorder and confusion. After a time of prayer, fellowship, and discussion, WOL leaders organized the WOL community of house churches that had spread all over China into seven pastoral regions (see Figure 3:1):

- Dongbei (Northeast) Pastoral District: Jilin, Liaoning, Heilongjiang.
- Huabei (North China): Inner Mongolia, Shanxi, Hebei.
- Coastal Regions: Shandong, Jiangsu, Anhui, Zhejiang, Fujian.
- Xibei (Northwest): Shaanxi, Gansu, Ningxia, Qinghai, Xinjiang.
- Xinan (Southwest): Sichuan, Yunnan, Guizhou, Tibet.
- Zhongnan (Mid-south): Hubei, Hunan, Jiangxi, Guangdong, Guangxi, Hainan.
- Zhongyuan (Midland): Henan and its surrounding areas.

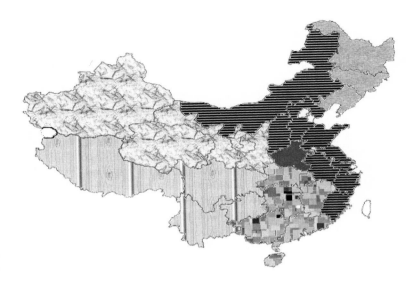

Figure 3.1. Seven Pastoral Regions of the WOL Church

In these seven pastoral regions, there was a conference in each respective region. Peter had a summing up: The church is one, just as the body is one, and yet consisting of three parts: (1) the Gospel Band, which was like the heavenly hosts, (2) theological education (TEs), which were like the heavenly military school, and (3) established churches, which were like the heavenly administrative units. These three parts were like the three legs of an ancient Chinese cooking vessel.[73] Looking at the church from this perspective, it was a lively and mobile church. A dynamic missiological cycle was created: It started with frontier evangelism, when itinerant evangelists were engaged in evangelistic ministry among people who had never heard of the gospel. When people came to faith and a house church was established among them, short-term training immediately followed when new believers were facilitated into Life/Truth meetings. Some dedicated believers, through recognition and recommendation of local elders and MGs, received further biblical and theological training, i.e. pre-TE and TE-1 and TE-2, and joined the Gospel Band and became MGs,. The Gospel Band, responsible for both Theological Education and coordinating evangelistic ministry of the WOL church, thus dispatched the MGs to frontier evangelism. Thus a new cycle started. With more and more people coming to faith, more and more house churches were established and added to the WOL community. With more believers dedicated themselves to theological training in preparation for ministry, more MGs were supplied to the Gospel Band and sent to frontier evangelism. The WOL kept expanding its network across the country as the cycle continued.[74] Figure 3.2 is an attempted illustration of the WOL dynamic missiological cycle.

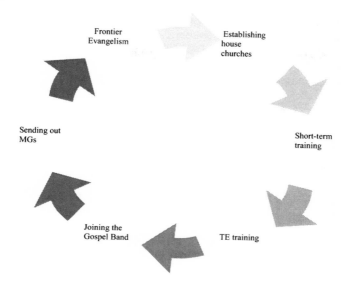

Figure 3.2. The WOL Dynamic Missiological Cycle

Through evangelism, a house church was established, with a size of, say, thirty, fifty, or a hundred. How was the church governed then? "The Holy Spirit would raise three to five, at most seven believers as the leaders of the church, among whom three were responsible for finance of the church, and the others for administration, caring for members, and other aspects of the church." Seven house churches formed a coworkers' meeting which met monthly. This meant that seven leaders from seven house churches would meet and have fellowship once a month, sharing relevant issues during the month, coordinating the work of the seven house churches, and discussing how the ministry could be further developed. There was also the representatives' meeting in which one to three selected members from the seven house churches participated.

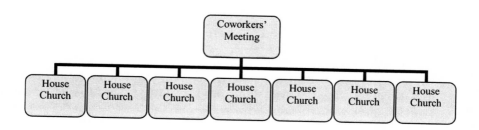

Figure 3.3. WOL Organization: Coworkers' Meeting

Then, seven coworkers' meetings formed an area. In some cases, an area can be further divided into a small area, a mid area, and a large area. An area meeting consisted of seven coworkers from each coworkers' meeting (abbreviated as CM in diagrams).   There was also the area representatives' meeting consisting of seven to twenty-one selected believers from each of the seven coworkers' meeting.

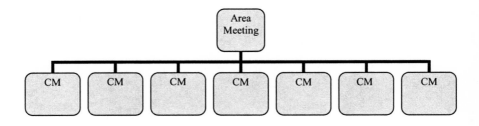

Figure 3.4. WOL Organization: Area Coworkers' Meeting

Seven areas formed a pastoral district, and seven pastoral districts formed a pastoral region. There was one to two annual general conference(s) involving representatives from all seven pastoral regions.

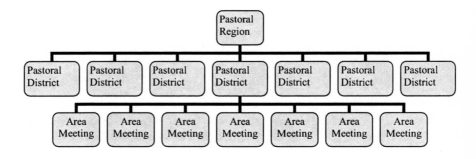

Figure 3.5. WOL Organization: Pastoral Region

Elected elders of the established house churches in each area meet monthly, which was called Area Conference. MGs who ministered in every pastoral region, district, and area met once a month, which was called System Meeting. There were two retreats for teachers in theological education annually. Depending on need, there were flexible joint meetings consisting of representatives from TE, Gospel Band, and established churches, in which they coordinated ministries of the whole WOL family. This is basically the framework of the WOL church organization. Figure 3.6 presents an overview of the WOL organizational structure.

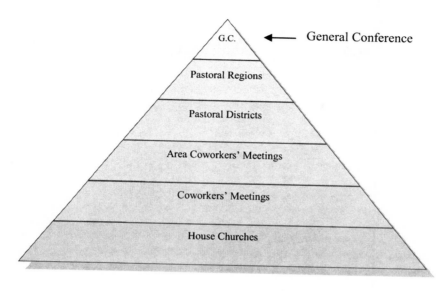

Figure 3.6. WOL Organization Overview

System of Theological Training

The training system started from evangelistic meeting, then moved on to Life Meeting, Truth meeting, Pre-TE, TE-1, TE-2, TE-3, TE-Sp and Graduate Class. There was also theological education among the established house churches in each area, starting with evangelistic meeting, Life meeting, Truth meeting, and gradually moving up the ladder. And then there was also training for pastoral and administrative elders of local house churches that were called Pillars' TE:[75] Pillars' Pre-TE, Pillars' TE-1, and Pillars' TE-2.This was summarized in poem that circulated among the WOL:

One church with three supporting legs
Seven principles and four lines
First fight with the Word of Life
Second fight with sanctification and victory
With prayer, repentance, and fellowship
Never stray from the principle of the Body.[76]

Throughout the 1990s, the WOL continued to grow and spread outward, based on their conviction of a New Testament centrifugal missiological model that the gospel was to be preached to all peoples all over the world. The task for the WOL community was then, first of all, to take the gospel to all the people in China.

The WOL network has now touched every province in China with the gospel and established hundreds of thousands house churches. Furthermore, the WOL has already crossed the national border and established churches, TE schools, and fellowships overseas, gearing toward the continuation of the Great Commission of preaching the gospel of Jesus Christ toward the end of the earth. For the WOL, this means to bring the gospel back to Jerusalem where the relay started two thousand years ago. The WOL community believe that they have taken the last baton in the gospel relay and are dashing toward the goal—Jerusalem.

The development continues in what they called "spiral development trend," which includes two cycle systems: an inward system and an outward system. Inwardly, the established house churches, through meetings of various forms, providing for the Word of Life and strengthening believers, so that the established churches become more mature and thriving. As a result, not only the established churches are able to meet their own needs, but also a successive birth of devoted workers will be added to the ministry of evangelism. Outwardly, through evangelistic outreach to the unreached, souls are gained for the Kingdom and new house churches are established. Those with calling will go through TE training and be included in the Gospel Band that will explore into new ground. This cycle continues until the gospel is preached to the end of the earth.[77]

The Gospel Band

The Gospel Band was one of the constituent parts of the structure of WOL, often referred to figuratively as one of the three supporting legs of an ancient Chinese cooking vessel. It is also one of the four development routes of the WOL as specified in the training manual: Route One: Local church pillars; Route Two: Administrative organization and fellowship meetings; Route Three: Developing the Gospel Band; Route Four: Partnership in ministry between the Gospel Band and regional established churches.[78] It is one of the secrets of fast growth of the WOL community in China.

The Role of the Gospel Band

The Gospel Band was first of all responsible for organizing and executing theological education among the WOL, which included the responsibilities of accepting students for theological training, training them, and eventually sending them out in mission to the unreached. Secondly, the Gospel Band had under it thousands of MGs who were doing the work of evangelism in various parts of the country constantly. Among these MGs were formed different evangelistic teams such as urban team, minority team, medical team, overseas team, special team, etc. Apart from evangelism, various teams of the Gospel Band also worked closely with the responsible elders of the established house churches in whatever area they were working, participated in the area fellowship meetings, and partnered in ministry.

An Evangelistic Center consisting of seven to ten elected MGs was formed in the Gospel Band, responsible for itinerant visitation, administration, supplying needs, organizing fellowship meetings and retreats, studying and investigating biblical and doctrinal issues, operating theological training, and producing Christian literature for WOL. Various evangelistic areas were divided according to different pastoral areas with elected evangelistic team leaders (two to four persons) as the leaders of each evangelistic area responsible for the ministry of the area. Ministry among each evangelistic area included operating theological training (local pillars' class) and various teachers' training; organizing area MGs retreats, operating evangelistic teams into the unreached areas, assisting the established house churches with charity work.

The goal of the itinerant evangelistic mission of the Gospel Band was to establish churches. In establishing new churches, the emphasis was on intensive training on the new life in Christ and evangelizing the surrounding area. When the local believers were trained and had experience in ministry, they could go through the TEs and join the Gospel Band, who would then be sent to the unreached areas to do evangelistic work and establish churches. In its work, the Gospel Band was always closely connected in ministry with the other two supporting legs of WOL structure: the established churches and theological education. Chao summarizes: (1) The Gospel Band establishes churches and is responsible for training new believers (on new life in Christ); (2) The established churches supply workers and support the ministry of theological training; (3) Training in theological education (Seminaries of the Fields) is for the purpose of furnishing itinerant evangelists (MGs) for the Gospel Band.[79]

Life and Ministry of the Messengers of the Gospel

All MGs were required to go through at least TE-2 before hands were laid on them and they were sent out to the mission fields. On sending the MGs out, the church gave rough directions of mission and it was the responsibility of the MGs themselves to find out Christian believers who were to receive them into their home and offer them opportunities to preach among them. To those who had not believed, the MGs would also persist in preaching to them the gospel message. Some would then come to faith and received the MGs into their homes. Sometimes the TSPM churches received the MGs also and offered them opportunities to preach in their services to thousands of people.[80]

Most, if not all, of the MGs were not married. They were often sent out in twos or threes as a team with a one-way train or bus ticket and minimum amount of money for food. They followed Jesus' teaching and trusted that God would provide for their physical need and protection. Prayer was their only tool in time of need and danger and many MGs could testify to the faithfulness of the Lord.[81]

When reaching a new area (Area A) the MGs were received by a believer or non believer into his/her home, they would start by inviting neighbors and friends through the host's social network, and share the gospel message. The team consisting two or three MGs would often divide the work among themselves: one preached, one led singing of hymns, and one taught basic

Christian doctrinal truth. When the number of converts in Area A reached around thirty to fifty, the team would leave for another area (Area B) to start the work all over again, while a new team was dispatched to Area A to do follow-up work of teaching and discipleship. This process usually lasted for about two to three months, but sometimes could go as far as six months, when believers in Area A were helped to root deep in the biblical truth and participated in ministry according to spiritual gifts. Seven coworkers would be elected in the process and formed a coworkers' meeting which was immediately incorporated into the Area Coworkers' Meeting in the WOL structure. The principle of WOL was: Where the work is started, there the workers will be raised.[82] Chao observes that the role of the MGs were quite like that of the apostles in the New Testament, who established churches, left to the care of the local believers and moved on to the next area.

Following is one of many stories of the MGs: Sister Mengzhao was sent to D County, Shaanxi Province. She was a primary school teacher before she was called into full-time ministry. As she was ministering there in D County, there arose rumors that she was a spy sent from Hong Kong to spread cult and deceive women. For a time, no one there dared to accommodate her and her co-worker any more. If they insisted on staying where they were already, they would incur trouble for the hospitality family (*Jie dai jia ting*). They moved out and stayed in the watchmans' straw hut in the crop fields, praying day and night for five consecutive days. They acknowledged themselves that, to fulfill this mission trip, they had totally obeyed the guidance of the Holy Spirit, and were sent out by the church in faith and prayer. And now they had nothing to fear but wait on God in prayer. When local villagers saw their determination, they were curious and came to talk to them. Sister Mongzhao said to them, "You have not even heard us preaching and yet decided that we are spreading cult. If you have listened to what we have to say to you and still think that we are cult, then we will leave here with a clear conscience. You see, we came here not to ask you for food or shelter, but for an opportunity to preach." Then leaders of the village agreed that they could preach. And when they started preaching, the Holy Spirit came down empowering their preaching and convicting people. Only then did they realize that Sister Mongzhao and her co-worker came from God who gave them such witness and power. So the gospel quickly spread in D County and people responded by dedicating their sons and daughters to preparation for ministry. And the second theological training school was established in D County.[83]

The Fruit of the Gospel Band

As one of the three supporting legs of the WOL (Established Churches, Theological Education, and the Gospel Band), the Gospel Band has been instrumental in the phenomenal growth of the WOL for the past two decades. The MGs are now working in every province of the country as well as overseas, with the primary goal of bringing the gospel back to Jerusalem. One simple fact highlights the work of the Gospel Band. In 1992, when Peter returned to where he was in Sichuan ten years ago to attend a coworkers meeting, one of the local coworkers told him, "Uncle, remember in 1982 when you and other MGs came to preach the gospel, there were no Christian believers here. People did not even know whether Jesus was a male or a female. After ten years of evangelism, today, every family knew the name of Jesus."[84]

In recent years, however, primary emphasis of the WOL community has been shifting from evangelistic outreach to pastoring the established churches.[85] Leaders of WOL felt the need to consolidate the work already done during the years, that is, to give more attention to teaching and discipleship. This is manifested in decreasing in production of MGs in comparison to the growing emphasis on Pillars' TE training programs.

The Role of Women in the WOL

Seventy percent of all the MGs in the WOL were women, who were working as diligently as their male coworkers.[86] These women devoted themselves to the Lord's work at the price of family, education, and comfort. They were indeed the "pillars" of the WOL, diligently doing evangelistic work, pastoral care, teaching, training, leading revival meetings, involving in hospitality ministry, etc. In a word, female coworkers were seen in every aspect of ministry in the WOL, even in top leadership circle. Most of the house church gatherings I participated during research, including Bible Studies, Sunday worship, fellowship meetings, testimony meetings, were led by women coworkers. However, on various leadership circles in the WOL organizational structures the role of women are not represented in proportion to the number of women coworkers in ministry. This is a common phenomenon not only among the WOL but also among other house church groups.[87]

Although it is difficult to come to a close estimate on the scale male/female composition of WOL by participating in a dozen of meetings, it is probably fair to say that the majority of believers in the WOL are woman. Seventy percent is probably a close representation of size of female composition in the WOL. In one of the Pillars' TEs that the author participated in, 60 percent of all students were female. In other house church meetings, however, females occupied about 70 percent of all attendance.

Finances and Financial Need

From the beginning, the WOL movement was a self-sponsored movement. Leaders and coworkers did not receive a salary. Expenses necessary for ministry such as travel, food, and materials and equipment for TEs come from the local Christians. Hospitality families serve as mission stations where local Christians bring things together for ministerial use accommodating and providing for coworkers' meetings of various levels, evangelistic and revival meetings, TE training, fellowship meetings, and so on. Some local Christians devote the income of their businesses such as small hotels and restaurants for church use, which provide substantial support for ministry.

Finance has been a needy area in the WOL. Coworkers have been enduring great financial difficulties as they faithfully serve in ministry. Sometimes support may come in from different avenues that help temporarily. For the past few years leaders of the WOL have been strategically planning on tent-making kind of businesses that would bring in some kind of revenue to finance the movement.

Unity Stage

In the midst of the new wave of extensive development among the WOL community in the mid-1980s, theological differences started to emerge due to influence from overseas missionary organizations and churches that started to minister among the house churches. As a result, the community split into several localities, with each developing its own network. This state of divided house church networks lasted until the mid-1990s when the breath of unity started to blow in the air. With the WOL community being one of the most active members of the unity appeal, the movement of unity is making noticeable progress. The work of the Spirit of God in this stage is undeniable.

Denominational Divisions

From 1983 to 1995, denominational differences started to emerge among the house churches that were originally under Peter's group. In a sense, this seemed to be directly related to the in-flux of many overseas organizations and missionaries. For instance, Brother R, the present leader of Fangcheng Fellowship, one of the largest house church networks centered in Henan Province, had originally been one of the coworkers in Peter's group in the '70s and early '80s.[88] According to Peter Xu and other senior elders, Brother R was sent by the church to go to Guangzhou to fetch Bibles and other Christian literature at a distributing station provided by an overseas Pentecostal group. In fellowship with leaders of the overseas group, Brother R embraced Pentecostalism and connected with believers with Pentecostal background across the country, and the group started to grow significantly with Brother R as one of the top leaders.

Another former WOL coworker, Brother X, became acquainted with the Bible-distributing station provided by Witness Lee of the Shouters Sect in Taiwan. Brother X embraced the Shouters practice and therefore brought back brochures/books on how to practice pietistic life written by Witness Lee. Many young believers received Lee's teaching on how to shout and practice pietism, etc. As a result, thousands of believers gathered together and shouted aloud to the point of disturbing public order. And the Shouters influence, especially introduced by Brother X quickly spread from Henan to other provinces, drawing large number of believers.[89]

With the rise of different denominational emphasis among groups of different localities, gaps started to be created in WOL. Revivals continued to take place in house churches, and each denominational group continued to spread and develop through the same organizational structure available. For example, in one town there were several house churches meeting and doing ministry, each affiliating with a different denomination. They would often critique one another in meetings, criticizing others as not "walking in the middle." Often believers living in the same village and yet belonging to different denominations did not speak to each other for fear of being contaminated by false teachings of other groups. Sometimes believers would rather speak to unbelievers than to believers of another denomination. Large house church groups competed and argued with one another, making it difficult for seekers to decide which one was orthodox and taught the truth. "Until 1995, the house churches in China had lost its witness of unity, and was also losing the space for the spreading of the gospel," Peter recalled.[90]

Efforts to Regain Unity of the Body

In 1995, former and current leaders of the WOL came together for fellowship and prayer. Recognizing the state of the house churches, they repented to God. "The Lord gave us a united body of Christ, and now it has been disintegrated to such a stage. What are we going to answer to the Lord when we eventually see Him?"[91] Peter recalls,

> God used Brother Yun to bring unity among the leaders of various house church networks. This was no easy task for years of silence between us had created unseen walls of bitterness and hostility. But God performed a series of miracles that lead to a meeting of the leaders of several house church networks in 1996. It was the first time many of us had seen each other for years. At that first meeting the Lord broke through our stubbornness and pride and there were many tears of repentance. We all confessed our bitterness to each other and asked for forgiveness.[92]

Since then, more fellowship meetings were organized across the house church networks as leaders started to work out issues and disagreements for the sake of the unity within the body of Christ.

Back to Jerusalem Movement

In the wave of the unity efforts among the house church networks, an ancient vision was rekindled and caught: Back to Jerusalem (BTJ)—to send out Chinese missionaries westward outside China and spread the gospel all the way back to Jerusalem.

The BTJ vision seems to have begun with the Jesus Family in Shandong Province, when, in the 1940s, this church started to send out workers "heading west into the Muslim nations on foot, intending to establish the kingdom of God in all the territories along the way."[93] The vision was continued by the

Northwest Spiritual Movement when the BTJ Evangelistic Band was formed and dispatched to the west of China.

At about the same period of time in the 1940s in Northwest Bible Institute in Shaanxi Province, west of Shandong Province, another BTJ Evangelistic Band was also established and went on mission towards the Xinjiang Autonomous Zone (in western China) in March 1947. The band was never able to enter Xinjiang because of the Civil War between the Nationalists and the Communists (1945–49). "All seemed lost. Like the children of Israel who were so close to the Promised Land that they could see it with their eyes, the Back to Jerusalem vision in the late 1940s and early 1950s was taken back into the wilderness, to await a time when the workers would be better equipped to handle the great task laid before them."[94]

When one of the early participants of BTJ movement in the 1940s providentially connected with the house churches leaders of the unity movement, the vision of bringing the gospel back to Jerusalem was readily embraced as God-given. Peter Xu affirms, "while he was dealing with the Chinese church and purifying us, God put the vision for Back to Jerusalem deep into the hearts of the house church leadership."[95]

For the participating house church networks, the basic strategic plan for the BTJ movement is to mobilize the churches in China and overseas to join in prayer and support of the BTJ movement, train and equip missionaries (with one hundred thousand trained BTJ missionaries as the goal), and send them out to evangelize all peoples and nations along the silk roads, westwards all the way back to Jerusalem, southwards to Southeast Asia, and southwest to South Asia, thus covering the three strongholds that have been resistant to the gospel—Islam, Buddhism, and Hinduism.[96]

Sinim Fellowship (希尼团契), Shenzhou Fellowship (神州团契), and BTJ Gospel Band (归回耶路撒冷福音使团)

In 1996, a fellowship meeting was called involving the leaders of Fangcheng Fellowship (both Brother R. and second generation leaders), Peter Xu, and several leaders from China Gospel Fellowship, Anhui Fellowship, and the Shouters. Together, the participants established "Sinim Fellowship" for the purpose of working toward unity. The name was taken from Isaiah 49:12, where the word Sinim has often been interpreted by many Bible scholars as referring to China. Peter Xu was elected as the president of the Fellowship.[97]

In 2001 Peter left China, which caused confusion among the leadership both in WOL and Sinim Fellowship. In 2002 Shenzhou Fellowship was established when part of the original leadership of Sinim Fellowship met in Hong Kong.[98] Peter was in Thailand at the time and was not informed of the meeting. Then in November 2002 Peter and Brother Yun arraigned a ten-day meeting in the Philippines, inviting leaders of the large house church networks, discussing how to further promote the work of "Back to Jerusalem." The meeting ended with the establishment of "Back to Jerusalem Gospel Band Sinim in and outside of China (归回耶路撒冷福音使团希尼在中外)."[99]

Several issues became clear at the meeting in the Philippines: First, both Shenzhou Fellowship and Back to Jerusalem Gospel Band were established on the basis of Sinim Fellowship, with its base in China, and branches in different overseas regions. Second, Sinim Fellowship continued to function. Third, Shenzhou Fellowship, with the support of five pastors, was established enlisting the Pentecostal house church networks in China. It is therefore an effort of unity among the Pentecostal house church networks.

Peter was much concerned about the inaccurate reports published overseas from observers of the church in China, which, he thinks, are prone to causing damage to the unity movement.

> Whether be it Sinim Fellowship or Shenzhou Fellowship, they are simply names. Sinim Fellowship continues to be recognized by both the fundamentalist and Pentecostal house church networks, while the newly founded Shenzhou Fellowship is only recognized by the Pentecostal house church networks. At least up to now, Pentecostal house church leaders continued to participate in Sinim Fellowship. David Aikman in his book mentioned that Shenzhou has replaced Sinim, which is not the case, and which might create opportunity for division within the unity movement.[100]

Challenges to the Churches in China

Today, the revival of the Chinese Church is far from over, but it is facing a lot of challenges. In the perception of the WOL Community, three challenges are prominent: First, in the wave of economic reform and the trend of urbanization in China, agricultural economy lags behind and the rural population struggle to make ends meet. As a result, rural workforce is drawn into cities where there are more job opportunities. Christian youth have also been among the workforce that pours into cities, and even some of the MGs and co-workers are also starting to follow suit. From a positive point of view, we can say that the rural house churches are encircling the cities and into the cities. However, in the stage of transition, rural churches are experiencing great shock when they start to lose in great numbers their young adult members. Second, the Chinese government continued to keep pressure on Christianity in China for the purpose of reducing its influence and keeping it under control, despite the recent influence of globalization in which human right is often appealed. Periodical campaigns often target unregistered house churches and their leaders. Third, since the 1980s, overseas mission organizations and churches have been in and out of China developing their own ministry with their own denominational emphases and agendas. Their ministry touched various areas of house churches with their theological emphases, attracting many followers, and at the same time, directly and indirectly creating denominational differences among house churches, making united fellowship even more difficult.

From another perspective, i.e. Anthony Wallace's theory of revitalization movement, the WOL could be identified as having coming through the stages of revitalization and established itself as one of the most dynamic Christian communities in China. In a way, the WOL has made it through to the "New Steady State," with an estimated twenty million Christians under its network. The challenge for this "New Steady State," though, as the WOL leadership consciously acknowledge themselves, is how the extensively stretched network of house churches can be stabilized. And this has been the focus of attention of the church for the past few years when ministry emphasis started to shift toward maintenance of the house churches within the network through Christian education. The seminary of the fields mentioned at the beginning of the book is one among many of such efforts. The purpose of this shift does not end at maintenance, though. Continuing the evangelistic expansion and bringing the gospel back to Jerusalem remain the goal for the WOL Church.

With the departure of Peter Xu from China in 2001, there has been some disagreement among the leadership circle of WOL. Some continued to look up to Peter as their spiritual leader and accepted his younger sister Deborah as substituting his role in WOL, while others retreated to the more conservative corner, reluctant to support Peter's call for unity among the house church networks. Two camps within the WOL have gradually surfaced, particularly among the senior elders: those who responded to Peter's call for unity among house churches and continued to support him as their leader, and those who did not. Among WOL coworkers and believers, those who support Peter Xu's leadership are often referred to as the "Unity Family"; while those who do not support the unity movement are called the "Hometown Family." Despite the disharmony within the WOL, the ministry continues, the structure functions, and the training systems continue to produce workers for the kingdom of God.

Conclusion

This chapter traces the emergence and development of the WOL movement in China through the storyline of its leader, Peter Xu. We have seen how the WOL coworkers identified the signs of the Spirit of God in their context and responded accordingly in each of the stages of development of the WOL community. This chapter does not claim to offer an exhaustive description of the WOL movement. Rather, it offers an overview of the development of the WOL movement for the past three decades. The following chapter analyzes the inner dynamics of the WOL movement through the lens of renewal movement, where more specific areas of the life and ministry of the WOL movement are treated.

Notes

1. Peter Xu, taped interview with author, Dec. 2004. Portions of the research data in this chapter on the history of the Word of Life movement was published in Yalin Xin, "Inner Dynamics of the Chinese House Church Movement," *Mission Studies* 25 no. 2 (Leiden, The Netherlands, Koninklijke Brill NV, 2008), 157–84.

2. Xu, interview.

3. Ibid.

4. Ibid.

5. Ibid.

6. The Great Leap Forward was an economic campaign called forth by the Chairman himself for a dramatic rise in industrial production in 1958. The entire Chinese population was mobilized to participate in the campaign. Unrealistic goals doomed the failure of the campaign. See also Michael Dillon, ed. *China: A Cultural and Historical Dictionary* (Richmond, Surrey: Curzon Press, 1998), 121–22.

7. "The Four Cleansing" was another political campaign which started in the early 1960s out of power struggle within the central government circle. It included "cleansing" in politics, economy, organizations, and ideology.

8. Xu, Interview.

9. Ibid.

10. "Floating population" was a specifically designated term by the Chinese government referring to people who left their hometown area, where they were registered, for means to survive and support the family, or for job opportunities. However, criminal acts such as stealing and robbing were often associated with the "floating population," which made them notorious.

11. People received food stamps from the local government bureau according to the size of the family in their legal residence. In order to purchase food from a store or restaurant, one needed to pay with both the proper amount of money as well as food stamps.

12. Xu, Interview.

13. Ibid.

14. Ibid.

15. Ibid.

16. Ibid.

17. Ibid.

18. Elder TG, Interview.

19. Xu, Interview. Cf. Sister H, interview.

20. Revival furnace is the term used by Peter Xu in interviews (with the author) in 2004 referring to the house churches that were experiencing revival at the time.

21. Xu. Interview.

22. Xu, interview. Cf. Elder TG, Interview.

23. Cf. Chao, *Purified by Fire*, 62-63.

24. Xu, interview. Cf. Elder TG, interview. Elder TR, interview.

25. Brother TY, interview with author, Mar. 2005.

26. Xu, interview. Cf. Brother TY, interview.

27. Brother Yun was one of the closest coworkers of Peter and the author of *Tian shang ren jian zheng—shen ai zhongguo* (*The Heavenly Man—God Loves China*) (China Care International Ltd., 2000).

28. Xu, interview. Cf. Elder TG, interview. Brother TY, interview.

29. Chao, *Purified by Fire*, 63.

30. Xu, interview. Cf. Brother P, interview with author, Mar. 2005.

31. One of the noted quotes from Maria Monsen, the Norwegian missionary to China in the first few decades of the twentieth century. See Maria Monsen, *A Present Help* (Translated from the Norwegian by Joy Guinness. London: China Inland Mission, 1960.). Miss Monsen's teaching and experience has often been proud encouragement to the Christians in Henan who embraced her legacies. Stories of her life and ministry, especially her role in Shandong Revival in the 1920s was often shared especially among Christian leaders in the WOL.

32. Xu, interview.

33. It is referred to as "Jerusalem Conference" in reports about the house churches in central China. Cf. *China Prayer Letter and Ministry Report* 82 (June 1987).

34. As the Chairman of the Communist Party as well as the Central Military Commission, Deng Xiaoping was best known for his economic reform and open door policy at the end of 1970s and beginning of 1980s.

35. Jonathan Chao, "House Church Seminary Training and Missions Strategy," *China Prayer Letter* 83 (1987): 3.

36. Xu, interview. Cf. Brother TY, interview.

37. Xu, interview.

38. Brother Yun, *The Heavenly Man* (China Care International Ltd., 2000), 26.

39. Cf. Yun, 23.

40. Xu, interview. Cf. Part 4 of WOL Manual II.

41. Xu, interview. Cf. Yun, 25.

42. Brother P, interview.

43. Marie Monsen, *A Wall of Fire*, translated by Joy Guinness (Salem, Ohio: Allegheny Publications, 2004), 82.

44. Yun, 22–24. Cf. Chao, "The House Church Movement," *China Prayer Letter* 82 (1978): 3; WOL Manual I & II.

45. Cf. Yun, 2000.

46. Xu, interview.

47. Ibid.

48. Xu, interview. Cf. Sister H, interview.

49. CCSC, "Report of the Seminaries of the Fields," *China and the Church* (Sept.–Oct. 1986).

50. *Shen xue* (Theological Education) was the term used by WOL referring to their various training schools or classes. These were intensive training sessions, usually 3–6 months in length. They were actually the "seminaries" of WOL, producing evangelists (MGs) and pastors/preachers.

51. The Chinese Church Research Center in Hong Kong first used term "the Seminary of the Field" in their follow-up report on the theological training among the house churches in China in 1986.

52. Xu, interview. Cf. Elder TR, interview; Elder TG, interview; Brother TY, interview.

53. CCSC, "Report, Part 1 & 2."

54. Cf. CCSC, "Report., Part 1 & 2."

55. Truth meeting was an intensive short-term gathering for new believers to consolidate their faith. The gathering included intensive biblical teachings, studying of the *Seven Principles*, personal and group devotions. It was also a time when new believers dedicated their lives to preparation for ministry.

56. Brother P, interview. Cf. CCSC, "Report," 14.

57. Cf. Chao, *Purified by Fire*, 91.

58. CCSC, "Report," 14, translated by author. Cf. Chao, *Purified by Fire*, 91–92.

59. Xu, interview. Cf. Elder TG, interview.

60. Xu, interview. Cf. Elder TG, interview; Brother J, interview.

61. Ibid.

62. Ibid.

63. Xu, interview.

64. Ibid.

65. Xu, interview. Cf. Elder TG, interview; Elder TR, interview; Brother J, interview; Chao, *Purified by Fire*, 90–91.

66. My interviewees included several former MGs as well as local pillars who had just come back from their seminary studies in the Philippines.

67. Chao, *Purified by Fire*, 84–85.

68. Jonathan Chao and Wanfang Zhuang, *A History of Protestant Christianity in China*, (Taipei: CMI Press, 1997), 522–23.

69. Jonathan Chao, "Press Release—April 25, 1988 Chinese Church Research Center," *China Prayer Letter and Ministry Report* No. 91 (May–June 1988): 8–9.

70. Chao and Zhuang, 522.

71. Elder TG, interview. Cf. Elder TR, interview; Brother TY, interview; Sister H, interview.

72. Cf. Chao and Zhuang, 523.

73. 鼎 is the Chinese character for the ancient cooking vessel. It is often used to symbolize firmness and steadiness. Cf. WOL Manual II: Part 4.

74. Xu, interview. Cf. WOL Manual.

75. According to the leaders of WOL, the term "pillar" was derived from Gal. 2:9 and 1 Tim 3:15 and were used to refer those who were engaged in pastoral ministry of the local house churches.

76. Xu, interview. Cf. Elder TG, interview; Brother P, interview.

77. Cf. WOL Manual II: Part 4.

78. Ibid.

79. Chao, *Purified by Fire*, 71.

80. Brother P, interview. Cf. Brother J, interview.

81. CCSC, "Secrets of the MGs, Part One," China and the Church 81 (Jan.–Feb. 1991).

82. Xu, interview. Cf. Brother P, interview; Brother J, interview; CCSC, "Secrets of the MGs."

83. Xu, interview. Cf. Elder TR, interview; Brother P, interview.

84. Xu, interview.

85. See Jonanthan Chao, "Da lu jidujiao fa zhan gai kuang" (A Brief Introduction of the Development of Christianity in China, 1996–2001), in *Xin jin huo chuan—Zhao Tian En mu shi ji nian wen ji* (The Undying Fire of the Burning Branches—A Posthumous Essay Collection of Dr. Jonathan Chao).Taipei, Taiwan: CMI Press, 2005), 151.

86. Chao, "The Changing Shape of the Church in China (1976–2002)," *China Ministry Report* 155 (2003), 1–4.

87. Cf. David Aikman, *Jesus in Beijing* (Washington, D.C.: Regnery Publishing, Inc., 2003), 3.

88. According to David Aikman (2003), Brother R. is "one of the best-known house church uncles in China" who has about 5 million Christians associated with his network. Brother R. was influenced by the "Pentecostal patterns of worship and prayer" introduced by Reverend Dennis Balcombe, an American pastor ministering in Hong Kong.

89. Xu, interview. Cf. Elder TG, interview; Elder TR, interview.

90. Xu, interview. Cf. Elder TG, interview.

91. Xu, interview. Cf. Yun, *The Heavenly Man*.

92. Paul Hattaway, *Back to Jerusalem* (Carlisle, UK: Piquant, 2003), 65.

93. Ibid., 40.

94. Ibid., 36.

95. Ibid., 67.

96. Brother P, interview. Cf. Hattaway, *Back to Jerusalem*.

97. Brother Yun and Paul Hattaway, *The Heavenly Man: The Remarkable True Story of Chinese Christian Brother Yun* (London: Monarch Books, 2002), 239. Cf. Aikman, 94.

98. Cf. Aikman, 94.

99. Xu, interview.
100. Xu, interview. Cf. Aikman, 94.

Chapter 4

Inner Dynamics of the Word of Life Movement

The previous chapter gives a brief historical description of the WOL movement from its origin to the present. We have seen that the movement has made significant impact on the Chinese population, recruiting millions of members in just a little more than three decades' time, sending evangelists to almost every province in China, and building a network that was able to sustain continuous growth.

The question of what has made the WOL a successful movement requires an investigation of its inner dynamic. Snyder's mediating model of church renewal provides such a framework for the evaluation of the WOL movement. This chapter examines the WOL movement from the perspective of Snyder's mediating model for church renewal. Such examination will identify whether the WOL movement demonstrates the ten marks Snyder suggests in his mediating model (refer to previous discussion on the model).

Rediscovering the Nature of the Gospel

Rediscovering the gospel is the foremost mark of Snyder's mediating model for church renewal and a "key element."[1] In his study of Pietism, Methodism, and Moravianism, Snyder observes that all three movements "made a 'new discovery' of the faith, or a rediscovery of aspects of the faith which were at the time obscured."[2] "This often constitutes a sort of experiential and conceptual paradigm shift in which the experience of God becomes central rather than secondary or absent. Often connected with this is a vision for the recovery of the dynamic of the New Testament church."[3]

The social and cultural unrest in China from the 1970s through the 1990s does not explain the emergence and growth of the WOL movement. Peter and his coworkers were the primary human agents who brought into being the WOL community of today. Significantly, these Christians of the WOL, in the given environment and time, with all its unfriendliness, "rediscovered" what was important for the church and its mission in the world and therefore engaged their focus and energy into it, and made a great difference.

In the history of the WOL movement, at least three stages of renewal can be clearly identified, all of which started with the discovery of a "new dynamic" that inspired leaders of WOL to come to a fresh understanding of the nature of the Christian faith and what it meant for Christian believers for that particular period of time in history. A "paradigm shift" took place. And the focus of ministry of the WOL church shifted accordingly.

Stage One: Suffering in Hope of the "Heavenly City"

The WOL movement started with the diligent ministry of a few saints, among whom Peter was rightfully the most recognized leader. Throughout his life and ministry, Peter, as well as his coworkers, has been significant in identifying such opportunities for a "paradigm shift," and he was able to communicate the vision to believers of WOL and thus set the movement on course. The first stage of renewal among the WOL was perhaps largely due to Peter's perception of the situation and his understanding of the needs of the time, in accordance with the Scripture.

In the 1950s, ecclesiastically speaking, the Chinese church was under tremendous pressure from the new regime and was forced to undergo change. This involved all churches being required to register with the TSPM as well as positive participation of all Christians in the repeated denunciation campaigns targeting those who had worked with foreign missionaries as well as those indigenous leaders who refused to associate themselves with the newly founded TSPM.[4]

Gradually, the church was losing its territory and impact in the Chinese society. By the beginning of the 1960s, even several years before the start of the Cultural Revolution in 1966, "fewer than 10 percent of the church's pre-1949 institutions were still employed for church use, with the rest either confiscated by the state or allocated to other work unit."[5] It gradually became extremely difficult for Christian believers to exercise their faith openly in terms of worshipping and having fellowship together, let alone sharing the gospel with others.

Then for the ten years from 1966 to 1976, all physical churches were completely shut down by the government.[6] Few dared to openly confess that they were followers of Christ. Socially, the whole Chinese population suffered because of the power struggle that was going on within the central government and the unrealistic introduction of economic policies such as the Great Leap Forward.

Perceiving the situation of the time, Peter, who felt called of God to share the good news to the Chinese people at a time when no one dared to mention the name of Christ as Savior apart from the "great savior Mao Zedong,"[7] went to the lost sheep of God, encouraging them in their suffering with the suffering of Jesus Christ on the cross for their sins and the sins of the whole world, and offering them hope of salvation. Peter said, "We suffer, but Christ suffered more, and for our sake so that we have hope in his return. If we suffer for Christ's sake, we are blessed for we are following his footsteps. It is our privilege and honor to have on our body the marks of his Cross."[8]

The writer of the book of Hebrews reflects on those ancient people of faith such as Enoch, Noah, Abraham, and Moses. "All these people were still living by faith when they died. They did not receive the things promised; they only saw them and welcomed them from a distance. And they admitted that they were aliens and strangers on earth. They were longing for a better country—a heavenly one. Therefore God is not ashamed to be called their God, for he has prepared a city for them" (Hebrews 11:13, 16). In the wave of fervent political and class struggle in the revolutionary China, people were close to despair and loss of all hope for a better life. The gospel of Jesus Christ who had died and was resurrected for the sins of the Chinese as well as the whole world rekindled the extinguishing fire among the people. Though still living in this seemingly hopeless society, there was the promised hope of eternity with God as promised in the Bible. The "furnaces of revival" served exactly for that purpose: to give people hope when there was none. "Hope transcended all pains and suffering in this world," as one believer affirms.

Stage Two: Centrality of the Cross

Change seemed to be an inevitable result in all spheres of the Chinese society after the establishment of the new regime in 1949. It was particular the case with the Christian religion and its practices, requiring the adjustment of the Christian community to the new environment.[9] In face of change, however, Christians made different choices: some chose to cooperate with the new regime, abiding its authority and leadership, while others chose not to do the same.[10] Whatever choices one made at the time, they involved great implications over time. Cooperation meant accepting the guidelines from the new regime in such matters as to the direction and the role of the church in China. Registration with the newly founded TSPM became the first obligation for the "cooperators," or "compromisers" as they were often referred to. Uncooperation, unfortunately, was not tolerated by the new regime, and those Christian leaders who chose to alienate themselves from the new regime and those "compromisers" of the church had had also to face the reality of being targeted and opposed.[11] These choices, as obvious as they were, gave momentum to the creation of the two Christian entities in China: the official TSPM church and the House Church.

Since devoting himself as an evangelist in 1960s, Peter Xu had been engaging himself to itinerant evangelistic ministry in Henan and surrounding regions. He felt something heavy on his heart, "a phenomenon," as he would call it, of differing reactions from the Christian community in China to the challenges of the new regime, which he describes: "Some died for the sake of the Lord; some were imprisoned; some escaped from China; some compromised their faith in fear; some betrayed the Lord and friends. Few dared to openly confess that Jesus is Savior."[12] Peter Xu started to question within himself over the root and cause of the phenomenon, which gradually shaped his theological reflection to a deeper level.

> The fact that, after the trials of the 1950s through the 1970s, some Christians went backsliding and some even recanted their faith, enables us to identify what a shaky foundation they built for themselves. And we cannot help wondering whether these Christians ever truly received the salvation through Jesus Christ. This provided us with historical reflection, probably the kind of insights one could only get in Communist countries. We therefore could not afford to take lightly faith, salvation truth, and experience. New life in Christ has to be established for any true Christian.[13]

Peter shared with his coworkers about his thought and they sought guidance and discernment from God in prayer. Toward the end of the 1970s, Peter and his coworkers started to shift their teaching emphasis to the theology of the cross (on the themes of *salvation through the cross* and *the way of the cross,* as well as *discerning the adulteress,* which became the first three principles of WOL's training manual that was compiled in the 1980s). In their reflection, leaders of WOL agreed that the nature of the gospel not only revealed the way of salvation through Jesus Christ, but also demanded that believers follow the way of the cross exemplified in Christ's incarnation, ministry, death and resurrection. In following the way of the cross, believers need to recognize the nature and destruction of the adulteress so that believers may be able to live a pure and holy life, as the bride of Christ completely devoted to him. A pure foundation of faith had to be laid before a believer could become a true disciple of Jesus Christ and start walking the way of the cross.

In the beginning of the 1980s, this theological shift was included in the first WOL Manual—*The Seven Principles* (in two volumes), as basic guide for teaching and ministry of the WOL church.

The first volume of the WOL manual lays out in a systematic manner biblical references, doctrines, and theological reflections on the topic of salvation through the cross. It includes twenty-one lessons in three units (over a hundred pages), covering, in Unit One, God's creation and redemption—the preparation for salvation; in Unit Two, the redemption of Christ—the fulfillment of salvation; in Unit Three, the Holy Spirit and redemption—the execution of salvation.[14]

The second volume of the manual continues to deal with the theme of the cross by exploring the biblical truth regarding the way of the cross:

> The way of the cross is the way of spiritual growth for saved Christians (cf. 1 Peter 1:6–7; Romans 8:17). On this way, there will be not only outside opposition, difficulties, and suffering (cf. Hebrews 10:32–36; 11:33–40), but also inside destroying, dealing with, breaking, losing, and denying (Mark 8:34; Luke 9:24; Romans 8:13; John 12:25); this way is the weeping valley (cf. Psalm 84:5–7) that Christians need to pass through on their way to Zion to meet God, and is also the overflowing cup of blessing, the valley of death with the presence of God, and above all, it is the only way through which Christians get to the God of glory (Isaiah 35:8; 43:1–2).[15]

In terms of the necessity of walking the way of the cross, the WOL Manual recognizes that it was exemplified by the Lord Jesus himself in word and deed (Matthew 5:12; Hebrews 11:32–38; Philipines 2:6–11; Hebrews 5:7–8; 1 Peter 2:20–24; 3:18), followed by the apostles (1 Corinthians 4:9–13; Acts 4:1–7, 13:21, 5:17–29,33,40–42, 6:8–14, 7:54,60, 9:23–25, 12:1–11, 13:50–52, 14:19, 16:19–26, 17:2,5–6, 18:12, 20:22–24, 21:12–13,30–36, 22:22–24, 23:13–15; 2 Corinthians 11:23–29; Hebrews 10:32, 13:3; 2 Timothy 1:11–12, 2:9; Colossians 1:24; Romans 8:35–39).[16]

It is evident that *salvation through the cross* and walking *the way of the cross* occupied the center of the WOL theology and practice. This recognition of the necessity to suffer and the willingness to suffer for Christ's name may provide crucial explanation to the phenomenal growth of the church in China.[17]

In the teachings and ministry of the WOL church, a continuity of conservative Christian influence, especially John Sung's legacy, can also be identified although the rebirth theme is much further developed and exercised in the WOL context. Theologically, such development manifests itself especially in the emphasis on the theme of *the way of the cross* as a necessary advancement for a believer who has experienced rebirth.

Stage Three: Unity among House Churches

China had been closed to the outside world since the beginning of the Communist regime. It was not until the 1980s when the new leader adopted an open-door policy as part of the economic reform. Seizing the opportunity, overseas churches and organizations started to make their way into China, involving in fellowship, training, and providing Christian literature. While house churches benefited from the support of their overseas brothers and sisters, one problem, however, almost immediately started to surface: denominationalism started to grow within the WOL community as some leaders started to embrace different denominational emphases and formed their own groups. As a result, what used to be one community of house churches split into several groups, with each persisting in its own theological emphasis. Over time, fellowship became impossible with fellow believers outside their respective group and theological crossfire started among the original "greater" WOL community.

Eventually these denominational groups within the WOL developed into several significant large house church networks. The situation went on basically until 1995 when leaders of the WOL repented before God for the damage this disunity had done to the body of Christ and asked God for opportunity to restore fellowship and unity in witness. Peter identifies the problem inhibiting unity among house churches: "When believers are united around a common goal, we can head there together, putting aside our petty differences. When we lose sight of our common vision, we stop looking forward and begin to look at each other. Soon we see each other's weaknesses and faults, and instead of fighting for the kingdom of God we start fighting each other."[18]

Although not everyone in the WOL community was ready to reconcile the broken relationships with former coworkers and therefore lagged behind in this effort for unity, the unity movement has brought genuine renewal among the house church community at large, thus making united witness, at least among the house church community in China, a reality and a blessing. Fellowship across the networks started to resume, and partnership in ministry, such as the BTJ movement, were established.

Evidently in the development of the WOL community in China, a rediscovery of the heart of the gospel ignited a paradigm shift, which sent a timely ripple of renewal across the WOL community and beyond. Without these paradigm shifts, it would be unimaginable that renewal would ever occur among the WOL community. It is therefore basic to the success of the WOL community that leaders of the WOL identified, by the Spirit, what was being neglected at certain points of the history of the Chinese church, and placed it high on the agenda. In this sense, it affirms Snyder's first point of the mediating model.

Existing as an *Ecclesiola*

According to Snyder, this form *ecclesiola* points to a "smaller, more intimate expression of the church within the church. It sees itself not as the true church in an exclusive sense, but as a form of the church which is necessary to the life of the larger whole, and which in turn needs the larger church in order to be complete." It also insists on the conviction that "the Christian faith can be fully experienced only in some such 'subecclesial' or small-church form."[19]

Because of the unique situation in which the WOL emerged, namely, the church emerged onto the China scene in a time when the church in China in its physical sense, i.e. believers meetings openly in church buildings or other premises, or any ministry or activity in the name of Christianity, was no more, the WOL did not rise out of a particular church denomination. In this sense it does not fit exactly the category Snyder describes in his mediating model, where renewal movements rise out of or within a larger church or denomination and bring renewal to the whole. In order to evaluate the WOL, then, it is necessary to look at it from a more relevant lens. In terms of the *ecclesiola in ecclesia*, the WOL can be viewed from at least the following perspectives.

First of all, in a more strict sense, the WOL movement did not come from Christian believers within a large congregation who had a conviction for the fuller expression of the Christian faith. The WOL was naturally formed by the "churchless" believers and converts during a time when there was no visible church.[20] In a broader sense, however, we can identify the WOL as part of the true Chinese Church, committed to renewing the Chinese Church and relighting the fire of revival of Christianity in China. Peter and his coworkers were conscious of the fact the WOL was part of the universal church of Jesus Christ. When asked of the name(s) of his church, Peter preferred either the WOL or the Church of Jesus Christ in China, by which he meant that the WOL was part of the Church of Jesus Christ in China.

Having gone through the 1950s and 1960s, Peter and his coworkers, in their experience, recognized the source of ill health of the Chinese Church even under the Communist rule. One was the external pressure from the government, as Philip Yuen-sang Leung rightfully puts it,

> the demand of the Communist government to create a uniform socialist culture that allowed little or no room for different points of view, hence the standardization, centralization, and nationalization policies in industry, agriculture and education, as well as in religion. This led to the shutting down of denominations, the expulsion of missionaries and foreign organizations, and the suppression of independent churches. The government supported the unified church, that is, the TSPM, at the expense of small independent churches, and unification, not unity, was the foundation of a politicized religious policy.[21]

The WOL Christians never felt detached from the Body of Christ even at times when there were fierce attacks on the WOL in terms of its orthodoxy from individuals in the leadership circle of the TSPM and CCC, as well as individuals from the house church community in China.[22] Leaders of the WOL always find the theological legacies of the first generation Chinese Christian leaders to be their proud inheritance. In fact, one of the earliest renewal light came from Peter's recognition of the internal factor that caused the ill health of the Chinese Church during the 1950s and 1960s. In his own words,

> we witnessed many theologians, Christian believers, and religious leaders fall from grace after the political movements since 1949. They either failed to stand up, or lost their faith and denied the Lord. Therefore, knowledge cannot save us. Confession with the mouth does not represent a spiritual relationship with the Lord. In face of this problem, we came before the Lord who shone light on us and inspired us so that we came to the understanding that the Word of God, as recorded in the Bible, was not bound by time, and it provided a relevant message for each period of time interpreted through the prophets. In the same way, the Bible also has a message for our time, which is a task for us, through our theological reflection which comes from spiritual practice, to discern, following the guidance of the Holy Spirit, what are the important messages for today. Salvation through the Cross and Walking the Way of the Cross address exactly the felt need of our time. The world presents a temptation, challenge, and test for Christians. James said, "Brothers, you should be joyful even in all the trials." Our new life in Christ is like the center point of a circle, vulnerable to the 360 radiant lines from the surrounding world. Unless we build a solid way of the Cross, we would not triumph over the world. This was the lesson we learned from the painful destruction of the Chinese Church before the revivals in the 1980s.[23]

This recognition explains the WOL church's emphasis on (Christian believers) establishing a solid relationship with Jesus Christ through experience of the rebirth. Later, such emphasis was more systematically developed in *the Seven Principles*.

Secondly, all the thousands upon thousands of the house churches within the WOL exist as *ecclesiolae*, which means that small house churches are the norms of worship and fellowship within the WOL. This would fit nicely the concept of *eccclesiola* if we consider the whole body of the WOL as the *ecclesia*. One may argue that the form of the WOL structure developed out of external pressure. This, however, is only partially true, for the WOL leaders, in their given environment, perceived, as enabled by the Holy Spirit, what was best for the church and its ministry. The fact is that these Christians spent a lot of time on their knees seeking the will of God.

Each individual house church functions exactly as a true and complete church in its own, with all the features of a true church, and yet it is part of the WOL house church network. Take one house church for example, the Grace Church, one of many house churches established through the ministry of the WOL Gospel Band in the 1990s. It has since grown into several house churches because of the growing number of converts that have been added to the church. The Grace Church, at its original meeting location in a small town in central China, has an attendance of around fifty regulars, meeting three to five times a week: Sunday worship, prayer meeting on Tuesday, Bible Study on Tuesday, testimony meeting on Thursday, and hymns and praises on Friday. There are five coworkers (like deacons) and one pillar (like a pastor), all of whom are raised from its own community of new converts. One coworker from Grace church is also a member of the Coworkers' Meeting which consists of seven representatives from seven house churches in the area and which meets once every month. Two other members from the Grace Church also participate the monthly Representatives' Meeting which consists of one to three selected members from each of the seven house churches in the Coworkers' Meeting. In the above mentioned meetings, the experience in ministry of each of the seven house churches would be shared, issues resolved, and further work coordinated. Through these meetings, the light of renewal is also shared among its members who, on the one hand, would bring it back to his/her own house church for reference, and on the other hand, would also report to the Area Meeting, and Pastoral District Meeting, and Pastoral Regional Meeting, etc.

In other words, Grace Church can be viewed as an *ecclesiola in ecclesia*, sending ripples of renewal wave to the whole body of the WOL community. It is the same with many other house churches in the WOL, functioning as *ecclesiola in ecclesia*. In this way the whole WOL network is then in motion of renewal.

When asked about the preference of the WOL house church structure versus the institutional big churches, several coworkers offered almost a unanimous answer: house churches provide more opportunity for believers to participate in the life and ministry of the Body of Christ. In terms of pastoral care house churches can meet the needs of their members more adequately. In terms of mission and evangelism, house churches are more efficient and therefore more readily to grow and multiply. For institutional churches, they have the privilege of being able to provide believers a free, safe, and long-term place to meet and worship. They, however, needs house churches to help pastoral care of its members.[24]

The unique Chinese situation has ruled out an automatic fit for this model. Denominational affiliation is not closely relevant to the emergence of the WOL community as it did not react against an institutional church or denomination. Rather the WOL church rose out of the concern for the health of the whole of Chinese Christianity and its structure facilitates renewal to the whole of the WOL community. In this sense, Snyder's model rightfully qualifies the WOL situation.

Small-Group Structure

In renewal movements believers intentionally made use of the "small communities within the local congregation" consisting of "a dozen or less persons who meet regularly once a week."[25] Snyder further provides guidelines for effective small groups and house meetings:

> Effective groups normally 1) meet weekly; 2) provide for adequate time (usually at least one and one-half to two hours); 3) meet consistently, each member seeing the group as one of the most fundamental commitments of the week; 4) meet over a long enough period of time (months or years) to build trust and a healing sense of community; 5) involve some combination of prayer, Bible study, and mutual sharing and encouragement; and 6) integrate themselves into the larger life of the church so that they nurture the congregation.[26]

As noted earlier, the WOL consists of house churches of anywhere between twenty to over a hundred believers meeting in the various villages and towns where people live. In the initial revival stage of the WOL during the early 1970s, through the work of the itinerant evangelists of the time, the lost sheep of God were found and gathered together for prayer, worship, and fellowship. Numbers grew from three to five believers to a dozen, and further into thirty to forty, and, in some cases, even up to a hundred. Initially, only believers met in prayer and fellowship. Later on, relatives and friends were invited to the meetings, to whom the gospel was shared. Itinerant evangelists would move on to the next destination when a house church was established, and would come back later in time to consolidate the church and encourage believers in an evangelistic itinerant circle covering a reachable area considering the fact that most of the time itinerant evangelists relied on bicycles, or simply their legs to cover the distances. After several itinerant circles, the house churches would grow significantly large and had to split into two or more house churches. This was the basic model of church planting of the time.[27]

Master-Apprentice Discipleship

The primary content of house church gathering during this time was prayer, studying the Bible, and preaching of the itinerant evangelists. When believers in a house church started to mature in faith, some committed Christians would dedicate themselves to the ministry as evangelists, teachers, or local pillars with the blessing of the itinerant evangelists and other coworkers. Traditional

Chinese way of apprenticeship involves the apprentice or the student formally requesting the master for acceptance through the necessary ritual. At the master's consent, the apprentice would start by observing the master in his assigned task as the master instructs where necessary. In the context of the WOL, this would often involve the laying of hands in prayer and affirmation before God. This was often done after a period of time of discipleship when committed believers followed the itinerant evangelists on the evangelistic tour and involved themselves in the work of the ministry.[28] In the Chinese educational context, where students were often encouraged to learn by heart and memorize the noted works of Chinese literature, or even the teachers' words, this master-apprentice relationship sometimes went as far as students copying and reciting the sermons of their leaders. When it comes to preaching opportunities in the house churches, young believers sometimes simply recite the leaders' sermons, or simply read from copied sermon manuscripts. The congregation, nonetheless, receives the messages wholeheartedly and responds with enthusiasm. Of course, later on in ministry as these young believers mature in faith and knowledge, they become less dependent on their leaders and more on the empowerment of the Holy Spirit.[29]

In fact one of the distinct features of the WOL community is that coworkers are not hesitant in articulating their theology of the cross and consistent in teaching and reflection. Everyone seems to be on the same page, affirming one another's experience.

As contextual as it is, the principle of the model is not a Chinese invention, for we find biblical precedent in Paul-Timothy discipleship experience.

Contextual Form

Much of the early form of house church within WOL remains over the years, although, in terms of form, house churches have gradually developed more diverse kind of meetings, and in terms of size, individual house churches have remained much the same. Today the house church gatherings within the WOL include approximately thirty to fifty believers and seekers. In more remote places of rural area, Sunday worship often draws a crowd of several hundreds, while other meetings during week often involve twenty to forty believers in different homes.

The small group kind of church life is not exclusive to the WOL. Majority of house church that affiliated with other networks share a similar feature. One researcher argues that in the Chinese context, "church life is often experienced in small groups that feature close relationships and family ties."[30] The WOL is no exception. The house churches, first of all, consist of immediate believing family members of the neighborhood: grandparents, parents, uncles, aunts, and children, and their friends or *Guan xi*.[31]

Songs and hymns are sung mostly in traditional Chinese tunes, often without the accompaniment of any musical instrument. One of the most popular Christian song writers, Xiao Min, is from Henan, the same province where the WOL got started. Though not formally trained as a musician, she has written over a thousand praise songs that are commonly known as "Canaan Hymns" series. These hymns are enthusiastically received by the Chinese Christians throughout the country including the WOL community. Kneeling in prayer as humble expression of approaching a holy God, often times on cold and hard floors, are generally practiced among the WOL Christians. Active participation of all members in the house church gatherings is encouraged and practiced by means of prayer, worship, praise, testimony, reflection, and service.

Theological Identity

The WOL links the house churches together through its unique structure. There is the distinct identity within the WOL community because the basis of the WOL teaching is *The Seven Principles,* a communal product of systematic study of the Scripture as it relates to Christian life and ministry. Most, if not all, of the preaching and teachings of the house churches within the WOL community are based on *The Seven Principles.* All believers need to go through the first two principles—*salvation through the cross* and *the way of the cross*—at the very beginning of their walk in faith. All the training in the seminaries of the fields of different levels revolves around *the Seven Principles.* It is the binding agent of the three constituent parts of the WOL movement: established churches, TE, and the Gospel Band. The special emphasis on "life" relationship with God through the experience of rebirth in Jesus Christ not only makes the WOL believers identifiable in the crowd, but also undergirds the vitality and growth of the WOL community. Revivals often start from one of the house churches in certain WOL pastoral area and spread to the neighboring areas and regions.

Variety of Meetings

The house churches normally meet at least a couple of times a week involving the whole respective congregation. Sunday worship is the primary event of the week when the whole local house church congregation show up for worship. Other meetings take place during weekdays, which would include prayer meetings, Bible Study, testimony meetings, hymns and praises meetings, etc. These are regular meetings that are called on weekly or bi-weekly. More meetings of different kinds are planned and scheduled as needed. As indicated in the WOL manual (2003), there are four primary kinds of meetings within the WOL network: regular meetings, spiritual formation meetings, holy occasions and coworkers' meetings (see Figure 4:1). Under each category there are a number of specific kinds of meetings.

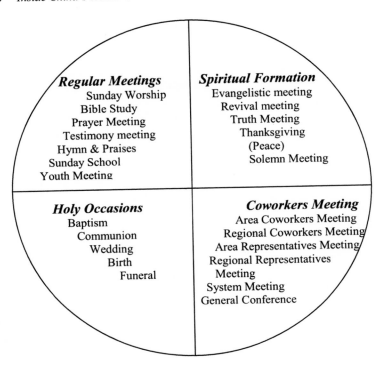

Figure 4.1: Variety of the WOL meetings

Sunday worship usually lasts at least two hours. Singing of hymns takes about half an hour to an hour (often starting well before the scheduled time for worship with believers arriving and immediately joining the singing), prayer for about half an hour, testimony sharing about twenty minutes to half an hour, and preaching for about an hour. Following is an example of a Sunday worship service of one of the WOL house churches in central China:

About forty to fifty people gathered at a house in a city in Henan for a Sunday worship, with approximately 70 percent of the attendance being women. More than half of women were forty plus years old. The scale was about the same for male attendance, with very few young men showing up. Those who had arrived earlier were already singing hymns with traditional Chinese melodies. This was followed by simultaneous prayer for about half an hour, with all kneeing on the floor, some with a cushion under their knees but most people kneeling without a cushion. After about half an hour of simultaneous prayer, the preacher concluded the prayer, and ending with the whole congregation reciting the Lord's Prayer.

Then there was a time of testimonies when people vied with each other in standing up to give testimonies of the grace of God they experienced in their lives and in others' lives in terms of healing of sickness, conversion experience, success in ministry, examples of transformation of lives, etc. The brother who took me to the meeting also stood up and gave his testimonies about how the Spirit of God provided opportunities for him to share the gospel to people on the street and how the Spirit worked in the hearts and minds of those who heard the gospel message so that they accepted it. Another lady shared about how her sister's health was miraculously restored after suffering a certain disease for years, she praised God for this healing. People attending the Sunday worship responded enthusiastically to the testimonies with "Amen." So, one after another, believers stood up and gave their testimonies and praises, and this went on for well over half an hour. If not for the local pillar who led the service to call it an end to the testimony time, this could go on and on.

After this, the preacher, a lady in her early thirties, started to preach a sermon, a very topical sermon about how believers should live by the Word of God instead of by the standard of this world. The attendance kept responding in Amen to the message.

Transformed Sense of Community

House church meetings tie believers close together across and beyond social networks. The fact that groups of people who are not necessarily related to one another by blood, and who do not share the same family name come together on a regular basis to have fellowship with one another and pray for one another is something phenomenal in a society where "each sweep only the snow in front his own yard and does not care about the frost on other people's roof."[32] Small-group type of meeting provides people with opportunities to speak out and interact with others which they do not have in other settings of daily life. Particularly for women, house churches become the place where they can let out their emotions and heart-felt needs in forms of prayer and praise to God.

Each house church within the WOL is a full church of Jesus Christ theologically and ecclesiologically, and yet it is not an independent church. Structurally, it is part of the whole community of the WOL. Each house church is closely knit into the web of the WOL organizational structure through regular fellowship meetings with other house churches within the WOL that take place in forms of coworkers meetings, representatives' meeting and special evangelistic meetings (often taking place during specific holidays such as the Chinese New Year when it is the least busy time for the rural farming population, and when many house churches in the area would participate in the ministry).[33] In this way, the WOL could keep the house churches affiliated with it, despite the fact that they might be hundreds or even thousands of miles apart from one another, in line with the vision of the movement ecclesiologically, theologically, and missiologically.

Limitations

Of course, this does not mean that everything takes place precisely according to the design of the WOL Manual. In fact, it does not. One simple fact is that the environment where the WOL finds itself is not a friendly one for the WOL to operate with freedom. All levels of the coworkers' meetings gather clandestinely and at temporary locations. At certain periods of time when the environment appears to be especially hostile, meetings have to be postponed, relocated, or cancelled. This is exactly what the author experienced during the field research in central China. Related to this factor is the observation that it is no easy task to organize such an extensive network of house churches that have spread all over the country. The fact that the WOL is a rural house church movement makes it particularly difficult. Sociologically speaking, because of the lack of mobility in the rural society in China, the rural population generally has a strong sense localism.[34] It is, therefore, a challenging task to maintain the cross-region house churches within the WOL network. Nonetheless, meetings go on, ministries go on, and renewal continues to impact the church.

Small group structure, in the case of the WOL community, house church structure, is the norm for the WOL community. In fact, house churches are the basic constituent parts of the larger WOL community. In terms of the function of the house church structure, it has surpassed the small group structure as it is understood in the West. For the WOL community, a house church is a church, part of the body of Christ. It is where believers meet, men and women, young and old, to worship, to study the Word of God, to fellowship with one another, to pray for the needy, to partake of the sacraments, to go out in mission, and so on.

Despite of the differences in concept between the WOL house church structure in comparison to what Snyder observes in his study of the three post-Reformation renewal movements, this study has found none but complementary elements. It is reaffirming the fact that Christianity is indeed a movement, where there twos or threes who gather together in the name of Jesus, there the church is.

Structural Link with the Institutional Church

As delineated in Chapter 1, in the case of China, unless registered with the TSPM, any Christian gatherings are considered illegal and therefore subject to opposition from the government. Churches registered (with TSPM) seem to fit best in the category of the institutional church. A majority of registered churches in urban areas have ordained ministers and staff, and services are scheduled regularly, opening to the public.

Thus, if we consider the TSPM as the institutional church, then the WOL does not have any formal structural links with the TSPM. In fact, as specified in the WOL manual, any act of mixture of religion and politics is regarded as idolatry, by which standard TSPM would be judged. True Christians are saved through the Cross, and would never compromise their faith for the sake of survival, but separate themselves from the world and worldly powers for the Lord, and walk *the way of the cross*. In preaching and teaching within the WOL network then, TSPM is often condemned and serves as an foil to the true church that is willing to suffer for the Lord because the Lord suffered for the world first.

In practice, however, there are exceptions, which are subject to the discernment and convictions of the coworkers involved. According to former MGs, when they were out in evangelistic outreach to a certain area or region, they were sometimes invited to speak at the local TSPM churches. When such opportunities opened up, they would gladly take them, addressing the believers in the TSPM churches.

> The Spirit of God worked with the house churches as well as the TSPM churches when he empowered out messages. People were convicted and confessed their sins, and they came before God in repentance. Revivals would visit the TSPM churches. Once we were sent to a certain area in the west part of China engaging ourselves in frontier evangelism. The Lord greatly blessed our ministry there, moving people into meetings after meetings and claiming people into his Kingdom. A great revival started among the newly established house churches. And people from all walks of life came participating in the blessings, among whom some were members of the local TSPM church. When words about the work of the Spirit of God were brought back to the TSPM church, leaders of the official church decided to be part of what God was doing through us and thus invited us to speak at the coming Sunday worship service at the local TSPM church. Led by the Spirit of God we went and spoke boldly on the messages of the Cross. The spirit came down and the whole congregation was greatly stirred. They had never heard of such a message before! People started to weep and repented their sins, and were eager to seek the new life in Christ. My co-workers and I had to stay behind for hours to encourage, confirm, pray and counsel with people.[35]

On the other hand, the WOL church emphasizes "interlink and fellowship" (one of *the Seven Principles* in the WOL Manual), although this principle was primarily implemented to consolidate the WOL community. Chao (2003) explains,

> In organizational terms, it means forming a "Pastoral District" out of thirty to fifty house meetings, each of which functions as a local church. Monthly meetings are conducted at the "district meetings," much like the meetings in the Presbyterian form of government. District ecclesiastical and mission affairs are taken care of by seven full time non-paid pastors. They deal with issues faced by members of the meetings points. Above the pastoral districts is "Conference Meetings," which are made up of two representatives from each pastoral district. These conferences would meet four to five times a years for a week or so. At these meetings, appointments of regional leaders are made, theological and pastoral conflicts are resolved, training of itinerant evangelists is decided and financed. The conferences are like Methodist conferences or synods in the Presbyterian system. Once a year, representatives from the regional conferences would gather together for fellowship, Bible study, and discussion on theological, ecclesiastical, and missiological issues followed by verbal resolutions. Decisions are then communicated to the various conferences and pastoral districts. The work of the (national) general conference is carried out by seven full-time non-paid itinerant evangelists or those selected from the church system. Recognition and assignment of pastoral leadership at the grassroots level are done at the district meetings. Theological education (such as setting up "seminaries of the fields"), theological differences, and planning for missionary expansion are done at the regional conference meeting.[36]

Later on, "interlink and fellowship" extended itself "outside the box" to include non-WOL house church networks. This was particularly so since 1995 when the call for unity among house churches was responded to positively by leaders of several large house church networks.[37] Since then, inter-network fellowships have been organized, particularly on the leadership level between the WOL and other large house church networks such as the Fangcheng Fellowship, China Gospel Fellowship, Anhui Network, and others.

A recent national inter-network coworkers' meeting was formed consisting of former MGs from various regions who affiliated with different house church networks with the intention to build what they call a "platform," from which ministry is coordinated for the best advancement of the evangelistic, training and pastoral ministry. Brother P says,

> We call this coworkers' meeting *"Tong lu ren hui"* ("Fellow Sojourners' Meeting") because we all had years of experience of MGs working in the frontiers of the fields and shared the same convictions that God had called us to forward his Kingdom on earth through preaching the gospel to the unreached peoples. This work will not and should not be the work of one house church network. It needs the participation of the whole church universally. In the context of China geographically, our vision has been that we build a platform from which there would be, first of all, fellowship among the coworkers of different networks and families, and then, coordination of the work of evangelism and resources. In this way, this platform would become one of supply and blessing, whereas if one area needs trained workers, other areas will supply, and if one area is short of resources, others will provide.[38]

In conclusion, whether or not the WOL movement is consistent with this mark of the mediating model depends on what one looks at the WOL church in relation to. In other words, in the case of the WOL church as an *ecclesiola*, who is the *ecclesia*?

When one takes the TSPM church as the institutional church, then the WOL church does not fit into Snyder's model because there is no structural link between the WOL church and the TSPM. Historically, one has never belonged to the other. Snyder's model, though, is valid in the long run, when possibilities of some kind of the link between the TSPM and the WOL community will eventually become a reality. When this happens, I believe, renewal will be more pervasive than what it is already. Sadly, for now, the two church bodies still remain separated.

Snyder's model would fit the WOL situation if we consider the individual house churches in relation to the whole of the WOL community. In this case, the house churches maintain close structural link with the WOL church. Even when we consider the WOL church in relation to the whole of the Chinese Church in general, there is certain structural link maintained, such as those house church networks involved in the Sinim Fellowship and BTJ movement.[39]

Commitment to the Unity, Vitality, and Wholeness of the Larger Church

According to Snyder, the renewal structure "will be concerned first of all with the life of that branch of the church which forms its most immediate context (for example, a denomination or a theological or ecclesiastical tradition), but it will also have a vision for the universal church and a concern for its unity and united witness."[40]

Although it may not have been specifically intended to at the beginning, in the process of its development, the WOL structure reflects exactly such commitment to the unity, vitality, and wholeness of the larger house church community. Such commitment can be clearly identified from their principles for ministry reflected in the WOL Manual.

Unity of the WOL Church

Unity comes close to being one of the most challenging tasks for the traditional Chinese, especially when we talk about the unity beyond traditional social network: family and kinship. The Chinese government seemingly succeeded in uniting the peoples of China through revolutions after revolutions, but such unity hardly had any root under the surface. The commune system collapsed disastrously in the 1960s. "The People's Commune" hardly created any sense of responsibility for one another in the community rather than enforced participation in labor together for the allocated grains after harvest each year. Therefore after the Cultural Revolution in 1976, the first things that the new government did were to reverse back to private ownership of property. Fields that used to be the property of the former commune now became family owned.

In the perspective of the cultural traditions of the Chinese rural people, it would be difficult to talk about unity in a house church network like the WOL with its millions of believers scattered in thousands upon thousands of house churches all over China. And yet the WOL basically achieved the "unity, vitality, and wholeness" through its unique organizational and ministerial structure that is committed to such ends.

Structurally speaking, on the one hand, each house church is a full church, an organic entity that is geared to the Great Commission, operating and developing in its local setting to its full capacity; on the other hand, each house church is part of the large whole of the WOL and therefore in communion and fellowship with the WOL by means of fellowship meetings of various kinds (such as area coworkers' meetings, Gospel Band and local churches fellowship meetings, etc.) in each locality, supplying workers to be trained through the TEs to the Gospel Band, and supporting the Gospel Band through finance and prayer. The illustration of the three supporting legs of an ancient Chinese cooking utensil referring to the close relationship of the established churches, TEs, and the Gospel Band precisely highlights the absolute necessity of unity. Unless the three legs are well coordinated, the whole pot would tip over.

Theologically speaking, in the mid 1980s, leaders and coworkers of the WOL, with the guidance of the Holy Spirit, started to reflect on theology and ministerial experience. Their theological and ministerial reflections were concluded and drafted in their first manual—*The Seven Principles*. Thus a unified theology and ministry guidelines were produced and put into practice within the WOL community even as it was already extending itself in cross-province mission and evangelism. *The Seven Principles* not only served as guidelines in ministry, principles in theology, and curriculum for TE training, but also served as a thread linking together the established house churches which scattered around the country.

Unity of House Church Networks

Then there was the period of ten years, from the mid-1980s to the mid-1990s, of separate development of house church networks from the same tree trunk of house churches. Brother Yun reflects on this piece of history:

> Throughout the 1970s there had been just one house church movement in China. There were no networks or organizations, just groups of passionate believers who came together to worship and study God's Word. The leaders all knew each other. God had brought them together during times of hardship. They learned to have fellowship and trust one another while shackled together in prison. After being released they worked together for the advancement of the gospel. In those early days we were truly unified...When China's borders started to open up in the early 1980s, many foreign Christians wanted to know how they could help the church in China. The first thing they did was smuggle Bibles to us from Hong Kong...However, after a few years these same mission organizations started putting other books at the top of the bags of Bibles. These were books about one particular denomination's theology, or teaching that focused on certain aspects of God's Word. This, I believe, was the start of disunity among many of China's house churches...Within a year or two, the house churches in China split into ten or twelve fragments. This was how so many different house church networks came into existence.[41]

All networks were growing significantly, and yet fellowship between them stopped because each clung to its own newly found denominational emphasis apart from the original WOL which emphasized the experience of rebirth. This situation went on basically until the mid-1990s when Brother Yun, who had been in partnership with Fangcheng house church network since the split, stood out and proposed the need for unity among house churches. Peter was the first to respond positively and took actions in reconciling the broken fellowship between former coworkers by washing their feet as humble expression of sincerity.[42] In so doing Peter exemplified in action not only what the Lord Jesus Christ had modeled but also what was taught in the seventh principle of the WOL manual: to interlink and fellowship.

Since 1995, therefore, the WOL, on the one hand, has been geared to developing its own ministry, which has spread across the country; on the other hand, many in WOL have caught up with the vision of unity of all house churches. Leaders of the house church networks involved call this unity effort the "unity movement." Sadly, some conservative leaders within the WOL have been reluctant to support the "unity movement." Some continue to hold grudge against the fact that, (1) some of the networks developed out of the split part of the WOL in the mid-1980s when they embraced some denominational emphasis brought in by overseas Christian missionaries and trainers; (2) these newly developed house church networks started to critique one another based on their own convictions of what the orthodox Christianity was.

Therefore, challenges and difficulties remain in this effort for unity among house churches. This problem became more evident after Peter left China in 2001, when a kind of two families started to be created among the WOL community: the Hometown Family and the Unity Family. Both families within the WOL continue their day to day ministries as specified in the manual, and yet the Hometown Family was less involved in the unity movement. This being sadly true, many second generation coworkers of the WOL are reluctant to be caught up in the conflict and started to fellowship across the denominational lines, coordinating TE training of various kinds in an inter-network manner. When asked about this move, several of these coworkers pointed out that the WOL Manual actually spells out clearly what the church is and how, as parts of the same body of Christ, Christians should have fellowship with one another just as churches should partner with one another to forward the work of the Kingdom.

> Before death, Christ prayed to God the Father for the unity of his disciples (John 17:11), which basically points to the unity in the Spirit as well as unity in outward manifestation (John 17:21). The unity comprises the unity of the church with Christ, Jewish and Gentile believers in Christ, and among Gentile believers themselves (Ezekiel 11:19–20; John 17:20–22; Eph. 4:4–6).[44]

The WOL Manual provides ample biblical references for unity:

> we serve the same God the father (Eph. 4:6; John 20:17); we are saved by the same God the Son (Eph. 1:7,10; 2:11–16); we are born again (baptized) through the same holy Spirit (Eph. 3:18; cf. Titus 3:5; Romans 6:3–4); we live according to the same Word of God (John 17:15-19; 1 Cor. 10:3–4); we are built on the same body (1 Cor. 10:16–17; 12:12–13; Eph. 2:19–22; 3:6); we are washed by the same love (1 John 4:7; Romans 5:5; Phillipines 2:1–2); we share the same hope (Eph. 4:4).[45]

In the paragraph on the universality and locality of the church the WOL Manual recognizes that dual characteristics of the church as being both universal and local. The church is universal, the manual contends, "in a broad sense," and it is "not limited by geography."

There is only one church in the universe, which is the "church of God," with Christ as the head and foundation (Eph. 1:22; 1 Cor. 3:11). In a more strict sense, what we call the church in a certain region should actually be called "the testimony of the Church of God in certain region," or "the organism of the Church of God in certain region." In a narrow sense, the church is indeed restricted by geography as it is engaged in the practical operation, ministry and worship. Only through the administrative system set up within each regional scope is the will of God for the Church expressed (2 Cor. 10:13–14). Therefore, the church in each respective locality should be its own administrative entity, just like the seven churches in Asia Minor, each being a lampstand on its own, answerable directly to the Lord (Rev. 1:11–13).[46]

In other words, the WOL Manual recognizes the universality of the church as the body of Christ while it also stresses that the ministry is for and realized in the local church.

The appeal for unity among house churches in China, which started in the mid-1990s, is an ongoing effort. The goal, however, is a combined effort to carry out the Great Commission, which, in terms of the role Chinese house church Christians perceived themselves, means to bring the gospel back to Jerusalem.

Peter relates the unity effort among the house churches since 1996 as jumpstarting the Back to Jerusalem Movement:

> I believe that meeting in 1996, and the ones that followed, were some of the most important events in the history of Christianity in China, because the Back to Jerusalem movement would never have gotten off the ground while the house churches remained divided. It was no coincidence that it was after 1996 that the details of the Back to Jerusalem vision began to fall into place.
>
> When we talk of this unity, it needs to be understood that the reason we came together was not for the sake of unity in itself. It was unity for the sake of fulfilling the common vision God had given us—the vision of taking the gospel back to Jerusalem, thus completing the Great Commission and hastening the return of our Lord! That is why we started our unified gatherings. Although various house churches still have different interpretations of some Scriptures and different practices, we recognize that we all share the common goal of sharing the good news with every person inside China and beyond.[47]

Back to Jerusalem

In the midst of the effort for unity among house churches a significant movement, the vision of bringing the gospel Back to Jerusalem (BTJ) was commonly shared, which involved prayers, financial support and manpower of all the house church networks participating in the unity movement. In the beginning of this millennium Peter left China and started to coordinate the BTJ movement from the U.S. Since then, Peter has traveled extensively in and out of the U. S., speaking in churches and organizations for the BTJ movement, gaining significant respect and support from Christians in the U.S. and beyond.

A significant point of this trans-national effort started at the establishment of BTJ Gospel Band in the Philippines in 2002. It was at this meeting that not only strategic planning was made, but also a common vision was shared among the participants that the BTJ movement needed the involvement of international Christian community. The movement is not just the Chinese task, although God has laid the burden on their hearts. It is the task of the universal Church of Christ, called to fulfill the Great Commission.[48] The BTJ Gospel Band was renamed the following year and formally registered in the U.S. as BTJ Gospel Mission.

Theologically fundamentalist influence continues to hinder the WOL community from opening its arms to accept one another in Christ because of the difference in theological/linguistic accents. With the fact that great efforts have been made by the WOL community to gear themselves toward unity among the house church community in China and united witness with the overseas churches, antagonistic contention toward the TSPM churches remains one of the biggest regrets in Chinese Christianity.

Mission-Oriented Structure

The WOL exists for mission! The entire structure is geared toward evangelism and training workers for the work of evangelism. From the evangelistic meetings to intensive training sessions, from TEs to joining the Gospel Band, the whole cycle becomes a dynamic polar train, constantly taking on and letting off passengers. In this cycle, new believers were able to be trained and molded into workers of the Kingdom according to their respective gifts. Therefore, some trained workers were let off as MGs, others as local Pillars, and still others as teachers, deacons, elders, and hospitality family personnel. In his interview with Paul Hattaway in 2003, Peter stated confidently,

> A strong church is one that is a spiritual baby-making center. Souls are being saved and discipled around the clock and the church is a hive of activity. There is no time for believers to sit around and argue with each other. They are too busy just trying to clean up all the mess these newborn babies make while simultaneously trying to prepare more bottles of milk to keep them fed![49]

Dynamic Motion of the WOL Structure

The basic and foundational structure of the WOL is the house churches, established through the evangelistic ministry of the MGs sent by the Gospel Band, which is closely related to and supported by TE (seminaries or training schools). Thus the Established Churches, TE, and the Gospel Band form a solid support for the whole WOL movement. The interaction between the three supporting legs inwardly and outwardly set the whole WOL community in motion. First, established churches support the ministry of the Gospel Band and TE financially, and work with them to provide care, discipleship and training for their members, i.e. through Life/Truth meetings, short-term trainings and TEs. Graduates from Pillars' TE come back to their own communities and become pastors of established house churches. Second, established house churches are also the source of supply of MGs to the Gospel Band that furthers frontier evangelism and establishes more house churches. Third, TE is responsible for providing training of various degrees and lengths preparing workers for service in different areas of ministry of the church. The three constituent parts of the WOL work closely together to keep the wheel spinning outward, thus enlarging the WOL network (see Figure 4.2).

Peter Xu summerizes, "He (God) showed us that spiritual life should be the foundation of our Christianity, building up the church is the center, and the training of workers is the point of breakthrough—the strategic place from where expansion can be carried out in all directions, radiating to every nation and people in the world."[50]

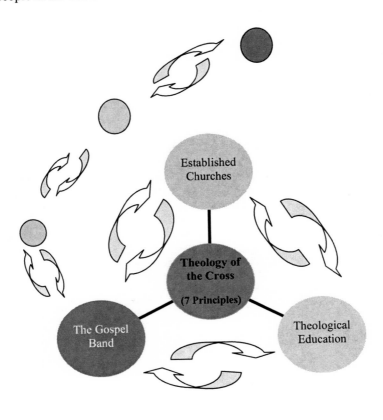

Figure 4.2: WOL Structure in Motion

Four Development Routes

The WOL Manual specifies four development routes along which ministries are developed:

- Route 1—Local church pillars: This line produces local church pillars to provide pastoral care for the local established churches so that churches may grow and, in turn, support TE and the Gospel Band, as follows:
  Life meeting → Truth meeting → Pillar's pre-TE → Pillar's TE → Local church

- Route 2—Organization and fellowship: This line develops along the available structure of the WOL for the consolidation of the structure and formation of leadership:
  Life Meetings → Truth Meetings → Meeting Points → small area Coworkers' Meeting → medium area Coworkers' Meeting → large area Coworkers' Meeting → Conferences

- Route 3—The Gospel Band: This line is geared to continuous yielding of trained MGs for the work of frontier evangelism:
  Life meetings → Truth meetings → Pre-TE → TE-1 → TE-2 → TE-3 → TE-Sp

- Route 4—The Gospel Band (GB) and Local House Churches (HC) Partnership in Ministry: Each team sent from the Gospel Band participates in fellowship meeting with leaders of the local established house churches so that partnership in ministry can be coordinated for mutual benefits:
  Life meeting → Truth meeting → GB+HC fellowship meeting → GB+HC fellowship meetings

According to Snyder, the renewal structure "senses keenly its specific purpose and mission, conceived in part as the renewal of the church and in part as the witness to the world."[51] As a renewal movement, the WOL community identifies the purpose and mission of its existence as renewal of the church, in this case, first the house church community and then the whole of Chinese Church, and evangelism, based on a renewed and united church, as the focus and emphasis of its mission. Although the WOL theology stresses the fulfillment of the Great Commission, the primary investment seems to be on evangelism, as reflected in the development of the unique WOL structure.

Covenant Based Community

The renewal movement, according to Snyder,

> sees itself as a visible form of the true church…a restricted community of people voluntarily committed to each other. Based on a well-understood covenant, it has the capability of exercising discipline, even to the point of exclusion, among its members. As a community the renewal prizes face-to-face relationships, mutuality, and interdependence. It especially stresses Scriptures which speak of *koinonia*, mutual encouragement, and

admonition within the body, and sees itself as a primary structure for experiencing these aspects of the church.[52]

One Community, Many Locations

Formal organization structure started to be in place since 1982 when the WOL was faced with the reality of ever increasing numbers of house churches under its umbrella, which implicated the church polity. A three-level structure was created: (1) pastoral area coworkers' meeting (consisting thirty to fifty house churches), (2) regional coworkers' meeting (consisting of ten pastoral areas), and (3) the general conference. Since the appearance of the three-level coworkers' meetings in 1982, the characteristics of a covenant based community became more and more distinct and functional. In the first year of the WOL structural organization, coworkers' meetings of various levels were able to settle doctrinal disputes among believers, restricting the emergence of possible heretic teaching, and ex-communicated false prophets and adulterers.[53]

At the top of the WOL organization structure is the general conference. Its task is to solve issues of heresy, disputes, and conflicting views among local churches in each region and area so that a unified truth will be reached. It also coordinates church affairs such as evangelism and missions, fellowship meetings, disciplines of the church, rules and regulations for coworkers, warning and punishment among believers of the WOL. Any coworkers, in local and regional coworkers' meetings or general conference, who do not seek diligently the Holy work, backslide, lose faith, commit crime, form own party, betray the Lord and friends, demonstrate unfit for the position, or are ex-communicated by the church, will be replaced at the decision of the conference."[54]

Fellowship among coworkers of all levels is vital in sustaining the covenantal community of the WOL. During their monthly meetings on each of the three levels of the WOL structure, the Word of God is always opened and studied, prayers is engaged, and issues in ministry are shared. Sometimes, doctrinal issues need to be settled through the study of the Word of God, and disciplines are enforced to certain members who violate the covenant as specified in the WOL coworkers' book of discipline.[55] Through these three levels of coworkers' meetings, theological and missional directions are channeled to the members of the WOL even in its pervasive network, so that the community of the WOL wherever it extends itself continues to manifest its distinct features.

Koinonia in the House Church

On the bottom level of the WOL structure is the house churches or meeting points. Here are the basic constituents of the WOL community. And here we have believers meeting in one place or another in twenties, thirties, and fifties, having communion together, praying together, singing hymns together, reading the Word of God together, fellowshipping with one another, helping each other, and witnessing together. Although the local pillar is the one who does most of the teaching and preaching on a weekly basis, believers can participate freely in such small group in different aspects of the respective meetings.

Brother D is the host of a hospitality family. He opens his apartment to receive coworkers, guests, and to store Christian literature. When there is a leadership meeting at his apartment, he would provide service such as preparing beds, cooking and serving food, keeping watch, and running chores. He would also go to any kind of meetings that he can spare time on and freely speaks out his opinion on such issues as, for example, theology and ministry. Whenever he has a chance, he would tell his testimonies at various kinds of house church meetings.

By participating in the meetings and ministry, believers take an active part in the life of the church as a new community. Various kinds of meetings are designed to encourage participation and bring out the *koinonia* kind of community. "Life" witness is also on the priority list that leaders of the WOL appeal its members to demonstrate in the community. Teachings of Wang Mingdao, first generation Chinese Christian leader, on moral and ethical conducts of Christian believers are hung high on the walls of the homes of the WOL believers.

Witnessing Community

As a covenanted community, the WOL is distinctive in that they are devoted to establishing churches all over the country emphasizing in its teaching the experience of rebirth and *the way of the cross*. Life testimony is one of the keys roles that the WOL plays in the Chinese society wherever there is a WOL house church. Testimonies are abundant in the local communities: An old lady who was known as a "tigeress," was converted through the evangelism of the WOL and experienced the illuminating power of the Holy Spirit that enabled her to see her true self. After that, she was totally changed from being extremely bullying to being gentle, living as a testimony of her faith. People in the neighborhood were amazed at how this Christian God can change such a seemingly hopeless person.[56] This kind of testimony has had great impact on the local population, astounding people with the power of Christianity to change.

In the rural areas of China, the WOL Christians become models of team work. They were devoted to doing charitable work in terms of helping those neighbors in need with food and clothing. Under the WOL there are also charitable kindergartens and nursing homes, all of which play a significant and noticeable role in the local community. Examples like these are natural manifestations of new life experienced by the WOL believers, which is something that features the WOL and explains their emphasis on the experience of rebirth or the way of the cross. There have also been appreciations shown by the local government to the good work of Christians. Villages with more Christians are usually known for low crime rate, where believers are regarded as more law-abiding citizens and ready to help those in need in the community. One of the former MGs the author interviewed used to be in charge of an elderly home before he and his wife were further trained in theology, after which they took up the responsibility of teaching and managing a seminary of the fields in one of the rural locations.

To summarize, the WOL is a distinct covenanted community with its distinct features in theology and ministry. It is consistent with historical renewal movements despite the significant difference in environment and time. The WOL community also lives out to a certain extent the biblical concept of *koinonia*. As such, this represents one of the essential characteristics of renewal movements.

Context for New Forms of Ministry and Leadership

Snyder contends that the experience of community within renewal movements contributes to the rise of "a practical stress on the gifts of the Spirit and the priesthood of believers."

> This consciousness combines with the natural need for leadership within the movement and the outward impulse of witness and service to produce both the opportunity and the enabling context for new forms of ministry. Similarly, it produces new leaders who arise not through the more restricted, established ecclesiastical channels (typically, education and ordination, restricted to males), but through practical experience and the shared life of the group. The renewal group provides both opportunities for leadership and service and a natural, practical environment for training new leaders.[57]

Contextual Leadership

WOL has been relatively effective in producing and reproducing evangelists, teachers, local pillars, hospitality families, deacons, elders, and leaders of local and regional levels. They have also developed unique kinds of environment for the rise, training, and exercise of contextual forms of ministry and leadership. Traditional Chinese way of master and apprentice is contextually adopted throughout the development of the WOL when devoted young believers learned from first-hand experience in ministry as followers and disciples of their senior leaders. To the extent that sometimes one of the leaders' sermons would be copied by the young disciples who then, in ministry practice, preached almost word by word to a different congregation. Sometimes, this would mean that some twenty or thirty young evangelists went in all directions to preach from the same sermon. And the result was most amazing: "When the same sermons were preached in different locations, with the work of the Holy Spirit, people were convicted of their sins and felt the need of repentance and seeking salvation."[58]

In the WOL training system, the same master-apprentice model is identified in the internship-kind of ministry involvement on the part of the TE graduates. For example, graduates of TE-1 would then be sent to lead Life/Truth meetings and Pre-TE training under the mentorship and support of more experienced coworkers for six to twelve months before they are called back for further TE training.

Rise of Leadership

The continuous flow of supply for those devoted to the work of the Kingdom from local house churches consolidates the foundation and construction of the WOL project. Any believer who, with the work of the Holy Spirit, is determined to dedicate himself/herself to the ministry of the WOL has the opportunity to be further trained through various TE programs in order to be a coworker sent by the WOL church to serve in its various capacities. This, however, does not mean that there is no supervision and guidance for those who seek to be involved in the ministry of the WOL. There are actually several stages of supervision involved in the process from selecting those who wish to be trained to the eventual sending out of graduates from the various TE programs.

First of all, local pillars, elders, and MGs working in the area are involved in observing, counseling, and selecting those who wish to be further trained for ministry in a local house church setting, and recommend those qualified to the appropriate TE program (i.e. TEs or local pillars TEs); then the responsible co-workers for each of the TE programs further examine the applicants holistically (biblically, spiritually, physically) before accepting them into the program. This often means spending a few days together involving interviews, group devotions, Bible content exam, etc. For those who are devoted to the ministry of Gospel Band, physical fitness is often one of the necessary requirements considering the challenge of frontier evangelism in China. Upon graduation, after living, studying, worshipping, praying, and fellowshipping together for three, six, or even twelve months, leaders (and teachers) of the TE program, leaders of the WOL, locally and regionally, are present to lay hands on each of the graduates and send them out to ministry according to their respective gifts.

The Role of TE in Leadership Formation

TEs in the WOL are particularly designed for the quick production of workers for the Kingdom of God. In *Truth Practical Curriculum* (WOL Manual II), the timetable for the TE training is referred to as for Workers Training Classes. Almost two decades after the TEs were initiated in the WOL, their timetables remained much the same, with significant attention given to spiritual formation of individual trainees as they feed on the Word of God. Many trainees go on to be leaders of the church after graduation. The following timetable is found in the appendix of the WOL Manual II as a guideline for all TE training classes of the WOL.

Timetable for Workers Training Classes (translated and adapted by author)

5:00 a.m.	Rise (watchful, punctuate, speedy, quiet)
5:15–7:15 a.m.	Devotional time (worship, Bible reading, prayer; state of mind: watchful, spiritual warfare, close fellowship)
7:30–8:00 a.m.	Breakfast (thankful, silent, meditative, hygienic)
8:00–8:30 a.m.	Worship (learning hymns, meditation, spiritual fellowship)
8:30–10:00 a.m.	1st Class (taking notes; concentrating and emphasizing application; keeping quiet in class and avoiding procrastination)
10:20–11:50 a.m.	2nd Class
12:00–12:30 p.m.	Lunch (thankful, silent/meditative, hygienic)
12:30–2:00 p.m.	Afternoon Break (keeping silent and avoiding disturbing others)
2:00–2:30 p.m.	Worship (singing hymns and meditating whole-heartedly)
2:30–4:00 p.m.	3rd Class (taking notes, concentrating and emphasizing application; keeping quiet in class and avoiding procrastination)
4:30–6:00 p.m.	4th Class
6:30–7:00 p.m.	Supper (thankful, silent/meditative, hygienic)
7:00–8:30 p.m.	Review (keeping quiet; reviewing what learned; doing homework)
8:30–9:30 p.m.	Evening Prayer (retrospective of the day, thanksgiving, and interceding)
10:00 p.m.	Bedtime (rest in time)

The Role of Coworkers' Meetings in Leadership Formation

The establishment of the coworkers' meetings in its organizational structure serves not only as an overall coordination of the work of the WOL in its various ministries, but also, more specifically, in the area of developing leadership personnel for ministry. It articulates, in the section on the Establishment of Coworkers' Meetings and Conferences, in the early draft of *the Seven Principles*, it specifies the responsibilities of the Coworkers' meetings as "to seriously identify and recommend potential coworkers from among believers," and "to guarantee the acceptance of coworkers God raises up in their local setting, so that church will continue to be under the fresh and lively guidance of God."[59]

Close Contact with the Poor

The WOL community consists of tens of thousands of house churches all over the country, united by its administrative structures within its network. Believers are spiritually bond by their relationship with the Lord and their theological conviction of the need to be born again in Christ. They are proud of being referred to by others as the born again family (community). Several times a week, and on special occasions such as public holidays, believers come together as a house church, to worship and edify one another in the Word of God. A community of WOL believers is evidently present and distinct in the larger residential community.

During the revival stage, those "furnaces of revival" in the central China area served as places of comfort and encouragement, and sometimes healing, for the poor peasants in rural China who dwelt on the margins of the turbulent society. "Prayers plus prayers, and the sick were healed; prayers plus prayers, and the evil spirits were scattered."[60] "In time of great turmoil in the Chinese society, people found something different with the Christian believers who were like salt and light of the world, something that attracted their attention and interest, so that they came forward for light and heat."[61]

Apart from the MGs who traveled to various parts of the country, engaging themselves in evangelism and establishing churches, the local established house churches are right among where believers are, which are, in the communities where they live and share with believers and non-believers alike. Majority WOL believers continue to do farming and engage in other professions as usual and are never detached from the community where they live. This gives these Christians opportunity to witness their faith to the people in the neighborhood. I personally know one brother, who was garbage cleaner in profession, a profession despised by many in the community, witnessed through casual conversations with people on the street, who became so interested and would stay on the topic of Christianity for twenty or more minutes. Another sister was highly looked up by her peers in the community, both believers and non-believers, as a mature Christian whom they could always come for advice on issues such as finding a proper job, dating, marriage, or family relationships.

As Snyder contends, "movements which appeal to and spread among the poor are both more radical and more socially transforming than those which do not,"[62] the WOL qualifies for this contention to a certain extent, at least, in that it has proved itself to be social transforming in its rural environment.

Due to the external limitations enforced on the House Church community, the WOL has not been able to involve in the society as a church as much as it would have desired to. Although there are a number of unofficial elderly homes and orphanages established and supported by the local WOL house churches, social involvement is still stingily promoted in the WOL community. We cannot put all the blames on their physical limitation as an underground church. The legacy of the fundamentalist camp that has been in deliberate tension with the liberal camp since the beginning of the 20th century may have played a role here. As a result, the weight is highly imbalanced toward the spiritual aspect of the spectrum on the scale of evangelism in comparison to social aspect. For the WOL, it is the "new life" found in Jesus Christ and the willingness to suffer for the sake of evangelization that has been much stressed in teaching and ministry.

In recent years, however, the WOL has made great effort to seek space to contribute to the local communities. "Given more freedom, we would like to be actively involved in the society as salt and light in the world. We had plans to set up more charitable centers for the poor, elderly, and orphans, but we have been limited from doing so."[63]

The WOL community, as it differs from some of the historical renewal communities, does not form new communities, although spiritually they are a new community, a community of followers of Jesus Christ. This is because, on the one hand, Christians of the WOL do not see the need to establish a physically separate community; on the other hand, the regime would hardly tolerate such communities. The Jesus Family that had existed until the beginning of the new regime in the 1950s when it was closed down serves as an example. The regime does not allow any form of community that is self organized.

Missiologically speaking, the WOL purposely spread its network extensively around the country, establishing house churches, area and regional coworker's meetings, so that this web of WOL continues to spread outward, drawing more and more people into the spiritual community. In this sense, the WOL will continue to be in close contact with the society and the poor.

Emphasis on the Spirit and the Word as the Bases of Authority

As a common characteristics found in Pietism, Moravianism and Methodism as movements of renewal, the renewal structure

> Stresses the norm of Scripture and the life of the Spirit and maintains both of these in some tension with the traditionalism of the institutional church. If it veers to the right or the left at this point, it will become either a highly legalistic sect or an enthusiastic cult liable to extreme or heretical beliefs. The renewal movement stresses the Spirit and the Word as the ultimate ground of authority, but within limits also recognizes the authority and traditions of the institutional church.[64]

Foundation to Renewal: Spirit and Word

The WOL church, as a movement of renewal, finds its source of power and guidance from the Word of God and the Holy Spirit. As an unregistered church, it does not submit to the authority of the TSPM, neither does it to the state regulation. Because of the stand of the WOL community, the WOL church becomes target of opposition. Yet this is exactly what propels the community to grow. When believers of the WOL follow the direction of the Holy Spirit and hold on the Word of God as the authority for living and ministry, the community naturally grows. Snyder contends,

> *The church has an inborn tendency to grow.* Growth is in its genes. Whatever its pathologies, every church has a vital urge toward its own health and renewal. The reason for this is simple, and simply profound: The church is the body of Christ. The very Spirit of Jesus is at work in his church, always prodding and drawing it toward life and renewal.[65]

The WOL manual recognizes the Bible as the "revelation from God, through men, to men." It is "the only infallible revelation of God to men." And the Bible is the "highest authority of all morality and faith. The whole Bible is God-breathed and the Holy Spirit preserves every thought, sentence, even every word from mis-spellings, omissions, and miscommunication (2 Peter 1:20–21)."[66] The manual also identifies the "dynamics of church growth as coming from the Holy Spirit, who inspires (Gal. 2:8; Acts 21:4), fills (Acts 2:4; 6:5; 7:55; 4:8, 31; 13:9), speaks (Acts 8:29; 10:19; 11:12; 13:2; 21:11), testifies (Acts 10:1-33; 8:26–35), prohibits (Acts 16:6–7), appoints (Acts 20:28), sends out (Acts 13:1, 4)."[67]

Leaders of the WOL identify their church structure, even their experience in the development of the WOL community, as following closely the biblical model. Just as Paul and his coworkers went on an itinerant evangelistic journey throughout Asia Minor and southern Europe, establishing churches, revisiting them to encourage and settle controversies, the WOL evangelists did likewise, making regular itinerant circles to consolidate the house churches they established. Just as persecution of Christians scattered believers in the early church resulted in the gospel being spread as Christians were on the run from persecution, the WOL leaders and coworkers experienced the same when the 1983 "Strike Hard" campaign targeted leaders of the unregistered churches in China. Peter reflects quoting Scripture, "All things work for the good of those who love God."

Statement of Faith

In 1998, leaders of four of the largest house churches networks in central China including the WOL church came together and drafted an official Statement of Faith of Chinese House Churches. In regard to the role of the Bible and the Holy Spirit, the Statement states:

1. The Bible
We believe that the 66 books of the Bible are inspired by God and that they were written by the prophets and apostles under the inspiration of the Holy Spirit. The bible is the complete truth and without error; no one is allowed to change it in any manner.

The Bible clearly states God's plan of redemption of mankind. The Bible is the highest standard of our faith, life and service. We are opposed to all those who deny the Bible [as the Word of God]; we are opposed to the view that the Bible out of date; we are opposed to the view that the Bible has errors, and we are opposed to those who believe only in selected sections of the Bible. We want to emphasize that the Scriptures must be interpreted in light of their historical context and within the overall context of Scriptural teachings. In seeking to understand Scripture, one must seek the leading of the Holy Spirit and follow the principle of interpreting Scripture by Scripture, not taking anything out of context. In interpreting Scripture one ought to consult the traditions of orthodox belief left by the church throughout her history. We are opposed to interpreting Scripture by one's own will, or by subjective spiritualization.

5. The Holy Spirit

We believe the Holy Spirit is the third person in the Trinity. He is the Spirit of God, the Spirit of Christ, the Spirit of truth, and the Spirit of holiness.

The Holy Spirit illuminates a person causing him to know sin and repent, know the truth, and to believe in Christ and so experience being born again onto salvation. The Holy Spirit leads believers to the truth, and gives them understanding of the truth, and enables them to obey Christ, thereby bearing abundant fruit of life. The Holy Spirit gives all kinds of power [to his servants] and manifests the mighty acts of God through signs and miracles. The Holy Spirit searches all things.

In Christ, God grants a diversity of gifts of the Holy Spirit to the church so as to manifest the glory of Christ. Through faith and thirsting, Christians can experience the outpouring and the filling of the Holy Spirit.

We do not believe in the cessation of signs, miracles or the termination of the gifts of the Holy Spirit after the apostolic period. We do not forbid speaking in tongues nor do we insist that everyone must speak in tongues. We do not use a criterion of speaking in tongues as the evidence of being saved. We refute the view that the Holy Spirit is not a person in the Trinity, but only a kind of influence. [68]

Spirit and Word in Ministry

In practice, the WOL leaders stress following the leading of the Holy Spirit as a general rule of ministry and mission. Young evangelists are modeled from the beginning of their preparation for ministry on how an intimate relationship is established with the Lord through prayer, Scripture reading, and daily practice of faith. When the young evangelists, after the TE training, are sent out to frontier evangelistic work, they then experience the Holy Spirit in the deepest personal way, especially at times when there is nothing else to rely on. In "the Secret of the MGs" (1991), it summarizes,

A MG, who receives commandment from God, is sent by God. When he/she is loyal and obedient to the commandment, he will be successful. A MG receives a message from God and preaches what God commands him/her instead of what pleases man. A MG must familiarize himself with the Word of God in order to understand His way and will. Only those who commit themselves to much scriptural reading and prayer can brighten their eyes of the heart and be appropriate to be used by the Lord. A MG receives supplies, light and strength from the Word of God. [69]

One former MG reflects,

At the beginning of our outreach, we felt like being pushed to the frontier, without adequate preparation for the ministry, very vulnerable indeed. When we encountered closed doors and scornful attitude, we did not have anything else to fall back on but God. We learned how to rely on God through prayer and discern the leading of the Holy Spirit. Miraculously, when we learned to rely on God, He cleared the way for us, and the gospel started to bear fruits.[70]

As mentioned earlier, Bible recitation is a required exercise for all trainees of various TE classes and encouraged for all believers of the WOL community. The result is often manifested in prayers when pervasive quote of scriptural verses accompanies each coworker. When asked about the role of the Bible, one coworker says, "The Bible is the sole dictionary that believers find the meaning and guidelines for life." Another adds, "The Bible is food for humans, without which one cannot survive." Still others hold the Bible as having the highest authority and final judgment of all things. "It is like a ruler, with which we can measure things."[71]

Indeed, the WOL maintains an emphasis on the Word of God and the Holy Spirit as the basis of authority in the life and ministry of the church. Such emphasis is reflected in all levels of the WOL church through its structure. There is the constant emphasis on the Spirit and the Word as the sole authority where the next move in ministry is directed. Because of such emphasis, the WOL structures itself in such a way that it has grown into what it is today.

Summary

This analysis has demonstrated the relevance of Snyder's mediating model as a perspective in studying the WOL movement, for the WOL movement, in the most part, exemplifies what Snyder proposes in his mediating model. Vice versa, Snyder's model provides useful tools by which the dynamics of the WOL church are clarified. The WOL movement has demonstrated itself to be a renewal movement within Chinese Christianity and is validated as such by Snyder's theory. For the sake of clarification, the following comparison shows the extent the WOL house church movement approximates the ten marks of the mediating model for church renewal. Because of the significant difference that exists in socio-political environments between China and the west, this figure does not claim to represent a tight fit in each of the marks. Rather, it is an attempt to generalize some of the common features that renewal movements share in a hope to identify the intercultural signs of the Spirit of God in renewing his church.

The following is a generalized identification of the consistency of the WOL movement with the historical Christian renewal movements in terms of common characteristics as identified and proposed by Snyder in the mediating model for church renewal.

1. The renewal movement "rediscovers" the gospel—highly consistent.
2. The renewal movement exists as an *ecclesiola*—less consistent.
3. The renewal movement uses some form of small-group structure—highly consistent.
4. The renewal movement has some structural link with the institutional church—less consistent.
5. The renewal structure is committed to the unity, vitality, and wholeness of the larger church—highly consistent.
6. The renewal structure is mission-orientated—highly consistent.
7. The renewal movement is especially conscious of being a distinct, covenant-based community—consistent.
8. The renewal movement provides the context for the rise, training, and exercise of new forms of ministry and leadership—consistent.
9. Members of the renewal movement remain in close daily contact with society, and especially with the poor—consistent.
10. The renewal movement maintains an emphasis on the Spirit and the Word as the basis of authority—highly consistent.

The two less consistent elements (2 and 4 above) identified are only to be seen as less consistent in a narrow sense because of the fact that the WOL movement did not grow out of an institutional church. As explained early in the chapter, the *ecclesiola in ecclesia* typology is applicable to the WOL house churches if we consider the whole of the Chinese Church as *ecclesia* in which the WOL church is a part, or the whole of the WOL church as *ecclesia* and the house churches within the WOL community as *ecclesiolae*. In any case, the WOL church would be consistent even in those two areas. As Snyder (1997) notes at the end of his mediating model,

> More importantly, if one's understanding of "church" includes broadly all the people of God in the various communions, all those who confess Jesus Christ as Savior and Lord, then such independent churches and sects may still be seen as *ecclesiolae* within the church of Christ, even though they are independent of any particular ecclesiastical structure larger than themselves.[72]

Snyder's mediating model includes most of the essential elements of renewal movements. We can see the consistency that the WOL house church movement has shown comparing with the historical renewal movements, a fact that helps us to more clearly identify the signs of the Spirit of God. There are, however, elements that can stand out more among the marks of the mediating model as well as some WOL-particular characteristics, which this study has found to be necessary elements of renewal. In the next chapter, these "new" elements will be introduced in addition to what Snyder's mediating model has offered us.

Notes

1. Howard Snyder, *Signs of the Spirit* (Eugene, Oregon: Wipf and Stock, 1997), 277.

2. Ibid., 269.

3. Ibid., 219.

4. Cf. Jonathan Chao and Wanfang Zhuang, *A History of Protestant Christianity in China: 1949–1997* (Taipei: CMI Press, 1997), 144–46; Jason Kindopp and Carol Lee Hamrin, eds., *God and Caesar in China: Policy Implications of Church-State Tensions* (Washington, D.C.: Brookings Institution Press, 2001), 123–24.

5. Kindopp and Lee, 124.

6. Cf. Chao and Zhuang, 189.

7. Chairman Mao was called the "great savior of the people" as in more than one of the praise songs for his role in the founding of the People's Republic of China.

8. Xu, interview.

9. Cf. Kindopp and Lee, 122–26.

10. Richard Bush, *Religion in Communist China* (Nashville, Tennessee: Abingdon Press, 1970), 214.

11. Bush, 214–19. Cf. Leslie Lyall, *China's Three Mighty Men* (London: OMF Books, 1973), 126–34.

12. Xu, interview.

13. Ibid.

14. Cf. WOL Manual I.

15. WOL Manual II, 36.

16. Ibid., 38–39.

17. Cf. Chao, *Purified by Fire*, 32.

18. Paul Hattaway, *Back to Jerusalem*, 66.

19. Snyder, *Signs of the Spirit*, 277.

20. From the early 1960s to the end of 1970s, all the church premises were either confiscated or put to other use by the state, and all Christian gatherings and activities were banned. The same situation also applies to other religious communities such as Buddhists, Taoists, and Muslims.

21. Philip Yuen-sang Leung, "Conversion, Commitment, and Culture," in *Christianity Reborn*, edited by Donald Lewis (Grand Rapids, Michigan: Wm. B. Eerdmans Publishing Company, 2004), 94.

22. Cf. Chao, "The Incident of Yongze Xu from the Perspective of the Contemporary Religious Policy and Legal System of the Chinese Government," *China and the Gospel* 21 (Nov. 1997); Aikman, 88.

23. Xu, interview.

24. Cf. Brother P, interview; Sister HE, interview; Brother J, interview.

25. Snyder, *Signs of the Spirit*, 277.

26. Ibid., 305–06.

27. Xu, interview. Cf. Chao, *Purified by Fire*, 62–63.

28. Cf. Chao, *Purified by Fire*, 63–64.

29. Cf. Brother P, interview.

30. Luke Wesley, *The Church in China: Persecuted, Pentecostal, and Powerful* (Baguio City, Philippines: AJPS Books, 2004), 35.

31. *Guan xi* means connections, a more prevalent network of relationship extending beyond family and kinship to include friends, colleagues, former schoolmates, etc. It is more popular in urban areas than rural areas.

32. Though this Chinese proverb denotes that people should not tab into others' business, the underlying rational suggests a highly family/kinship prioritized relationship in the Chinese society, where each family/clan takes care of its own members.

33. Cf. Discussion on the structure of the WOL church in Chapter 3.

34. Cf. Kalun Leung, *Gai ge kai fang yi lai de zhongguo nong cun jiao hui* (The Rural Churches of Mainland China since 1978) (Hong Kong: Alliance Bible Seminary, 1999).

35. Brother P, interview.

36. Chao, "The Changing Shape of the Church in China (1976–2002)," *China Ministry Report* 155 (2003):2–3.

37. Ibid., 1-4.

38. Brother P, interview.

39. Cf. Discussion on Unity Stage of the WOL church in Chapter 3.

40. Snyder, *Signs of the Spirit*, 278.

41. Brother Yun and Pau Hattaway, *The Heavenly Man*, (London and Grand Rapids: Monarch Books, 2002), 232–34.

42. Cf. Yun and Hattaway, 236.

43. Cf. Hattaway, *Back to Jerusalem*.

44. WOL Manual II, 36.

45. Ibid., 36–37.

46. Ibid., 37.

47. Hattaway, *Back to Jerusalem*, 66.

48. Xu, interview.

49. Hattaway, *Back to Jerusalem*, 66–67.

50. Ibid., 67.

51. Snyder, *Signs of the Spirit*, 278.

52. Ibid., 279.

53. Chao, *Purified by Fire*, 66–68.

54. Cf. CCSC, "Report, Part 1 & 2."

55. Ibid.

56. Elder TR, interview.

57. Snyder, *Signs of the Spirit*, 279.

58. Brother P, interview.

59. CCSC, "Report, Part 2," 8.

60. Brother J, interview.

61. Xu, interview.

62. Snyder, *Signs of the Spirit*, 280.

63. Brother P, interview.

64. Snyder, *Signs of the Spirit*, 280.

65. Ibid., 300.

66. WOL Manual I, 3.

67. WOL Manual II, 38.

68. Jonathan Chao, trans., "Chinese House Church Confession of Faith," *China Prayer Letter and Ministry Report* 149 (Nov. 1998–Feb. 1999): 2–4.

69. CCSC, "The Secrets of the MGs, Part One," *China and the Church* 81 (1991): 13–14.

70. Sister HE, interview.

71. Brother L et al, interview.

72. Snyder, *Signs of the Spirit*, 281.

Chapter 5

Toward a Theology of Renewal for the Chinese Church

The previous chapter analyzes the WOL community with Snyder's mediating model of church renewal. We have found that most of the characteristics are consistent with those of the WOL while several others do not closely fit into the WOL experience, primarily due to difference in socio-political environment. In addition, there are elements, some of which are culturally specific to the Chinese experience, existing in the WOL community that are fundamental to its renewal, that Snyder's model does not thoroughly discuss. Based on the study of the WOL movement, this chapter attempts to nuance Snyder's model, identify some of the significant elements in the renewal of the WOL community, and develop a theology of renewal for the future of the Chinese church.

Amplifying the Mediating Model for Chinese Church Renewal

This section attempts, as a result of the study of the WOL movement, with reference to studies on Christian renewal and revitalization movements, to clarify some emerging issues that Snyder's mediating model does not specify or deal with. It is not an attempt, however, to add to Snyder's model for church renewal in a universal sense. Rather, these elements are highlighted because they are prominent in the life and ministry of the WOL community as a significant movement of renewal in China. As such, the clarifications made to the mediating model for church renewal are primarily for the sake of the Chinese Church. Whether or not these clarifications are valid for the global church will be a matter of further observation and test in time.

Back to the Heart of the Gospel

The experience of the WOL community points us back to the basics of the gospel: "No one can see the kingdom of God unless he is born again" (John 3:3). Absolute necessity of reconciled relationship with God is seen as the entrance requirement in the WOL community. As discussed in the early chapters, the WOL church stresses in its ministry the experience of being born again for every seeker and believer, through the specifically designed intensive meetings, i.e., evangelistic meetings, "Life meetings" and "Truth meetings." In the theology of the WOL church, establishing such "life" relationship is absolutely foundational to the Christian life journey in Christ as members of the body of Christ.

First of all, according to the WOL Manual, such emphasis has a biblical foundation: "No one can enter the kingdom of God unless he is born of water and the Spirit" (John 3:5); our spiritual life comes from "the last Adam, a life-giving spirit" (1 Cor. 15:45). To be born again is to be united with Christ (Rom. 6:3–5; 2 Cor. 5:17; Eph. 2:10); Our new life comes from the power of the resurrected Christ (1 Peter 1:3). We become sons and daughters of God (John 1:12, 13; 1 John 3:1), new creation (2 Cor. 5:17), and temple of the Holy Spirit (2 Cor. 6:19). "Without the new life in Christ, a believer can not walk the way of the cross. Vice versa, walking the way of the cross is the natural result of (owning) spiritual life."[1]

Secondly, we can see the influence of theological reflections from the first generation of Christian leaders in China such as Watchman Nee. In *Sit, Walk, Stand*, Nee reflects,

> Christian life does not begin with walking; it begins with sitting. The Christian era began with Christ, of whom we are told that, when He had made purification of sins, He "sat down on the right hand of the Majesty on high" (Heb. 1:3). With equal truth we can say that the individual Christian life begins with a man "in Christ"—that is to say, when by faith we see ourselves seated together with Him in the heavens. Most Christians make the mistake of trying to walk in order to be able to sit, but that is a reversal of the true order. The Christian life from start to finish is based upon this principle of utter dependence upon the Lord Jesus.[2]

In other words, the WOL theology can be seen as part of the contextual Chinese theological reflection, based on what the community of believers receives from the Holy Spirit in reading the Scripture and through ministerial practice. The history of Christianity in China has seen significant church growth with Nee's Little Flock and today in the WOL community as believers inherit from the best of heritages of their forefathers of faith.

Such understanding seems consistent with what Richard Lovelace proposes as the primary elements of continuous renewal: Justification, sanctification, the indwelling Spirit, and authority in spiritual conflict.[3] Lovelace finds those elements as biblical and essential in continuous renewal.[4] For him, these elements are the primary elements in the dynamics of spiritual life, from which other "dimensions of our existence in Christ" derive.

Therefore, it is useful to incorporate Lovelace's proposal of primary elements into Snyder's mediating model so that some of the core elements are placed in their right places in the model. The experience of the WOL community—in this case, it's theological and structural emphasis—has already shown us the necessity of prioritizing certain elements as the springboard for other aspects of life of the church to be launched onto their right tracks. Although such prioritization is implied in Snyder's model, this study has found it necessary to make it more explicit. In this case, then, it is the "life" relationship with God that needs to be established, deep in every believer's heart, as the start of the Christian journey.

Lovelace defines the heart of the gospel as those factors that

> answer most immediately the urgent hunger and thirst for righteousness awakened in the individual who has come into the light concerning the nature of the true God and his or her own sinful condition...the good news of the reconciliation Christ accomplished through his death and resurrection.[5]

Elevating this specific element in the mediating model as one of the primary elements of church renewal helps clarify what the "heart of the gospel" means, when used in a model of renewal for Chinese Christianity. For this primary element of renewal, I am using the terminology that is commonly used in the WOL community: "Life," which means a genuine reconciled relationship with God established through the experience of rebirth in Jesus Christ. This enriches the description of the first mark of a mediating model as identified by Snyder (1997). This should also be a primary element in both personal and corporate renewal as individual believers and the congregation as a whole continues to experience the freshness of life in Christ everyday, living and ministering in his perfect will.

Corporate and Dependent Prayer

As Christians, we can never underestimate the significance and power of prayer. The Bible provides abundant examples of corporate and dependent prayer from the life of the Israelites in the Old Testament and Christians (Jews and Gentiles) in the New Testament which testify to the importance of this ministry.

At the dedication of the temple, Solomon led the whole assembly of Israel in prayer to the Lord, asking the Lord to "forgive the sin your people Israel" and restore them when they make "supplication" in this temple (1 King 8:33–34). In restoring the city walls, Nehemiah led the Israelites in corporate prayer to the Lord for protection from the plot of their enemies (Nehemiah 4:9). The whole of Psalms provides examples of both individual and corporate prayer to God. It includes recognition of God's presence with his people (46), plea for forgiveness (51), cry for help (54, 109, 143), trust in God (56), prayer for protection (59, 64), hymn of thanksgiving (65, 67), prayer in suffering (69), prayer for the nation (85), recognition of God's sovereignty and justice (93, 94), and prayer of praise (145, 146, 147, 148, 149, 150).

In the New Testament, prayer becomes even more evidently significant in the teaching of Jesus and the life and ministry of the followers of Jesus. In Matthew 18:19–20, Jesus said, "I tell you that if two of you on earth agree about anything you ask for, it will be done for you by my Father in heaven. For where two or three come together in my name, there am I with them." The Apostles "joined constantly in prayer" in Jerusalem after Jesus' ascension (Acts 1:14). After Pentecost, the Christians "devoted themselves to the apostles' teaching and to the fellowship, to the breaking of bread and to prayer" (Acts 2:42). Acts 4 records that believers came together and "raised their voices together in prayer to God" (4:24), and "after they prayed, the place where they were meeting was shaken" and "they were all filled with the Holy Spirit and spoke the word of God boldly" (4:31). When Peter was in chains, "the church was earnestly praying to God for him" (Acts 18:5).

Prayer, both personal and corporate, is one of the secrets of the WOL community of believers in their daily walk with God. As we have noted from the above exegesis of Scriptural teaching on prayer, corporate and dependent prayer is not a WOL invention. Believers in the WOL church are simply obedient to the teachings of the Bible. The element of corporate prayer that is evident in the life of the WOL church is not exclusive of the necessity and function of personal prayer. Rather, corporate prayer stands out in the WOL community as a distinctive and powerful manifestation of the intimate and dependent relationship of the community of believers as the bride of Christ. It is a conscious gathering of the community of believers on a regular basis, not just for intercessory prayer, but for seeking God and his will as a body, and being dependent on his supply of power and resources for all aspects of life and ministry.

As a rural church movement, consisting of the marginalized portion of the Chinese society, the WOL community is a gathering of, in comparison with their urban counterparts, country folks, with less education, less information, less contact with the outside world, and, in terms of Christianity, with less exposure to systematic theology. These are all true, which makes it possible for the WOL community to become what it is today—the biggest church community in China, even with the fact that it is considered illegal and therefore restricted by the state.

Among all the factors that contribute to the phenomenal growth of the WOL community, corporate and dependent prayer plays an inseparable and essential role. Since the beginning, it has been part of the life of the WOL community. As such, corporate and dependent prayer goes much further than weekly prayer intercessory meetings as commonly practiced in the churches in the West. It is in addition to personal prayer time with God. It is seeking God as a community, repenting together, praising God corporately, seeking directions and power. Such prayer exemplifies what Eugene Rubingh states, "Prayer equips us for mission and enables us to boldly recommend Jesus. In our very powerlessness we find power from God. In our obvious weakness we receive strength. In our despair we find hope."[6]

Corporate prayer, in terms of the WOL house church community, manifests itself in a variety of forms and involves different numbers of participants. The

WOL Manual specifies four kinds of contextual prayer meetings: prayer class/mountain, early-morning prayer meeting, whole day prayer chain, and regular prayer meeting.[7] A prayer meeting is often pre-planned but can also be spontaneous as needed. There are prayer meetings involving more than a hundred believers; there are also times when only a few believers gather together to pray.

A glimpse of the author's research experience sheds some light on this factor. After receiving the author into one of the hospitality families, local coworkers started to come and greet the author. This was not prearranged. A brief self-introduction was immediately followed by a time of corporate prayer, when everyone went on their knees, praising God for the opportunity of fellowship, asking him for protection of the hospitality family, visitors and coworkers present, and seeking his will for the meeting. At the end of the day, coworkers gathered together once again for a time of prayer (well over an hour).

Early next morning at about 6 a.m. the author found that the three coworkers who had also stayed at the hospitality family were already on their knees praying silently. As the author joined them, they started to pray out loud, first together, then one after another. This went on until about 7 a.m. when the Lord's Prayer was said together as a concluding prayer. Early morning (5 a.m. to 7 a.m.) prayer is a daily devotion of coworkers of the WOL.

The same afternoon, another simultaneous prayer meeting was summoned in the hospitality family when more coworkers showed up. For the next two hours, believers prayed first together (with each one saying his or her own prayer), then one after another. Everyone knelt on the cold, hard floor for the entire prayer session. At the finish of the night, another one-hour prayer involved all those present at the hospitality family before sleep.

At the underground seminary, students engaged in small-group prayer for two hours every morning before breakfast.[8] At the beginning of the class in the afternoon, there was again a time of prayer involving the whole student body for well over half an hour. For the underground seminaries, daily corporate and dependent prayer is absolutely essential for both students and teachers. They trust the safety and operation of the seminaries to God and are able to continue their preparation in faith under such extreme circumstances. Of course, these seminaries are also daily prayed for by the local house churches and the larger WOL community.

Corporate prayer plays a significant role in the growth of the WOL community of believers, who are sensitive to the voice of God, seeking God's wisdom, finding unity, and receiving power in prayer. When coming together in prayer, believers are in awe before the holy God, examining themselves as a community and humbly asking God for the forgiveness of sins, individually and corporately. Humbleness before God is one of the marks of the WOL community.

Chao (2000) identifies the prayer movement of believers as one of the secrets of the rapid growth of the Chinese Church: "Believers' only dependence is God, and the only means is by prayer. And therefore a movement of prayer was started in the house churches. Until today, most house churches continue to gather daily at 5 am for a two-hour prayer, asking God for protection, guidance, power and the spread of the gospel."[9]

Although we cannot grasp fully the mystery of corporate and dependent prayer, it is biblically grounded and practically demonstrated. In corporate and dependent prayer, we humble ourselves as a community of believers before God, in unity, recognizing who he is, finding his heart for the world, renewing our vision and passion for mission, and receiving power and wisdom for ministry.

Speedy Production of Workers for Service

One of the clear marks of the WOL training structure is the quick turnout of workers into service. In terms of ordained ministry in the TSPM church, candidates need to complete the M.Div. degree and perhaps a period of internship before they can be officially ordained. This is not the case with the WOL community. Most of its members do not have undergraduate degrees, which immediately prevents them from entering into a graduate degree such as a M.Div. program, even if it is available in the context of China. The fact is that the thirteen officially sanctioned seminaries in China do not accept any non-TSPM church recommended students.

Within the environment given, the WOL church, based on its understanding of the scriptural teaching about the priesthood of all believers, developed its own biblical and theological training programs for its members. A typical local pillar's (pastor's) training would normally take about six months, in which period students are gathered together in one of the underground seminary locations with little contact with outsiders for the entire time. In six months, the hours spent on study add up to about the same number of hours for a three-year degree program at an overseas seminary.[10]

Two dynamic cycles directly result from this quick turnout of the WOL training system. One is the continuous supply of MGs for the Gospel Band; the other is dynamic growth of the local house churches. In his study of the WOL community Chao offers a concise description of the two dynamic cycles:

> In the process of establishing churches, itinerant evangelists are responsible for conducting five to seven days discipleship training, after which they would encourage the participants to dedicate themselves for Christian service. Those with clear calling will then be sent to the seminaries to receive a three-month training and, upon graduation, join the Gospel Band and be sent out on itinerant evangelistic journey with experienced MGs. More churches will be established through the ministry of these new MGs, who will be responsible for the conducting revival meetings, preaching and teaching of the newly established churches, until more believers devote themselves to the training to be MGs. And the cycle goes on.[11]
>
> Among the students of the seminaries of the fields, some are already involved in the local house church service before the seminary training. In other words, the seminaries of the fields offer further training to those workers. When these workers are called out to receive training in the seminaries, there arise, in their place, a new generation of workers who continue the ministry of the local house churches. As these churches grow, more devoted workers are

called to seminary training, and more new generations of workers would emerge from the local house churches. And the ministry continues.[12]

It is clear that the WOL training system differs from overseas seminary education in that it takes much less time to produce and send out a worker for ministry. Unique environment forces leaders of the WOL to think strategically in terms of how a continuous supply of MGs and local pillars can be made available to meet the enormous need. This training system has been working really well for the WOL community over the years, making it possible for the network to continue to spread in China. It will be a significant factor in the continuous growth of the WOL community in the future.

The future face of Chinese Christianity is yet to be known. There might be possibilities that organization and structure of the house church community will inevitably evolve. Given the success of the WOL training system, it should be kept as one of the most practical and dynamic elements of all church renewal in China, and maybe applicable to overseas church as well. Questions will be asked as to what extent that the present length of seminary training is necessary and adequate, and who are qualified to provide and receive training. In this area, I believe, the New Testament has provided more affirmation to the WOL training system than denial.

"Rhetoric Framing"

In his study on social movements, Gregory Leffel proposes a framework consisting of six variables by which he analyzes social and religious movements. These six variables can provide another way of looking at renewal movements as a social and religious movements, and draw out insights as complimentary to the mediating model for church renewal. In the case of the WOL house church movement, rhetoric framing is one of the elements that Snyder does not deal with in his mediating model, and yet can be very useful in evaluating the movement concerning this important aspect of life. Leffel highlights that rhetoric framing is the "conceptual architecture" of a movement, an "ideological variable."

> Movements seek to redefine reality as much as they seek to disrupt or change political and social structures. The ways in which their grievances are names, and a positive vision for the future is put forward, play an essential role in motivating and sustaining movement activism. Ideas must be shaped, or "framed," in ways that articulate dissatisfaction with existing social life and that define the terms of engagement with the opposition. A movement's rhetorical frames (see the discussion of collective action frames, master frames, and general movement above) must connect with existing cultural themes so that the movement is rooted deeply within an existing social history. They must also create a new language that unites the movement within its own intellectual, emotional, and moral life world. The skill of movement participants in crafting a powerful thought world, and in promoting and defending its message in public is essential to a movement's success.[13]

As we have seen, the WOL contextual theology was formed in ministry as believers read the Word of God in dialogue with the context. Believers were challenged by the phenomenon of the Chinese Church at the time and prompted to reflect theologically over the perceived needs: the shaky foundations some believers demonstrated in the context of opposition and persecution, and the emergence of false teaching that confused people. As they reflected the Word of God, the Holy Spirit guided believers to formulate *the Seven Principles* that seemed to be able to address the needs of the time. They drafted the principles in their first "Jerusalem Conference," and continued the effort until approximately two years later when the historical document—*the Seven Principles*, which may well be the first significant theological document of the house church community, was born.

How did leaders channel *the Seven Principles* to the many thousands of house churches, then? It was actually immediately put in use in the WOL training system. Starting from "Life meetings" and "Truth meetings," all the way up to the TEs, which means that, from the basic level of local house church believers to the TE training of MGs, every believer in the WOL need to go through, to differentiated extent and degree, *the Seven Principles*. At the local house church level, though, after the intensive seven to fifteen-day "Life" and "Truth meetings," there would be continuous teaching on the topic on a regular basis. In my interview with the coworkers of the church on the question of WOL manual, everyone was able to spell out a concise content of *the Seven Principles* without hesitation.

Obviously, the WOL church is able to communicate its theology, through its unique training systems, to all of its members, in intensive meetings at the start, sustained then through regular weekly house church teachings. The TEs, on the other hand, train students in a more systematic and detailed manner, so that, when these students graduate and are sent out as MGs or local pillars, they are equipped to articulate the WOL theology in their teaching and preaching.

Furthermore, *the Seven Principles* as the WOL theology is set at the core of the WOL engine transmitting power to the three constituents of the WOL community. As such, it sustains the movement and cements the community together with a strong identity (see Figure 5.1).

The WOL theology of the cross as implicitly narrated in *the Seven Principles* represents a set of guidelines for personal and corporate spiritual renewal and ministry. It is the axle of the WOL movement. For the past 20 years, it has underpinned the movement as it went through outward pressures in the 1980s and 1990s, and projects itself into the twenty-first century. Despites changes and controversies revolving leadership and revival meetings, the WOL community stands strong on the China soil, continuing to bear witness in the Chinese society and engage in frontier evangelism, with its theology of the cross as its distinct identity.

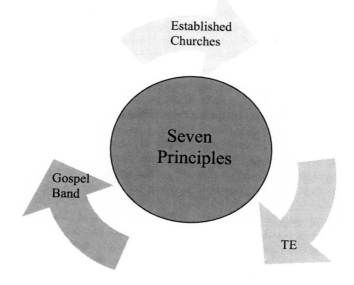

Figure 5.1: Three Constituents of the WOL in Relation to Its Theology

Because of the essential role of redefining reality and promoting it to the public, rhetorical framing lies at the heart of success or failure of a movement. In the study of renewal movements, rhetoric framing should be one of elements that need to be examined closely. Insights of renewal can be readily identified in the movement's articulation of the redefined reality and how it promotes and defends its message in public. [14]

WOL Uniqueness and Contribution

The WOL church, as an indigenous Chinese church that emerged onto the China scene since the 1970s, has grown to be the largest house church community in China with its distinctive characteristics. Consciously and unconsciously, believers of the WOL incorporated certain cultural elements into their ministry. In the study of the WOL movement, some of the features appear to be culturally specific to the Chinese situation in time and space, and can be helpful for the future of the Chinese Church in general.

Gaining/Maintaining New Reality in Community

Based on the understanding of the rural Chinese cultural features and borrowing from the heritage of the first generation Chinese evangelists and

Christian leaders such as John Sung, Watchman Nee, and Wang Mingdao, the WOL leaders and coworkers designed the unique intensive meetings, such as evangelistic meetings (three to five days), "Life meetings" (seven days) and "Truth meetings" (seven to fifteen days), all of which have become a constituent part of the initial steps to faith and service for the WOL believers. These meetings provided a context where the arrangements of the themes for these intensive meetings are deliberate and well reasoned for the Chinese mind, and where seekers and believers come in direct contact and communication with the new subjective reality. And because all participants to the meetings are required to stay in the meeting premises for whole time without any contact with outside, whether it is five days or seven days, when seekers and young believers alike live with the MGs and other house church coworkers under the same roof, this seems to create a kenosis effect that allows the maximum refill of new reality. As a result, these meetings appear to have left a long-lasting effect on the participants.

"Reality is socially defined," as Peter Berger and Thomas Luckmann observe in *The Social Construction of Reality*, "But the definitions are always embodied, that is, concrete individuals and groups of individuals serve as definers of reality."[15] In these intensive meetings, though short as a matter of fact, seekers and believers are encountered with the new reality brought to them by the MGs and coworkers of the local churches who are strong adherents of the Christian faith, as "definers of reality," day and night, in prayer, in worship, in confession, in singing, in meditating and in counseling. Through preaching, conversation and counseling, participants to these meetings adopt the new reality and begin to internalize it, a process that will maintain the new reality as they re-socialize themselves into the community of WOL believers in house churches and TEs.

From another perspective, this intensive meeting for those who have just come to faith can be seen as a binding experience, just like a new-born infant becomes bonded with his parents. In "Bonding and the Missionary Task," the authors notes:

> The excitement and adrenalin levels of both the child and his parents are at peak. The senses of the infant are being stimulated by a multitude of new sights, new sounds, new smells, new positions, new environment and new ways of being held. Yet, at that particular time, he is equipped with an extraordinary ability to respond to these unusual circumstances.[16]

We can, then, easily identify the parallels between the infant's bonding with the parents and new believers bonding with the new reality. The first five, seven, or fifteen days immersed in the new faith community will more likely yield a long-lasting bond of faith.

"Since socialization is never complete and the contents it internalizes face continuing threats to their subjective reality, every viable society must develop procedures of reality-maintenance to safeguard a measure of symmetry between objective and subjective reality."[17] The house church structure provides such a "reality-maintenance" of the new reality encountered. For instance, house churches in Henan meet daily: hymn & praises on Monday, Bible study on Tuesday, prayer meeting on Wednesday, discipleship training on Thursday, evangelistic meeting on Friday, worship on Saturday and Sunday.[18] And of course the teaching would generally be based on *the Seven Principles*. Thus, the language of the new faith is reinforced and the new reality consolidated in the ongoing house church meetings.

George Hunter III, in *The Celtic Way of Evangelism* (2000), provides a succinct summary of insights from Peter Berger's *The Social Construction of Reality* that validates the WOL experience:

> (1) A person's view of Reality is largely shaped, and maintained, within the community into which one has been *socialized*. (2) In a pluralistic society, the possibility of conversion, that is, changing the way one perceives essential Reality, is opened up through *conversations* with people who live with a contrasting view of Reality, and (3) one adopts and internalizes the new worldview through *resocialization* into a community sharing that new worldview.[19]

Centrality of the Theology of the Cross

As delineated in the third chapter of this book, the cross is one of the major themes in the theological reflection of the WOL community and it has played a significant role in the growth and development of the network. Leaders of the WOL church identify it as foundational to the explosive expansion of the WOL network, and critical to the effectiveness of its evangelistic ministry across China. Chinese church observer such as Jonathan Chao has also affirmed that the theology of the cross underpinned the growth of the WOL community.[20]

The WOL Manual clearly articulates that, at the cross, not only sin is forgiven, and salvation was made possible to all, but also the way of the cross is exemplified by Christ to all who are to follow him. Therefore, on the one hand, one needs to connect to the life in Christ through repentance, confession and rebirth; on the other hand, as a natural projection from rebirth, one needs to walk the way of the cross, which is "the way of suffering, and dealing, which is destroying the old self in Adam and creating a new man in Christ. It is a way of life. Because 'we must go through many hardships to enter the kingdom of God' (Acts 14:22)."[21]

In the immediate context of the WOL church, though, at least two themes from this theology are prominently relevant to believers, providing guidance and support to the community of believers.

Model in Suffering

In his research on the house churches in central China, Chao analyzes, "To believers, suffering is not accidental. It is to share in the suffering of Christ so that they will also share in his glory."[22] Indeed, in interviews relating to the issue of suffering, the community of the WOL church provide a consistent understanding. "We suffer because Christ suffered first. He is our big brother, our model. 'The Son of Man came not to be served but to serve, and to give his life a ransom for many' (Mark 10:45). He manifests to us the necessity of walking the way of the cross."[23] "It is the only way that leads to the kingdom of God, and it is the way that Christ had to walk. In the same way, as disciples of Christ, we need to also walk the same way of the cross and suffer for his sake."[23]

The theme of Jesus as a model in suffering is also evident in *the Seven Principles*, especially the first two principles, *salvation through the cross* and *the way of the cross*, that give so much attention to the incarnation, ministry, suffering, death, and resurrection of Christ and how it is necessary, as disciples of Christ, to share in his suffering.[25] As Bosch (1993) states, "What is true of the Master's mission is true of the disciples' also. The difference between the Pauline mission and that of his opponents in Corinth lies in the cross—not only Christ's, but also the missionary's."[26]

Promise in Suffering.

According to *the Seven Principles, the way of the cross* is a prerequisite and guarantee to fruitful spiritual life and ministry. And this way is the way of suffering. As modeled by Christ, suffering is necessary and should not be shun by followers of Christ. The suffering that believers endure in walking the way of the cross will eventually lead to victory in Christ. The victory is already affirmed even when believers still suffer temporarily. Unless believers walk *the way of the cross*, they will only backslide at times of temptation and opposition.[27] Indeed as the Scripture promises, "And the God of all grace, who called you to his eternal glory in Christ, after you have suffered a little while, will himself restore you and make you strong, firm and steadfast" (1 Peter 5:10). This insight has helped the WOL believers recognize the need for renewal in the Chinese Church and is one of the primary elements they have identified as essential in personal and corporate renewal.

The WOL theology of the cross is the fruit of the devoted Christians laboring under an unfavorable system and in an unfriendly environment as they reflect on the Word of God. It is the reflection of both their ministerial practice and life experience. As a theological response of the WOL community to the unique Chinese context, it serves as a contextual Chinese theology that addresses the needs of the WOL community and can be relevant to the Chinese Church in general as well as to the larger hermeneutical community.

WOL Itinerant Evangelistic Model

Itinerant evangelism is not a model invented by the WOL evangelists. It is basically a New Testament model, a fact much appreciated and recognized by the WOL evangelists, for they hold the Bible as having absolute authority in all of life and ministry of the church. In fact, in the WOL Manual, it upholds the biblical model of mission as the model to follow: "the establishment and development of the early church in Acts is the model for the churches today."[28]

Identification with the New Testament model

As believers of the Bible, the WOL leaders and coworkers identify themselves with the Christians in the early church, from whose experience they borrow to enrich their own. This, first of all, has helped believers to firmly root their faith in the promise of God even in time when opposition was no less than what their fellow believers endured two millenniums ago because they find encourage and affirmation from the experience of the early church. Secondly, at a time when no other reference could be found on evangelism and church planting, the WOL believers did not hesitate to simply adopt the New Testament model, trusting that this was God's special provision for the Chinese Church in that situation.

Spread of the gospel

Believers of the WOL community identify their situation with that of the early church as recorded in Acts. When persecution started, believers were scattered throughout Judea and Samaria," and "preached the word wherever they went" (Acts 8). And as a result, the gospel spread among the regions and churches were established. In the similar manner, persecution broke out in the early 1980s forcing leaders and coworkers on the run from arrest. As these Christians scattered, they brought the gospel with them and continued ministry. As a result, many house churches were established in the neighboring provinces and the network started to extend outward.[29]

Itinerant evangelism

According the book of Acts, Paul and his workers went on itinerant evangelistic trips to Asia Minor and Europe, preaching the gospel, establishing churches, teaching believers, and revisiting the churches they established to teach and encourage Christians.[30] This model was adopted by the WOL evangelists to great effectiveness. The WOL itinerant evangelistic model therefore has biblical precedent. What Paul and his coworkers practiced in mission then, the believers of the WOL practice now. As Paul took one or two disciples on itinerant trips, so does the WOL evangelistic team (usually consisting of two to three MGs). An illustration is helpful here for the sake of comparison (see Figure 5.2).

New Testament Model	WOL Model
Persecution scattered believers (Acts 6:8–9:31)	*"Severe Punishment" campaign in 1983 scattered believers*
Scattered believers evangelized and established churches in Judea, Galilee and Samaria (Acts 8–9)	*WOL believers fled to neighboring provinces of Anhui, Shandong, Shanxi, Shaanxi, Hubei and Hunan and established churches there (Chao 2003:1)*
The church in Antioch became a missionary sending church	*The WOL church is a missionary sending community of house churches*
Paul and his coworkers made itinerant evangelistic trips in Asia Minor and Europe	*The WOL MGs engage in itinerant evangelistic trips to all provinces of China*
Paul exemplified discipleship modeling and training in ministry	*The WOL emphasized in its TE training system master/apprentice model of discipleship*
Jerusalem conference was called to settle controversies and coordinate ministry	*First house church "Jerusalem Conference" was convened in 1982, when some heretics were excommunicated and the Seven Principles was drafted*
The Great Commission (Matt. 28:18–20) represents a centrifugal model of mission	*The WOL church keeps reaching out to the unevangelized areas in China*

Figure 5.2: New Testament Parallels to WOL Itinerant Evangelistic Model

Contextual development

In their following the New Testament model of mission and ministry, the WOL leaders have also paid attention to the contextual issues that gradually emerge in ministry. For instance, as the community of believers continued to grow, there emerged the great need for discipleship and care for the newly established house churches. If the MGs stay for extended time teaching and caring for the house churches, there would be short of MGs for frontier evangelism. The WOL leaders and coworkers then came together in fellowship and prayer, seeking wisdom from God. Two significant structures came into being: the WOL organizational structure and TE training system.[31]

These structures provide essential support for the effectiveness of the work of the Gospel Band in its coordination of sending MGs in outreach. In terms of the contextual development from the New Testament model, the three constituent parts, namely established churches, theological education and the Gospel Band, form a dynamic cyclic development, so that the three parts support and coordinate with each other as the whole movement advances.

The supply of MGs in relation to house church maturity

A continuous supply of MGs comes directly from the local established house churches, through TE training, to the Gospel Band that will then decide, according to needs, where to send the MGs for frontier evangelism. Established house churches, in supplying MGs to the Gospel Band, are in a continuous cycle of identifying and raising up more devoted Christians for service at the churches, from whom a future supply of MGs are ensured. This forms a dynamic cycle that leads to both the growing numbers of MGs in frontier evangelism and believers actively in service at the local house church level.

The Gospel Band in partnership with local house churches

MGs form close fellowship with area coworkers' meetings. This is one of the Four Development Routes in the WOL structure.[32] In this way, the work of the area can be coordinated, such as MGs providing necessary training to the house churches in need, and the support for the MGs can be raised. On the one hand, the local churches are strengthened and believers mature in faith through the labor of the MGs, and, as a result, on the other hand, the work of the Gospel Band is supported through these churches.

Many churches claim or seek to follow more or less a biblical model in ministry. The WOL church, however, demonstrates a closer engagement with the biblical model in dialogue with context. We have seen the usefulness of the Gospel Band system in the WOL house church movement and how it contributes to the spread of the network throughout the country from the beginning of the movement to present. If it is based on a biblical model of evangelization and it is effective in the China context, the Gospel Band system can be useful for the rest of the Chinese Church community as well. In fact, its validity is already testified by several other house church networks in central China that adopt a similar itinerant evangelistic model.[33]

A Model of Renewal for the Chinese Church

Based on the above study, a more clarified model of renewal seems to be evident that can be useful as a reference for the present and future of the Chinese Church in general. The situation of the Protestant churches in China, however, is still quite complicated, with implications pertaining to both the house church networks and the TSPM church. The attempted model of renewal for the Chinese church does not claim to be representative of the Chinese church. Rather, it can be regarded as a tool for evaluation. As a proposed model of renewal for the Chinese church, it should contain at least the following elements.

"Life" as Prerequisite

As Snyder suggests in the mediating model, a rediscovery of the gospel is a "key element" in renewal movements that leads to a "new paradigm of the Gospel and of the church."[34] For the WOL church such rediscovery of the gospel is exactly what has become a driving force for the church to spread among the rural population, which is a genuine reconciled spiritual ("life") relationship in Christ. "Life" is prerequisite to genuine Christian life and renewal, and foundational to effective ministry. From this "life" relationship, justification becomes reality, sanctification is initiated, and the Holy Spirit dwells in and empowers.[35] It is the beginning and primary element in personal and corporate renewal and growth.

As prerequisite to meaningful Christian renewal, believers in the WOL community are called to look beyond the blessings of salvation promised in the gospel, to examine themselves in relationship to God who loves them so much as to die on the cross for the redemption of sins. With the work of the Holy Spirit, sins are confessed and forgiven, the love of God is experienced, and the sinners are released from the law of sin and death by the Spirit of life. "Everything old has passed away; see, everything has become new!" (2 Cor. 5:17b). This is the beginning of renewal, from personal to corporate, from individual to community. A community of believers experiencing renewal is empowered by the Spirit of God in ministry, and will inevitably spread the ripple of renewal outward to the neighborhood, counties and regions, as the examples of the WOL house church movement attest. Without "life," there is no foundation to renewal by the Spirit, and, as Scripture warns, it would be like the house built on sand. When rain and wind beat against it, "it fell with a great crash" (Matt. 7:26–27).

The Word and Spirit as Authority

Historically, renewal movements stressed "the Spirit and the Word as the ultimate ground of authority" which often means tension with the traditions of the institutional church.[36] This is essential if the movement continues to bring renewal to the whole church. Since the beginning of the WOL church believers have been holding the Bible and the Holy Spirit as the ultimate authority in their ministry. The tension, however, is not so much with the traditions of the institutional church in the case of the WOL church. It is, rather, a protest against the general ill health of the church in China. The impact of the WOL house church movement is obvious, a fact that testifies the validity of this element in renewal.

The very nature of the Bible as the inspired Word of God and the Spirit as "Counselor" who illuminates and empowers believers highlight the importance of this element as essential in renewal. As the Spirit guides, Christians should always read the Word afresh every day and ground their ministry on the principles laid out in the Bible while interacting with their context. In renewal movements, it is especially important that Christians open themselves to the teaching of the Bible as illuminated by the Spirit, so that those dead traditions and structures that have become blockade to ministry can be identified and transformed. Genuine renewal cannot persist unless it is grounded in Word and Spirit.

Corporate and Dependent Prayer as Power

Since both Old and New Testament present to us abundant examples of corporate and dependent prayers in various contexts, Christians are called to acknowledge themselves to the mystery and dynamics of such prayers, and actively engage themselves in this ministry. Believers in the WOL community have experienced the amazing power from God in corporate and dependent prayer in their effort of renewal as they often face the seemingly insurmountable obstacle of taking the gospel to every part of China and back to Jerusalem. They, however, find encouragement in the Word of God and affirmation from the experience of the early Church. Lovelace notes:

> Facing the formidable and largely unexpected task of evangelizing the whole world for the Messiah, the early church went to prayer, waiting for Jesus to pour out his Spirit to empower them for this task (Acts 1:13-14). Only the every presence of the risen Lord could equip them to move outward in mission. And this movement could only be maintained through a continual dependence on him, receiving divine direction and encouragement in prayer.[37]

What's more, in corporate prayer, we find God's heart and desires for the church and the world at large as well as better understand our own needs as a community of faith. Historically in renewal movements prayer has always played an important role. The Moravians engaged in "a round-the-clock prayer meeting" for renewal and mission. Jonathan Edwards and his coworkers developed the "concerts of prayer" that was instrumental in expanding the awakening.[38]

Suffering as a Mark of Discipleship

Suffering is the proud mark of the WOL Christians because they see it an honor to suffer as disciples of Christ. Chao (2000) notes in his observation of the ten elements of the rapids church growth in China:

> The life of Chinese believers and churches becomes even richer because of suffering. Suffering helps them to embody more closely the experience of suffering, dying and resurrecting with the Lord. Because of suffering, the church is renewed and transformed. Because of suffering, believers become strong and firm, gaining power from the Lord, engaging in evangelism, and establishing churches.[39]

The two dimensions of suffering (external and internal) delineated in *the Seven Principles* present us both a spiritual insight and a contextual understanding on the necessity of suffering. Coworkers serving in the WOL house churches readily embrace suffering as part of their commitment and conviction. Suffering, then, has become a mark of followers of Christ and something believers feel privileged to endure. This seems to affirm the Apostle Paul's charge to Timothy and the Ephesian church at large.[40] Lesslie Newbigin notes, "This suffering is not the passive acceptance of evil; it is the primary form of witness against it. It is the way in which we follow Jesus along the way of the cross."[41]

The emphasis on the internal dimension of suffering of dealing with the old self in the process of sanctification has contributed to the yielding of many faithful and devoted workers of the kingdom within the WOL community, and it will continue to address the needs of the community and beyond. It can be an element translatable cross-culturally as we are all called to strive to take off the old self and put on the new one.[42] This element is important especially for the Chinese situation with its socio-political characteristics, but also can serve as a mirror to Christians in other cultures and environments to constantly examine themselves as they partnership with God in mission.

House Church as Basic Structure

"The most basic meetings of the Christian community should be in homes. Homes often provide ideal settings for fellowship, study, prayer, small-group worship and evangelism. The biblical pattern seems to be 'the church in your house.'"[43] Even with the difference in orientation, the WOL structure is consistent in function with the small group structure in historical renewal movements. As analyzed above, each house church within the WOL network is an *ecclesiola*—"a smaller, more intimate expression of the church within the church." It provides the context for believers to experience *koinonia*, "mutual encouragement, and admonition within the body."[44] As small group structure was essential in the renewal movements historically, the house church structure should continue to serve the needs of the Chinese Church. This is an important model for the institutional TSPM church that are in need of the house church structure to provide adequate pastoral care as well as for members to participate and experience *koinonia* rather than Sunday church-goers.

Snyder (2004) proposes three criteria for evaluating church structure, which will be helpful in safeguarding the quest for structural validity:

> First, church structure must be biblically valid. That is, church structure must be compatible with the nature and form of the gospel and of the church as biblically presented.
> Second, church structure must be culturally viable. Structure must be compatible with the cultural forms of the society in which the church finds itself.
> Third, church structure must be temporally flexible. It must be open to modification from time to time as changing circumstance warrant.[45]

Transformed Sense of Community as Goal

In *The Community of the King*, Snyder highlights four biblical bases for the priority of community: "(1) the concept of the people of God, (2) the model of Christ with his disciples, (3) the example of the early church and (4) the explicit teachings of Jesus and the apostles."[46] Following the New Testament model of Christian life, the WOL house church structure offers us a picture of organic movement of messianic community, linking believers together in close fellowship, practicing *koinonia*, engaging in evangelism, witnessing in worship and service, and thus transcending the traditional Chinese family-centered solidarity. The presence of this new community of faith alone bears powerful witness in its surrounding.

With the biblical model as primary reference, a continuous transformation is needed within the new community with the Word and Spirit as authority, where spiritual gifts are recognized and exercised, fellowship and community become enhanced, love and support are experienced, believers are equipped for service, and, as a result, the community of faith is enlarged. It involves both going-out (reaching out in service and evangelism) and welcoming-in (drawing people to the new community and transform them in the process). Figure 5.3 illustrates the concept of the transformed community.

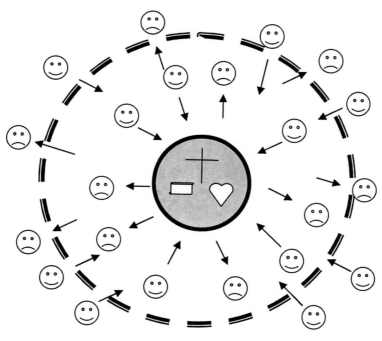

Figure 5.3: Transformed community in witness

Active Discipleship as Imperative

Making disciples lies in the core of the so-called Great Commission of Jesus in Matthew's Gospel (Matt. 28:19–20). The activities involved in the task of discipleship include going (28:19), baptizing (28:19), and teaching (28:20). As followers of Christ, all Christians are called to go out, bringing people under the Lordship of the triune God, and teach them the Word of God. "The result of this process would be obedient disciples (28:20)."[47]

As discipleship lies at the heart of the Believers' Church,[48] so is it a key element of renewal in the WOL structure that provides such an environment and opportunity for active discipleship. The expansion of the WOL network highlights the validity of such structure. The fact is, however, there has always been need for workers equipped for this ministry despite the emphasis on discipleship training through the training system and through the house church structure. One obvious external disadvantage is the illegal status of the church which implicates direct limitation on its seminary operation. The growth of the WOL community seems to be much faster than what the supply of workers can handle. The church has realized the need and is paying more attention to training and mobilizing believers for service at the house church level. This will be a key element in the future of the WOL community as a movement of renewal.

Since the WOL structure notably facilitates the disciple-making process of the faith community, it can be referenced by the larger Christian community in China. The house church provides the most viable environment for family members, kins, neighbors, and friends to be responsive to the gospel calling and become equipped for service in God's kingdom. As a model of discipleship, it is both biblical and culturally viable. The advantages of the house church structure for discipleship is nicely summarized by Arn and Arn (1998):

1. *Oikos* Relationship Are a Natural Network.
2. *Oikos* Members Are Receptive.
3. *Oikos* Relationships Allow for Natural Sharing.
4. *Oikos* Relationships Support the New Christian.
5. *Oikos* Relationships Effectively Assimilate Converts.
6. *Oikos* Relationships Tend to Win Entire Families.
7. *Oikos* Relationships Provide New Contacts.[49]

Mission as Evangelism and Transformation

The sense of mission has always been strong within the WOL community. The church makes the Great Commission the responsibility of every believer from the beginning of his/her Christian walk,[50] a factor that is inseparable from its remarkable growth over the past three decades. The scope of mission, in the case of the WOL, and as a recommendation to the greater Chinese church community, could be broader enough to address human needs in a holistic way.

At Wheaton Conference in 1983, the Consultation on the Church in Response to Human Need produced the following statement:

According to the biblical view of human life, then, transformation is the change from a condition of human existence contrary to God's purposes to one in which people are able to enjoy fullness of life in harmony with God (Jn 10:10; Col 3:8–15; Eph. 4:13). This transformation can only take place through the obedience of individuals and communities to the Gospel of Jesus Christ, whose power changes the lives of men and women by releasing them from the guilt, power and consequences of sin, enabling them to respond with love toward God and towards others (Rom 5:5) and making them 'new creatures in Chris' (2 Cor 5:17).[51]

As much as the WOL Christians have been involved in the social transformation of its local environment, mission as evangelism is still weightier on the scale compared to social involvement. It is, therefore, a biblical demand that the WOL rethink of mission as both evangelism and transformation, or, more accurately, transformation as projection of evangelism. Christians should be concerned not only with bringing the lordship of Christ to the world, but also Christ's love and involvement. The church's mission in the world should involve both the proclamation and demonstration of the gospel, which include evangelization, response to immediate human needs, and work toward social transformation.

Biblical and Contextual Leadership as Model

A biblical model of leadership is suggested by Snyder that includes the three components: "leadership based on the Scriptural qualifications of character and giftedness; pastoral leadership defined primarily as equipping for ministry; and team or plural leadership in each congregation." Snyder also lists some of the key biblical passages on leadership: Acts 6:1–4, 20:28; 1 Cor. 12:1–28; Eph. 4:7–16; 1 Tim. 3:1–13; 2 Tim. 2:2; Titus 1:5–9; Heb. 13:17; James 5:13–16; and 1 Peter 5:1–3.[52] This provides essential biblical foundation for leadership and can be used as criteria of evaluation on the formation and role of Christian leadership.

In constructing contextual theology, Stephen Bevans (1992) proposes that the following elements as essential: "the spirit and message of the gospel; the tradition of the Christian people; the culture in which one is theologizing; and social change in that culture."[53] Developing effective Christian leadership needs also take the above elements into consideration. There is no one single model of leadership that applies to all cultures and environments. Ministry works best when it interacts with the context, a task of contextualization.

In terms of leadership formation, the WOL structure generally facilitates the growth and development of diverse leadership teams that, through seeking God's will in the selection process, the community recognize that the Spirit entrusts the gifts necessary for the life and ministry of the church. Biblical qualifications such as what is specified in 1 Timothy 3:1–13 and Titus 1:5–9 are listed as guidelines in the selection of leaders for service in the WOL community.

Nonetheless, in the Chinese cultural context, leadership still tends to be viewed as primarily the responsibilities of the male, especially in the higher level leadership circles. This tendency is also reflected in the WOL community, as well as in the rest of the Christian community in China. With the significant cultural change in China, leadership will best serve the community when (1) it takes the teaching of the Bible as essential guidelines, such as the scriptural qualifications for leadership, (2) recognizes that spiritual gifts are what qualify believers for leadership, as Snyder (2004) notes that "God's plan, his *oikonomia*, for leadership" is that he "provides for leadership in the church through the exercise of the gifts of the Spirit," and (3) interacts with the context, paying attention to cultural characteristics and social change and discerning what model best serves the community of faith. "The goal is the edification of the church and thereby the glorification of God and the accomplishing of his cosmic plan."[54]

Interlink and Fellowship as Practice

Unity within the Body of believers evidently taught in the Bible that calls for a mutual dependence and fellowship within the body of Christ. "For we were all baptized by one Spirit into one body" (1 Cor 12:13a). Snyder states,

> Total independence of local congregations is not the biblical pattern, for there is one body of Christ, not multiple bodies. The body metaphor of 1 Corinthians 12 legitimately applies to the whole church, not just to local churches. Churches need each other, and this is true at least as much today as in New Testament days.[55]

The WOL church bases its principle of interlink and fellowship (one of *the Seven Principles*) on the Scripture that teaches the importance of fellowship and partnership in ministry (Acts 2:42, 44–46; Rom 12:4-5; Eph 2:20–21; 4:16) as they reflect on their ministry experience.[56] Through interlink and fellowship, the WOL church is able to extend its house church network and expand its mission frontier. Within the network, coworkers' meetings of all kinds and levels are responsible for keeping the communication flow, channeling renewal ripples to the whole network, and thus sustaining the network. There is also the inter-network fellowship that serves to coordinate ministry jointly, such as the Sinim Fellowship that mobilizes the BTJ movement and the Fellow Sojourners Meeting that coordinates training and ministry of several house church networks in different regions of China.[57]

Kingdom as Framework

Snyder notes that, "The reality of the kingdom gives the church both an overarching theological framework for its life and also practical handles for holding the various dimensions of the kingdom creatively together. The kingdom tells us that God is the God of 'all things in heaven and on earth' (Eph 1:10), and that, in God's kingdom plan, all dimensions of reality are in fact part of one total web."[58] This presents us a "kingdom balance" in the "relationship between the priority of evangelism and justice."[59]

In the effort of renewal, the WOL church has shown us the struggle in maintaining such "kingdom balance." This, however, is exactly the area that the Chinese Church in general should work on, so that in our fervor for evangelism we do not forget social justice; vice versa, in our involvement in social justice we do not neglect evangelism.

We are partakers of God's grand scheme of reconciliation of all things to himself. Since God's plan is to restore the creation, with which he was so pleased when he created, through reconciliation so that human will live under his perfect will and sin will be dealt with and exists no more, our mission will inevitably touch all dimensions of life that have been affected by the fall, including the corrupted human heart and mind, the social injustice, and the scarred environment. All of these challenge us, in our zeal for mission, to work under the framework of the kingdom plan, working out practically in evangelism, service, love, care, social justice and peace.

Summary

Employing Snyder's mediating model for church renewal in the study of the WOL house church movement in China, this study has affirmed the applicability of the model for studying movement of renewal in a cross-cultural manner. Indeed, this mediating model, as the author claims, is "useful in comparing and evaluating various renewal movements, including contemporary ones."[60] By nuancing the mediating model, this study hopes to contribute insights from the experience of the WOL movement to the hermeneutical community, as an attempt to enrich our learning and experience as we continue to serve God's kingdom.

The suggested model of renewal for the Chinese church summarizes learning from the WOL house church movement of renewal as it is consistent with characteristics of renewal movements in history identified by Snyder in *Signs of the Spirit*. As a model of renewal, it specifies only the key elements that are applicable to the renewal of the church in China.

A word has to be said of the role of the Holy Spirit in renewal. In the study of renewal movements, we should never neglect God's role. The Spirit of God does what the Scripture promises he would do: he is with his people (Haggai 2:5), leads his people on level ground (Ps. 143:10), empowers (Judges 6:34), chooses leadership for the church (Acts 20:28), guides the church in decision-making (Acts 15:28), elects and sends evangelists (13:2, 4), directs the work of evangelism (Acts 8:29, 39), lives in us (John 14:16–17), grants us new life (John 3:5-6, Titus 3:5), helps us understand God's love (Rom. 5:5), empowers us to testify Jesus (Acts 1:8, 6:9–10), helps us discern truth (1John 4:1–6), comforts us (Acts 9:31), controls us (Rom. 8:9), gives us joy and peace (Rom. 14:17), fellowships with us (Philippians 2:1), grants us spiritual gifts (1 Cor. 12:4–11), sanctifies us (2 Thess. 2:13), and gives life to our mortal bodies (Rom. 8:11).

o

While recognizing the role of the Holy Spirit as the ultimate cause of renewal, this study examines the human response to the leading of the Spirit of God in renewal and identifies elements that are important to the continuous dynamics of the life of the church. Through the examination of these elements, the signs of the Spirit of God in renewing his church also become clear to us. In other words, by the experience of the historical renewal movements and the present WOL movement, we have come to a closer understanding of the role of the Holy Spirit in equipping believers for service and renewing the church. Through this study we also understand better our role as servants of God in his kingdom. God "saves us through the washing of the rebirth and renewal by the Holy Spirit" (Titus 3:5), and desires us to be transformed by the renewing of our mind (Rom. 12:2). We are, therefore, called to be sensitive to the guidance of the Holy Spirit in our life and ministry so that our individual and corporate life will be renewed day by day.

Notes

1. WOL Manual II, 1.

2. Watchman Nee, *Sit, Stand, Walk* (Bombay: Gospel Literature Service, 1957), 11–12.

3. Cf. Richard Lovelace, *Dynamics of Spiritual Life* (Downers Grove, Illinois: Inter-Varsity Press, 1979), 75.

4. Ibid., 74.

5. Ibid., 93.

6. Eugene Rubingh, "Twice Blessed: Biblical Perspectives on Prayer," in *The Praying Church Sourcebook*, 2nd ed., by Alvin J. Vander Griend (Grand Rapids, Michigan: CRC Publications, 1996), 27.

7. Cf. WOL Manual II.

8. Cf. CCSC, "Report Report on the Seminaries of the Fields," *China and the Church* (Sept.–Dec. 1986).

9. Jonathan Chao, "Bi puo ku nan yu jiao hui zeng zhang" (Opposition and Surrering in Relation to Church Growth), in *Xin jin huo chuan* (The Undying Fire of the Burning Branches) (Taipei: CMI Press, 2005), 83

10. Cf. Chao, *Purified by Fire*, 92.

11. Chao, *Purified by Fire*, 73.

12. Ibid., 93.

13. Gregory Leffel, *Faith Seeking Action* (Lanham, Maryland: Scarecrow Press, Inc., 2007), 59–60.

14. Cf. Leffel, *Faith Seeking Action*.

15. Peter Berger and Thomas Luckmann, *The Social Construction of Reality: A Treatise in the Sociology of knowledge* (New York: Anchor Books, 1967), 116.

16. Thomas Brewster and Elizabeth Brewster, *Bonding and the Missionary Task: Establishing a Sense of Belonging* (Pasadena, California: Lingua House Ministries, 1982), 452–53.

17. Berger and Luckmann, 147.

18. Cf. Chao, *Purified by Fire*, 11.

19. Goerge Hunter III, *The Celtic Way of Evangelism* (Nashville, Tennessee: Abingdon Press), 99–100.

20. Cf. Chao,2000

21. WOL Manual II, 1.

22. Chao, *Purified by Fire*, 35.

23. Elder TG, interview.

24. Elder TR, interview.

25. Cf. WOL Manual I & II.

26. David Bosch, "Reflections on Biblical Models of Mission," in *Toward the Twenty-first Century in Christian Mission*, edited by James Phillips and Robert Coote (Grand Rapids, Michigan: Eerdmans, 1993), 182–83.

27. Cf. WOL Manual I & II.

28. WOL Manual II, 52.

29. Cf. Chao, "The Changing Shape of the Church in China (1976–2002)," *China Ministry Report* 155 (2003), 1–4.

30. Cf. WOL Manual II, 52–57.

31. Cf. Chapter 3 for more detailed discussion of the two structures.

32. Four Development Routes: 1) local church pillars; 2) administration and fellowship; 3) Gospel Band; 4) GB/local churches partnership in ministry. See also discussion on the Four Development Routes in Chapter 4.

33.House church networks, especially those started off in central China share a similar missiological pattern, i.e. the itinerant evangelistic model. It is particular so with those networks that have grown out of the split from the WOL in the mid-1980s.

34. Howard Snyder, *Signs of the Spirit* (Eugene, Oregon: Wipf and Stock, 1997), 276.

35. Richard Lovelace, *Dynamics of Spiritual Life* (Downers Grove, Illinois: Inter-Varsity Press, 1979).

36. Snyder, *Signs of the Spirit*, 280.

37. Richard Lovelace, *Renewal As a Way of Life* (Eugene, Oregon: Wipf and Stock Publishers, 2002), 170.

38. Cf. Richard Lovelace, *Dynamics of Spiritual Life: An Evangelical Theology of Renewal* (Downers Grove, Illinois: Inter-Varsity Press, 1979), 151–60.

39. Chao, "Opposition and Suffering," 82.

40. Cf. 2 Tim. 1:8, 2:3, 3:11, 4:5.

41. Leslie Newbigin, *The Open Secret: An Introduction to the Theology of Mission*, revised ed. (Grand Rapids, Michigan: Eerdmans, 1991), 107.

42. Cf. Eph. 4:22; Col. 2:11, 3:9.

43. Howard Snyder, *Kingdom, Church, and World* (Eugene, Oregon, Wipf and Stock Publishers, 1980), 40.

44. Snyder, *Signs of the Spirit*, 277–79.

45. Howard Snyder, *The Community of the King*, revised ed. (Downers Grove, Illinois: InterVarsity Press, 2004), 160–63.

46. Ibid., 90–91.

47. John Harvey, "Mission in Matthew," in *Mission in the New Testament*, edited by William J. Larkin Jr. and Joel F. Williams (Maryknoll, New York: Orbis Books, 1998), 133.

48. Cf. Donald Durnbaugh, *The Believers' Church* (New York: The Macmillan Company, 1968), 210.

49. Win Arn and Charles Arn, *The Master's Plan for Making Disciples*, 2nd ed. (Grand Rapids, Michigan: Baker Books, 1998), 49–53.

50. See Chapter 3 for discussion on the system of training in the WOL.

51. As quoted in Vinay Samuel and Chris Sugden, eds., *Mission as Transformation: A Theology of the Whole Bible* (Carlisle, UK: Regnum Books, 1999), x.

52. Snyder, *Signs of the Spirit*, 308.

53. Stephen Bevans, *Models of Contextual Theology* (Maryknoll, New York: Orbis Books, 1992), 1.

54. Snyder, *The Community of the King*, 112.

55. Ibid., 169.

56. At the moment, the WOL house church community interlinks and has fellowship primarily with some of the significant large house church networks such as those involved in Sinim Fellowship. Cf. WOL Manual II for reflection on the biblical principle of interlink and fellowship.

57. Fellow Sojourners' Meeting (*Tong lu ren hui*) was established in recent years by the former MGs who are serving in leadership positions in both the WOL church and other house church networks, for fellowship and coordination of ministry in a inter-network manner. For example, a WOL based underground seminary may train students from other house church networks.

58. Snyder,. *Kingdom, Church, and World,* 82–83.

59. Snyder, *Signs of the Spirit*, 280.

Chapter 6

Conclusions and Recommendations

This book has, in the previous chapters, offered a historical description of the Word of Life movement in China, engaged in analytical examination of the movement using Snyder's mediating model for church renewal, and proposed a theology of renewal for the Chinese church. In this final chapter, this book gives a few general conclusions, recognizes some of the challenges and opportunities with regard to the WOL community, identifies the missiological contribution of this study, and proposes suggestions for further study concerning the WOL movement.

General Conclusions

The study of the WOL movement has provided not only a familiarity with the movement itself, but also insights in identifying the signs of the Spirit of God in renewing his church. Following are some general conclusions of this study categorized in three aspects: the usefulness of the mediating model for church renewal, signs of the Spirit of God in renewal, and the role of human agents in renewal.

The Mediating Model for Church Renewal

This study first of all demonstrates the qualifications of the model as a theoretical framework for the study of the WOL as a movement of renewal cross-culturally, through which the WOL movement is evaluated and analyzed. Thus the mediating model can be further used and tested universally for the study of church renewal in all cultures and situations, historically and contemporarily.

Signs of the Spirit of God in Renewal

Although this study is based on the research data on the human experience, it nevertheless testifies to the work of the Spirit of God in renewal. The Holy Spirit is the primary initiator in renewal, with humans as agents and participants. It is God's desire that the image of God be renewed, individually and corporately, a process in which the Holy Spirit acts in many special ways, through election and empowerment, leading and directing, illuminating and comforting. The shared experience of renewal of the WOL movement and historical Christian renewal movements helps reveal how the Spirit of God works in renewing his church that has become less of what it should be, whether it is trapped lifeless in the institutional routines, or compromises to earthly powers at the sacrifice of Christian integrity, or simply loses focus on the fundamentals of the gospel.

The Holy Spirit is always where God's people are, ready to bring change in the church toward life and vitality. God is "I AM," consistent and unchanging in what he is and in his promises. He will bless his people and multiply their numbers if they remain faithful to him and sensitive to his voice.

The Role of Human Agents in Renewal

This study further affirms the indisputably significance on the part of the human response to the leading of the Spirit of God in renewal. The Spirit of God guides and leads the church out of his unchanging good purpose. The church is the body of Christ, and therefore, life, vitality, and growth is promised. God, however, chooses to invite his people on the journey with him instead of enforcing his will on them. It is, thus, essential that Christians identify the signs of work of the Spirit of God and be obedient to his leading. Historically, faithful servants of God such as Philipp Spener, Count Zinzendorf, and John Wesley, were able to follow the signs of the Spirit of God for their time and context, and became partners with God in bringing significant renewal to the church. Today, the active participation of men and women called to service in the WOL movement, who, being sensitive to the guidance of the Holy Spirit, structure themselves in such a way that contributes to the continuous dynamics of the life of the church, offers us insights as how we can be better servants of God in his Kingdom.

Missiological Contributions of the Study

First of all, this study contributes to our knowledge of the church in China by offering a historical description of the Word of Life movement in China for the past three decades. As such it provides a relatively detailed account of the development of the WOL community through the labor of the faithful men and women who, called by God, become agents of God in renewal, instrumental in the explosive growth of the community throughout the country.

Second, this study analyzes the dynamics of the movement from the perspective of renewal movement, using the mediating model for church renewal proposed by Snyder (1997) as the major framework guiding the analysis. Such analysis results in identifying the common characteristics between the WOL movement and historical renewal movements, as well as features that are culturally specific to the Chinese situation.

Third, in evaluating and amplifying the mediating model for church renewal based on the study of the WOL movement in China, this study incorporates learnings and insights from Richard Lovelace (on theology of renewal), Peter Berger (on sociology of knowledge), and Gregory Leffel (on social movements) and proposes a model of renewal for the Chinese church, which, on the basis of the mediating model for church renewal, pays attention to the unique experience of the WOL movement.

Challenges and Opportunities

Empowered by of the Holy Spirit, the WOL movement in China touched a significant portion of the population with the gospel message, and is instrumental in bringing millions of souls under the lordship of Jesus Christ. The three decades of development is a story of the power of the Holy Spirit, as well as the diligent and devoted ministry of the faithful believers. In the study of the WOL movement, we identify a further affirmation of the signs of God in renewing his church and active response from His people in following His will. The story and experience of the WOL Christians undoubtedly contribute to the understanding of the hermeneutical community, testifying His faithfulness in renewing the Church. As the hermeneutical circle continues to enlarge, we are getting closer to knowing the heart of God.

As this research reveals, nonetheless, it has not been a smooth development historically in the case of the WOL movement. There have been challenges and obstacles all along the way and some of them are still present even as new challenges continue to emerge. How the WOL is prepared to meet the challenges and turn those into opportunities will be significant to the future of the movement.

Challenges

Within many internal factors that present challenge to the WOL movement, the loss of its members, especially its youth, to migration, is one of the primary challenges to the continuous growth of the community, even with the fact that there has always been shortage of coworkers to minister in various levels of the WOL community ever since its formation three decades ago.

An agricultural nation, China had contained 80 percent of her one billion inhabitants in the vast rural areas of China up to the end of 1970s. Since then, with the state economic reform and open policy called forth by the new leader, China has become gradually industrialized and urbanized. As a result, one of world's largest population migration was immediately underway. In approximately twenty years since the beginning of 1980s, about 100 million from the rural population have been added to the urban population in China. The exit of rural population has proven to be a great challenge for the WOL community that has grown out of the rural context. Many young believers, including some coworkers, because of the lack of job opportunities in the rural context, have left for the cities for means of making a living and supporting the families. The WOL community has experienced an immediate shortage of young believers and coworkers, without whose presence the community feel "a withdraw of burning wood from the fire." Of course this problem is not exclusive to the WOL community, as other rural house church communities have also been affected by this demographic change caused by the urbanization trend in China. At any rate, the effect of this loss is intimately and evidently felt.

This challenge is further aggravated by the fact that those involved in ministry in all levels of the WOL structure, that is, from individual house churches within the network, to area, regional coworker's meetings, consist primarily of Christians in their twenties, thirties, and forties. These age groups are naturally among the most affected in this demographic transition. As a result, pastoral shortage among the vast community of the WOL house churches is posing one of biggest challenges.

Opportunities

On the other hand, the influx of rural Christians in the cities seems to naturally create opportunities for the gospel to spread as these young believers settle themselves into the various neighborhoods. In terms of church affiliation, there seem to be several options available: urban house churches, which can often be categorized as traditional house churches and young professionals' fellowship, and the TSPM churches. The fact, however, is that it is still a challenging task for these young believers to identify themselves with the urban counterparts due to their marginal economic status as *Min gong*, a term that is commonly used to refer to migrant workers who normally take on jobs rejected by the urban dwellers.[1] Inferior political and economic status itself can create great internal obstacle in witnessing, let alone the effect of the external discriminative attitude from the urban dwellers toward *Min gong*. While some rural Christians are able to attend worship services or other forms of gathering in either the urban house churches or TSPM churches, they, however, feel nowhere at home.

What's more, on the part of the urban house churches, cultural differences, compounded with an attitude of suspicion toward Christian *Min gong*, especially those from rural house church networks, such as the WOL, seem to play a role in the degree of openness in receiving the rural Christians. Even with these obstacles, however, urban Christian population has been significantly increased simply due to the presence of the rural Christians.

The WOL community is very much conscious of the situation their migrant brothers and sisters are facing. Issues and reports are constantly brought back to the churches back home, which are shared in community and lifted up in prayers. How the WOL community responds to the challenge and opportunity given for the best advancement of the gospel is the issue at stake. Can loss be turned into gain?

Missiological Recommendations

The impact of urbanization in China is so great that it inevitably touched the general rural population including the WOL community that has grown in the pervasive rural China areas. There are no quick fixes for this social problem, a fact that the WOL community faces squarely. With the younger believers gone, the task of ministry will inevitably fall on the shoulder of the senior adult believers as well as the remaining young believers. This may explains why the focus of the WOL ministry is transiting from frontier evangelism to consolidating established churches and discipleship training in recent years.

Coordination is absolutely necessary between the WOL and the urban churches. At the moment, it is still a challenging task because no significant fellowship link exists between the WOL and the urban house churches. The unity movement basically involves only the rural house church networks, particularly those that developed from the split of the original WOL community. Challenging as it is, the WOL needs to put this need high on their agenda and find ways to establish the much needed "interlink and fellowship," one of *the Seven Principles* of the WOL theology.

Several ways can be suggested as to deal with the problem: 1) that the WOL church actively proposes fellowship with the urban churches so that the need can be recognized and addressed. This would mean that, in actively receiving and understanding the rural Christians, the urban house churches will be able to provide relevant pastoral care for the rural Christians, and in turn, rural Christians could then find themselves "at home" in the urban house churches and participate in ministry according to their respective spirit gifts. In mutuality, *koinonia* is practiced, growth is experienced, and vitality is sustained; 2) Christian *Min gong* from the WOL community may organize their own house churches in the cities where they now work and live. This is exactly what some young believers have done in the past few years. A community of faith will eventually form and be salt and light to their surrounding world, especially to the *Min gong* community. These *Min gong* churches, to a significant degree, maintain marks of the rural churches and therefore have the natural affinity to the *Min gong* community. A significant Christian movement may well be ignited among the urban poor. In due time, people will be attracted to the gathering and fellowship will start with the urban churches. As a consequence, renewal may extend to the urban churches through the WOL *Min gong*.[2]

Pervasive coordination in ministry across networks needs to be initiated among the house church community, not only the present participating house church networks, but also the urban house church networks and "families." This can be done through fellowship meetings of various levels, one of which is the

Tong lu ren hui (Fellow Sojourners' Meeting), the platform established by former MGs for the coordination of ministry across house church networks. More of these kinds of platforms are highly recommended that involve urban churches as well. This will not only channel the ripple of renewal but also enlarge the scope of the unity movement.

Suggestions for Further Study

This study targets primarily at the identification of the signs of the renewal revolving around the WOL movement. It focuses on the characteristics identified by Snyder in the mediating model for church renewal. As such, this study reveals the dynamics in the WOL as a movement of renewal, and verifies the validity of the common characteristics of renewal movements identified by Snyder in *Signs of the Spirit* (1997).

Quantitative Study of the WOL movement

An indepth statistical study of the WOL community has not been done. Many of the numbers that appear in the literature today are not empirically verified. Such research will be a challenging task in itself, given the underground nature of the WOL movement, which probably means that statistical record concerning membership is not kept in written forms. Even the figures from the top leadership of the WOL concerning the number of believers affiliated with the church are not seriously researched. Rather, they are approximated according to the report from regional and area coworkers' meetings. Apart from this, there may also be the tendency of "double counting"—that the WOL might have included some of the house churches that actually are affiliated with other networks that grow out of the split of the original WOL community. The same observation may also be valid for the statistics given by other house church networks.

Contextual Change and Its Implications

The trend of urbanization in China has obviously affected the WOL community. The question of the extent that the WOL has suffered or benefited from this social factor is one that is well worthy of research and observation. First of all, the extent of loss of members to the urbanization process in China causes the WOL community an immediate shortage of young believers in the community as well as young coworkers, especially MGs whose primary task is frontier evangelism for the continuation of the expansion of the WOL community in China as well as outside China.

Secondly, the influx of young believers of the WOL into the cities supplies new strength to the urban churches, despite of the fact that there has not been as much link between the WOL *Min gong* and the urban churches as might be desired. This phenomenon is undergoing change, consciously and unconsciously.

It remains to be seen how the WOL structure can continue to function well with this new change even as it may continue to consolidate it. It is possible to speculate the future development of the WOL church through in-depth research done in this area.

Back to Jerusalem Movement

Since the 1990s the WOL church has been actively involved in preparing and mobilizing resources for the BTJ project, a vision shared by many in the Chinese Church. The WOL community regards BTJ as part of its calling to fulfill the Great Commission, that to evangelize the Muslim nations, Hindu nations, and Buddhist nations through the three routes of the Silk Roads from China. BTJ has seemingly become a missiological driving force for the WOL even as the community continues its evangelistic outreach within the national boundary.

Though still in the fledgling stage of development, BTJ movement has already raised some consciousness and support from the global church. How the BTJ has impacted the WOL community, which started as a rural church movement, as it prepares to go international in a significant way? What are some of the internal and external implications? Does BTJ signify a new stage of development in the WOL as a movement of renewal in and outside China? These are just a few suggestions for further research as we anticipate to be amazed by the Spirit of God in fulfilling his salvation plan through his servants.

As a concluding word, the WOL movement offers an insightful model of renewal for the church in China through its shared experience and yet unique response. It is not a perfect church or movement and has its weaknesses and faults that need to be dealt with. It is, however, a community much blessed by God because it seeks after God's heart and finds the signs of the Spirit of God at work in renewing the church.

Notes

1. *Min gong* (literarily meaning "peasant worker") is one of the several most commonly used terms referring to migrant workers in China. In southern part of the country, *Da gong zai* is preferred for male migrant worker, and *Da gong mei* is used to refer to female migrant worker. Regretfully, these terms often connote elements of discrimination.

2. Cf. Yalin Xin, "The Future of Christianity in China," *The Asbury Journal* 64 no. 1 (2009), 80.

Bibliography (English Language)

Abraham, William J. *The Logic of Renewal*. Grand Rapids, Michigan: W. B. Eerdmans Publishing Co., 2003.

Adeney, David H. "Inside China's Churches." *Christianity Today* 36 (1992): 21–23.

_____. *The Long March of the Chinese Church*. Ventura, California: Regal Books, 1985.

Aikman, David. *Jesus in Beijing*. Washington, DC: Regnery Publishing, Inc., 2003.

Anderson, Gerald H. *Asian Voices in Christian Theology*. Maryknoll, New York: Orbis Books, 1976.

_____. *Christ and Crisis in Southeast Asia*. New York: Friendship Press, 1969.

_____, ed. *Christ and Crisis in Southeast Asia*. New York: Friendship Press, 1968.

Anderson, Gerald H., and Peter G. Gowing. "Bulwark of the Church in Asia." In *Christ and Crisis in Southeast Asia*, edited by Gerald H. Anderson, 135–62. New York: Friendship Press, 1968.

Arn, Win, and Charles Arn. *The Master's Plan for Making Disciples*, 2nd ed. Grand Rapids, Michigan: Baker Books, 1998.

Asia Theological Association. *Voice of the Church in Asia*. Hong Kong: Asia Theological Association, 1975.

Baker, Gilbert. *The Church on Asian Frontiers*. Westminster: Church Information Office, 1963.

Barnett, Suzanne W., and John K. Fairbank, eds. *Christianity in China: Early Protestant Missionary Writings*. Cambridge, Massachussett: The Committee on American-East Asian Relations of the Department of History in collaboration with The Council on East Asian Studies/Harvard University, 1985.

Barth, Karl. *The Church and the Churches*. Foreword by William G. Rusch. Grand Rapids, Michigan: Eerdmans Publishing Company, 2005.

Bays, Daniel H. "Chinese Popular Religion and Christianity Before and After the 1949 Revolution: A Retrospective View." *Fides et Historia* XXIII:1 (1991): 69–77.

_____, ed. *Christianity in China: From the Eighteenth Century to the Present.* Standford, California: Stanford University Press, 1996.

_____. "The Growth of Independent Christianity." In *Christianity in China: From the Eighteenth Century to the Present,* edited by Daniel H. Bays, 307–16. Stanford, California: Stanford University Press, 1996.

Beaver, R. Pierce. "Rufus Anderson 1796-1880: To Evangelize, Not Civilize." In *Mission Legacies: Biographical Studies of Leaders of the Modern Missionary Movement.* Gerald H. Anderson et al., eds. Pp. 548–53. Maryknoll, New York: Orbis Books, 1994.

Berger, Peter L., and Thomas Luckmann. *The Social Construction of Reality: A Treatise in the Sociology of knowledge.* New York: Anchor Books, 1966.

Bevans, Stephen B. *Models of Contextual Theology.* Maryknoll, New York: Orbis Books, 1992.

Bieler, Stacey, and Dick Andrews. *China at Your Doorstep: Christian Friendships with Mainland Chinese.* Downers Grove, Illinois: Intervarsity Press, 1987.

Bloesch, Donald G. *Wellspring of Renewal: Promise in Christian Communal Life.* Grand Rapids, Michigan: Eerdmans Publishing Company, 1974.

Bodde, Derk. *Essays on Chinese Civilization.* Princeton, New Jersey: Princeton University Press, 1981.

Boff, Leonardo, and Virgil Elizondo, eds. *Any Room for Christ in Asia?* Maryknoll, New York: Orbis Books, 1993.

Bonavia, David. *The Chinese.* Middlesex, England: Penguin Books, 1981.

Bong, Rin Ro. *Urban Ministry in Asia.* Taichung, Taiwan: Asia Theological Association, 1989.

Bosch, David. "Reflections on Biblical Models of Mission." In *Toward the Twenty-first Century in Christian Mission,* edited by James M Phillips and Robert T. Coote, 175–92. Grand Rapids, Michigan: Eerdmans, 1993.

Brewster, E. Thomas, and Elizabeth S. Brewster. *Bonding and the Missionary Task: Establishing a Sense of Belonging.* Pasadena, California: Lingua House Ministries, 1982.

Brother CH. Interview notes by author. China. March, 2005.

Brother J. Interview notes by author. China. March, 2005.

Brother L et al. Interview notes by author. China. March, 2005.

Brother P. Interview notes by author. China. March, 2005.

Brother TY. Interview notes by author. China. March, 2005.

Brother Yun, and Paul Hattaway. *The Heavenly Man: The Remarkable True Story of Chinese Christian Brother Yun.* London and Grand Rapids: Monarch Books, 2002.

Brown, Thompson G. *Christianity in the People's Republic,* revised ed. Atlanta, Georgia: John Knox Press, 1986.

Burkhardt, V. R. *Chinese Creeds & Customs,* Vol. II. Hong Kong: The South China Morning Post, Ltd, 1955.

_____. *Chinese Creeds & Customs,* Vol. III. Third ed. Hong Kong: The South China Morning Post, Ltd, 1960.

Bush, Richard C. *Religion in Communist China*. Nashville, Tennessee: Abingdon Press, 1970.

Cao, Shengjie, et al. *Selected Essays on Theological Thinking Construction*. Shanghai, China: China Protestant Christian Association, 2004.

Chao, Jonathan. "The Changing Shape of the Church in China (1976–2002)." *China Ministry Report* 155 (2003): 1–4.

_____, ed. *The China Mission Handbook*. Hong Kong: Chinese Church Research Center, 1989.

_____. *China's Religious Policy and Christian Missions*. Hong Kong: China Graduate School of Theology, 1977.

_____. "China's Revival Meetings and Tears—An Analysis of 'Sheng ming hui.'" *China Prayer Letter and Ministry Report* 125 (1993): 1–3.

_____. "The Church in China Today: Officially Registered Churches and House Churches *China Prayer Letter and Ministry Report* 112 (1997): 5–7.

_____. "Chinese House Church Confession of Faith," *China Prayer Letter and Ministry Report* 149 (Nov. 1998–Feb. 1999): 2–4..

_____. "Han Wenzhao Slanders House Church Leader." *China Prayer Letter and Ministry Report* 112 *(1997)*: 1–2. (1997e)

_____. "The House Church Movement: Its Beginning and Structural Development." *China Prayer Letter and Ministry Report* 82 (1987): 1–3.

_____. "House Church Seminary Training and Missions Strategy." *China Prayer Letter* 83 (1987): 1–2.

_____. "Seminary of the Field: A Model for Mission." *China Prayer Letter and Ministry Report* 74 (1986): 1, 6.

Charbonnier, Jean M.E.P. "China 1993: Openness: Its Cultural Implications." *Tripod* 75 (2005): 5–25.

Chen, Susan, and Claudia Chang, eds. *The Undying Fire of the Burning Branches: A Posthumous Essay Collection of Dr. Jonathan Chao*. Taipei, Taiwan: China Ministries International, 2005.

Ch'en, Jerome. *China and the West*. Bloomington and London: Indiana University Press, 1979.

Ching, Julia. *Mysticism and Kingship in China: The Heart of Chinese Wisdom*. New York, New York: Cambridge University Press, 1997.

Christian Study Center on Chinese Religion and Culture (CSCCRC). "The True Jesus Church Yesterday and Today, Part 1." *Bridge* 62 (December 1993): 5.

Chung, Wai-keung. "Qinqing (Familial Love and Familial Relationship) Mission Theology for the Chinese: An Interdisciplinary Study." Ph.D Dissertation. Reformed Theological Seminary, Jackson, Mississippi, 2000.

Clark, William H. *The Church in China—Its Vitality; Its Future?* New York: Council Press, 1977.

Cliff, Norman H. *Fierce the Conflict: The Moving Stories of How Eight Chinese Christians Suffered for Jesus Christ and Remained Faithful*. Dundas, Ontario: Joshua Press, 2001.

_____. "Watchman Nee--Church Planter and Preacher of Holiness," *Evangelical Review of Theology* 8 no.2 (1984): 289–97.

Cohen, Paul A. *China Unbound: Evolving Perspectives on the Chinese Past.* New York, NY: RoutledgeCurzon, 2003.

Confucius [Kong Zi]. *Analects.* Arthur Waley, trans. New York: Vintage Books, 1938.

Cooley, Frank L. *Indonesia: Church & Society.* New York: Friendship Press, 1968.

Coulson, Gail V. *The Enduring Church: Christians in China and Hong Kong.* New York: Friendship Press, 1991.

Cooley, Frank L. "Social Revolution and Christian Renewal." In *Christ and Crisis in Southeast Asia,* edited by Gerald H. Anderson, 107–134. New York: Friendship Press, 1968.

Creel, H. G. *Chinese Thought: From Confucius to Mao Tse-tung.* Chicago, Illinois: The University of Chicago Press, 1953.

Crook, Isabel, and David Crook. *Ten Mile Inn: Mass Movement in a Chinese Village.* New York, New York: Random House, Inc., 1979.

Crouch, Archie R., et al. *Christianity in China: A Scholars' Guide to Resources in the Libraries and Archives of the United States.* Armonk, New York: M. E. Sharpe, 1989.

Cuddihy, Kathy, ed. *Christianity for China: Foundation for Dialogue.* Hong Kong: Centre of Asian Studies, University of Hong Kong, 1991.

David, M. D. *Western Colonialism in Asia and Christianity.* Bombay: Himalaya Publishing House, 1988.

Das, Man Singh, and Panos D. Bardis, eds. *The Family in Asia.* London, England: George Allen & Unwin Ltd., 1979.

De Bary, William Theodore, and Irene Bloom. *Sources of Chinese Tradition: From Earliest to 1600.* New York, New York: Columbia University Press, 1999.

De Bary, William Theodore, and Richard Lufrano. *Sources of Chinese Tradition: From 1600 Through the Twentieth Century,* second edition. New York, New York: Columbia University Press, 1999.

Digan, Parig. *Churches in Contestation: Asian Christian Social Protest.* Maryknoll, New York: Orbis Books, 1984.

Dillon, Michael, ed. *China: A Cultural and Historical Dictionary.* Richmond, Surrey: Curzon Press, 1998.

Durnbaugh, Donald F. *The Believers' Church: The History and Character of Radical Protestantism.* New York, New York: The Macmillan Company, 1968.

_____. *Fruit of the Vine: A History of the Brethren, 1708–1995.* Elgin, Illinois: Brethren Press, 1997.

Eberhard, Wolfram. *The Local Cultures of South and East China.* Leiden, Netherlands: E. J. Brill, 1968.

Ebrey, Patricia Buckley. *Cambridge Illustrated History of China.* London, England: Cambridge University Press, 1996.

Elder TG. Interview notes by author. Henan, China. March, 2005.

Elder TR. Interview notes by author. Henan, China. March, 2005.

England, John C., ed. *Living Theology in Asia*. Maryknoll, New York: Orbis Books, 1981.

Fairbank, John King. *China: A New History*. Cambridge, Massachussetts: The Belknap Press of Harvard University Press, 1992.

Finney, Charles Grandison. *Lectures on Revivals of Religion*, edited by William G Mcloughlin. Cambridge, Massachusetts: The Belknap Press of Harvard University Press, 1960.

Francis, T. Dayanandan, and Franklyn J. Balasundaram. *Asian Expressions of Christian Commitment*. Madras: Christian Literature Society, 1992.

Fung, Raymond. *Household of God on China's Soil*. Geneva: World Council of Churches, 1982.

Gamer, Robert E., ed. *Understanding Contemporary China*. Boulder, Colorado: Lynne Rienner Publishers, 2003.

Gerlach, Luther P., and Virginia H. Hine. *People, Power, Change: Movements of Social Transformation*. Indianapolis: Bobbs-Merrill, 1970.

Gernet, Jacques. *China and the Christian Impact: A Conflict of Cultures*, translated by Jane Lloyd. Cambridge, England: Cambridge University Press, 1985.

_____. *A History of Chinese Civilization*. Translated by J. R. Foster and Charles Hartman. Cambridge, UK: Cambridge University Press, 1996.

Gih, Andrew. *"Launch Out into the Deep!"—Tales of Revival Through China's Famous Bethel Evangelistic Bands and Further Messages*. London & Edinburgh: Marshall, Morgan & Scott, Ltd., 1938.

Gillman, Ian, and Hans-Joachim Klimkeit. *Christians in Asia before 1500*. Ann Arbor, Michigan: The University of Michigan Press, 1999.

Guang. "My Visit to 'The Jesus Family'." *Bridge* 34 (1989): 16–19.

Gunde, Richard. *Culture and Customs of China*. Westport, Cincinnatti: Greenwood Press, 2002.

Hartzell, Richard W. *Harmony in Conflict: Active Adaptation to Life in Present-day Chinese Society*. Taipei, Taiwan: Caves Books, Ltd., 1988.

Harvey, John D. "Mission in Matthew." In *Mission in the New Testament: An Evangelical Approach*, edited by William J. Larkin Jr. and Joel F. Williams. Maryknoll, New York: Orbis Books, 1998.

Harvey, Thomas A. *Acquainted with Grief: Wang Mingdao's Stand for the Persecuted Church in China*. Grand Rapids, Michigan: Brazos Press, 2002.

Hattaway, Paul. *Back to Jerusalem*. Carlisle, UK: Piquant, 2003.

_____. *Operation China: Introducing All the Peoples of China*. Pasadena, California: William Carey Library, 2000.

Hattaway, Paul, and Joy Hattaway. "From the Front Lines with Paul & Joy Hattaway." *Asia Harvest* 2 (March 2002): 2–11.

Hellerman, Joseph H. *The Ancient Church as Family*. Minneapolis, Minnesota: Augsburg Fortress Press, 2001.

Highbaugh, Irma. *Family Life in West China*. New York, New York: Agricultural Missions, Inc., 1948.

Hoke, Donald E. *The Church in Asia*. Chicago, Illinois: Moody Press, 1975.

Hook, Brian, general ed. *The Cambridge Encyclopedia of China*. Cambridge, New York, Melbourne: Cambridge University Press, 1982.

Hsu, Francis L. K. *Americans & Chinese: Passage to Differences.* Honolulu, Hawaii: The University Press of Hawaii, 1981.

_____. *Under the Ancestors' Shadow: Kinship, Personality, and Social Mobility in Village China.* Garden City, New York: Anchor Books, 1967.

Hu, Wenzhong, and Cornelius L. Grove. *Encountering the Chinese: A Guide for Americans.* Yarmouth, Maine: Intercultural Press, Inc., 1999.

Hunsberger, George R. *Evangelical Dictionary of World Missions.* A. Scott Moreau, ed. Grand Rapids, Michigan: Baker Books, 2000.

Hunter, Alan, and Chan Kim Kwong. *Protestantism in Contemporary China.* Cambridge, UK: Cambridge University Press, 1993.

_____. *A Strong Movement in the Making for Protestants in China 1990.* Cambridge: Cambridge University Press, 1993.

Hunter, Alan, and Don Rimmington, eds. *All under Heaven: Chinese Tradition and Christian Life in the People's Republic of China.* Kempen Netherlands: J. H. Kok, 1991.

Hunter, George G. *The Celtic Way of Evangelism: How Christianity Can Reach the West...Again.* Nashville, Tennessee: Abingdon Press, 2000.

Hwa, Yung. *Theology and Mission in the Asian Church.* D.Miss dissertation. Wilmore, Kentucky: Asbury Theological Seminary, 1994.

Jones, Francis P. *The Church in Communist China: A Protestant Appraisal.* New York, New York: Friendship Press, 1962.

Jones, Francis P., ed. *Documents of the Three-Self Patriotic Movement.* New York: Far Eastern Office, Division of Foreign Missions, NCCC-USA, 1963.

Johnstone, Patrick, Robyn J Johnstone, and Jason Mandryk. *Operation World,* 21st Century Edition. Cumbria, UK: Paternoster Lifestyle, 2001.

Kan, Baoping. "Theology in the Contemporary Chinese Context." *Word & World* XVII no.2 (1997): 161–67.

Kang, Thomas Hosuck. *Confucius and Confucianism: Questions and Answers.* Washington, D. C.: Confucian Publications, 1997.

Kauffman, Paul E. *China, the Emerging Challenge: A Christian Perspective.* Grand Rapids, Michigan: Baker Book House, 1982.

_____. *Through China's Door.* Hong Kong: Asian Outreach, 1977.

Kennedy, Diane, O.P. "A Contextual Theology of Leadership," *Theological Education* (Oct., 2000): 63–72.

Kindopp, Jason, and Carol Lee Hamrin, eds. *God and Caesar in China: Policy Implications of Church-State Tensions.* Washington, D.C.: Brookings Institution Press, 2001.

Kinnear, Angus. *Against the Tide: The Story of Watchman Nee.* Wheaton, Illinois: Tyndale House Publishers, 1973.

Kraft, Charles H. *Anthropology for Christian Witness.* Maryknoll, New York: Orbis Books, 1996.

_____. *Christianity in Culture: A Study in Dynamic Biblical Theologizing in Cross-Cultural Perspective.* Maryknoll, New York: Orbis Books, 1979.

Kung, Hans, and Julia Ching. *Christianity and Chinese Religions.* New York: Doubleday, 1989.

Kwok, Pui-lan. *Discovering the Bible in the Non-Biblical World.* New York: Orbis Books, 1995.

Kyoung Bae Min. "Christianity in Korea." In *Christianity in Asia: North-East Asia*, edited by T. K. Thomas. Singapore: Christian Conference of Asia, 1979.

LaFleur, Robert A. *China: A Global Studies handbook.* Santa Barbara, California: ABC CLIO, Inc., 2003.

Lam, Anthony. "China's Underground Movements: Meaning and Resolution." Norman Walling, trans. *Tripod* 110 (1999): 5–18.

Lam, Wing-hung. *Chinese Theology in Construction.* Hong Kong: Tien Dao Publishing House, Ltd., 1980.

_____. *Wang Ming-tao and the Chinese Church.* Hong Kong: China Graduate School of Theology, 1982.

Lambert, Tony. *China's Christian Millions: The Costly Revival.* London, UK: Monarch Books, 1998.

_____. "Counting Christians in China: A Cautionary Report." *International Bulletin of Missionary Research* 27 (Jan., 2003): 6–10.

_____. *The Resurrection of the Chinese Church.* Sevenoaks, Kent, UK: Hodder and Stoughton, 1991.

_____. *The Resurrection of the Chinese Church.* Wheaton, Illinois: OMF IHQ, Ltd., 1994.

Latourette, Kenneth Scott. *Chinese, Their History and Culture.* New York: The Macmillan Company, 1946.

_____. *A History of Christian Missions in China.* New York: The Macmillan Company, 1929.

_____. *A History of Modern China.* London, Batimore: Penguin Books, 1954.

_____. *The Twentieth Century Outside Europe—The Americas, the pacific, Asia, and Africa: the Emerging World Christian Community.* New York, New York: Harper & Row, Publishers, 1962.

Lawrence, Carl. *The Church in China.* Minneapolis, Minnesota: Bethany House Publishers, 1985.

Lee, Chun Kwan. *The Theology of Revival in the Chinese Christian Church, 1900–1949: Its Emergence and Impact.* Ph.D Diss. Westminster Theological Seminary, Philadelphia, Pennsylvania, 1988.

Leffel, Gregory P. *Faith Seeking Action: Mission, Social Movement, and the Church in Motion.* Lanham, Maryland: Scarecrow Press, Inc., 2007.

Leung, Beatrice, and John D. Young. *Christianity in China: Foundations for Dialogue.* Hong Kong: Centre of Asian Studies, University of Hong Kong, 1991.

Leung, Ka-lun. *Far Ahead and Lagging Behind: Studies in Contextual Hermeneutics and Theology.* Hong Kong: Alliance Bible Seminary, 2003.

Leung, Philip Yuen-sang, "Conversion, Commitment, and Culture: Christian Experience in China, 1949–99." In *Christianity Reborn: The Global Expansion of Evangelicalism in the Twentieth Century*, edited by Donald Lewis. Grand Rapids, Michigan: Wm. B. Eerdmans Publishing Company, 2004.

Li, Xinyuan. *Theological Construction—or Destruction?: An Analysis of the Theology of Bishop K. H. Ting (Ding Guangxun)*. Streamwood, Illinois: Christian Life Press, Inc., 2003.

Lian, Xi. *The Conversion of Missionaries: Liberalism in American Protestant Missions in China, 1907–1932*. University Park, Pennsylvania: The Pennsylvania State University Press, 1996.

Lin, Chi-ping, ed. *Christianity and Indigenization in China*. Taipei, Taiwan: Cosmic Light Media Publishers, 1990.

Lin, Melissa Manhong. "A modern Chinese Journey of Inculturation." *International Review of Mission* 87 (1998): 9–24.

Lin, Peter C., ed. *Indigenization of Christianity in China*. Taipei, Taiwan: Cosmos Light Publishing Co., 1990.

Ling, Oi Ki. *The Changing Role of the British Protestant Missionaries in China, 1945-1952*. Cranbury, New Jersey: Associated University Press, 1996.

Lipton, Edward P. *Religious Freedom in Asia*. Hauppauge, New York: Nova Science Publishers, Inc., 2002.

Lovelace, Richard F. *Dynamics of Spiritual Life: An Evangelical Theology of Renewal*. Downers Grove, Illinois: Inter-Varsity Press, 1979.

_____. *Renewal As a Way of Life—A Guidebbok for Spiritual Growth*. Eugene, Oregon: Wipf and Stock Publishers, 2002.

Lyall, Leslie T. *China's Three Mighty Men*. London: OMF Books, 1973.

_____. *God Reigns in China*. London: Hodder & SAtoughton, 1985.

_____. *John Sung*. London: China Inland Mission, 1954.

_____. *The Phoenix Rises*. Singapore: Overseas Missionary Fellowship Ltd., 1992.

_____. *Urgent Harvest*. Chicago, Illinois: Moody Press, 1964.

Ma, Andrew Chi Sing. *Toward a Contextual Theology of Suffering: The Chinese Christian Perspective since 1949*. Ph.D Dissertation. Fuller Theological Seminary, Pasadena, California, 2005.

Mackerras, Colin. *China's ethnic Minorities and Globalisation*. New York, New York: RoutledgeCurzon, 2003.

Magnuson, Norris A. "Church Renewal," in *Evangelical Dictionary of Theology*, edited by Walter A. Elwell, 934–36. Grand Rapids, Michigan: Baker Books, 1984.

McAleavy, Henry. *The Modern History of China*. New York, New York: Praeger Publishers, 1967.

McGavran, Donald A. *The Bridges of God: A Study in the Strategy of Missions*. London: World Dominion Press, 1955.

_____. *Understanding Church Growth*, revised ed. Grand Rapids, Michigan: Eerdmans Publishing Company, 1980.

McKenzie, Peter. *The Christians: Their Beliefs and Practices*. Nashville, Tennessee: Abingdon Press, 1988.

McLoughlin, William G. *Modern Revivalism: Charles Grandison Finney to Billy Graham*. New York: Ronald Press Co., 1959.

_____. *Revivals, Awakenings, and Reform: An Essay on Religion and Social Change in America, 1607–1977*. Chicago, Illinois: The University of Chicago Press, 1978.

Merwin, Wallace C., and Francis P. Jones, eds. *Documents of the Three-Self Movement: Source Materials for the Study of the Protestant Church in Communist China*. New York, New York: Far Eastern Office, National Council of the Churches of Christ in the U.S.A, 1963.

Minamiki, George, S.J. *The Chinese Rites Controversy from Its Beginnings to Modern Times*. Chicago, Illinois: Loyola Universtiy Press, 1985.

Moffet, Samuel H. *A History of Christianity in Asia, Vol. I: Beginnings to 1500*. Maryknoll, NY: Orbis Books, 1998.

_____. *A History of Christianity in Asia, Vol. II: 1500–1900*. Maryknoll, NY: Orbis Books, 2005.

Moise, Edwin E. *Modern China: A History*. Essex, England: Longman Group Limited, 1994.

Monsen, Marie. *Awakening: Revival in China, a Work of the Holy Spirit*, translated by Joy Guinness (1961). London, Great Britain: China Inland Mission, 1959.

_____. *A Wall of Fire*, translated by Joy Guinness. Salem, Ohio: Allegheny Publications, 2004.

Moore, Charles A., ed. *The Chinese Mind: Essentials of Chinese Philosophy and Culture*. Honolulu, Hawaii: East-West Center Press, 1967.

Moreau, A. Scott, ed. *Evangelical Dictionary of World Mission*. Grand Rapids, Michigan: Baker Books, 2000.

Mosher, Steven W. *Broken Earth: The Rural Chinese*. New York, New York: The Free Press, 1983.

Mueller, Wilhelm K., SVD. "China's Christians: Catalysts of Social Change." *Tripod* 126 (2002): 5–21.

Myrdal, Jan. *Return to a Chinese Village*. New York, New York: Pantheon Books, 1984.

Nee, Watchman. *Changed into His Likeness*. Eastbourne, Sussex: Victory Press., 1967.

_____. *Concerning Our Missions*. Shanghai, China: The Gospel Book Room, 1938.

_____. *A Living Sacrifice*. New York: Christian Fellowship Publishers, Inc., 1972.

_____. *Love Not the World*. Eastbourne, Sussex: Victory Press, 1968.

_____. *The Messenger of the Cross*. New York: Christian Fellowship Publishers, Inc., 1980.

_____. *The Normal Christian Life*, revised ed. Washington D.C.: International Students Press, 1962.

_____. *The Prayer Ministry of the Church*. New York: Christian Fellowship Publishers, Inc., 1973.

_____. *The Spiritual Man*, Vol. 1. New York: Christian Fellowship Publishers, Inc., 1968.

_____. *The Release of the Spirit*. Cloverdale, IN: Sure Foundation, 1965.

_____. *Sit, Stand, Walk.* Bombay: Gospel Literature Service, 1957.

_____. *Spiritual Authority.* New York: Christian Fellowship Publishers, Inc., 1972.

Neill, Stephen. *A History of Christian Missions.* New York, New York: Penguin Books USA Ltd, 1986.

Newbigin, Lesslie. *The Open Secret: An Introduction to the Theology of Mission,* revised ed. Grand Rapids, Michigan: Eerdmans, 1991.

Orr, J. Edwin. *Campus Aflame: A History of Evangelical Awakenings in Collegiate Communities.* Wheaton, Illinois: International Awakening Press, 1994.

_____. *Evangelical Awakenings in Africa.* Minneapolis, Minnesota: Bethany Fellowship, Inc., 1975.

_____. *The Flaming Tongue: The Impact of Twentieth Century Rivivals.* Chicago, Illinois: Moody Press, 1973.

_____. *Second Evangelical Awakening.* London, UK: Marshall, Morgan & Scott, 1955.

_____. *Through Blood and Fire in China.* London & Edinburgh: Marshall, Morgan & Scott, Ltd., 1939.

Parish, William L., and Martin K. Whyte. *Village and Family in Contemporary China.* Chicago, Illinois: The University of Chicago Press, 1978.

Paterson, Ross. *The Continuing Heartcry for China.* Tonbridge, England: Sovereign World Ltd., 1999.

Patterson, George N. *Christianity in Communist China.* Waco, Texas: Word Books, Publisher, 1969.

Peale, John S. *The Love of God in China: Can One Be Both Chinese and Christian?* Lincoln, NE: iUniverse, Inc., 2005.

Rausch, Thomas P. *Radical Christian Communities.* Collegeville, MN: Liturgical Press, 1990.

Rees, D. Vaughan. The 'Jesus Family' in Communist China. Devon, UK: The Paternoster Press, 1959.

Ren, Jiyu. *The Book of Lao Zi.* Translated by He Guanghu, Gao Shining, Song Lidao and Xu Junyao. Beijing, China: Foreign Languages Press, 1993.

Riss, Richard M. *A Survey of 20th-Century Revival Movements in North America.* Peabody, MA: Hendrickson, 1988.

Roberts, J. A. G. *A Concise History of China.* Cambridge, Massachussett: Harard University Press, 1996.

Robinson, Louise, and Frank T. Cartwright. *Chinese in Dispersion.* New York: Interchurch Center, 1962.

Rubingh, Eugene. "Twice Blessed: Biblical Perspectives on Prayer." In *The Praying Church Sourcebook,* second ed. Alvin J. Vander Griend. Grand Rapids, Michigan: CRC Publications, 1996.

Rubinstein, Murray A. *The Protestant Community on Modern Taiwan: Mission, Seminary, and Church.* Armonk, New York: An East Gate Book, 1991.

Samuel, Vinay, and Chris Sugden, eds. *Mission as Transformation: A Theology of the Whole Bible.* Carlisle, UK: Regnum Books, 1999.

Sheng, Stephen L. *The Diaries of John Sung: An Autobiography.* Translated by Stephen L. Sheng. Brighten, Michigan: Luke H. Sheng & Stephen L. Sheng, 1995.

Sherley-Price, Leo. *Confucius and Christ.* Westminster, London: Dacre Press, 1951.

Shih, Lei. "Unity in the Chinese Church Revisited." Translated by Norman Walling. *Tripod* 117 (2000): 5–22.

Sih, Paul K. T. *The Chinese Culture and Christianity.* Reprinted issue of *AMERICAN BENEDICTINE REVIEW,* Vol. III No. 3 (Autumn, 1952).

Sister DG. Interview notes by author. China. March, 2005.

Sister HE. Interview notes by author. China. March, 2005.

Slote, Walter H., and George A. DeVos, eds. *Confucianism and the Family.* Albany, New York: State University of New York Press, 1998.

Smith, A. J. *Jesus Lifting Chinese,* or, *Marvelous Spiritual Awakenings in China.* Cincinnati, Ohio: God's Bible School and Missionary Training Home, 1929.

Smith, Carl T. *Chinese Christians: Elites, Middlemen, and the Church in Hong Kong.* New York: Oxford University Press, 1985.

Snyder, Howard A. "Church Growth Must Be Based on a Biblical Vision of the Church as the Vital Community of the Kingdom of God." In *Evaluating the Church Growth Movement—Five Views,* edited by Gary L. McIntosh. Grand Rapids, Michigan: Zondervan, 2004.

———. *The Community of the King,* revised. ed. Downers Grove, Illinois: Inter-Varsity Press, 2004.

———. *Kingdom, Church, and World: Biblical Themes for Today.* Eugene, Oregon: Wipf and Stock Publishers, 1985.

———. *Liberating the Church: The Ecology of Church and Kingdom.* Downers Grove, Illinois: Inter-Varsity Press, 1982.

———. "Marks of Evangelical Ecclesiology." In *Evangelical Ecclesiology: Reality or Illusion?* John G. Stackhouse, Jr., ed. Grand Rapids, Michigan: Baker Academic, 2003.

———. *Models of the Kingdom.* Nashville, Tennessee: Abingdon Press, 1991.

———. *Radical Renewal: the Problem of Wineskins Today.* Houston, Texas: Touch Publication, 1996.

———. *Signs of the Spirit: How God Reshapes the Church.* Eugene, Oregon: Wipf and Stock, 1997.

———. "Survey of Renewal Movements." Syllabus. Wilmore, Kentucky: Asbury Theological Seminary, 2003.

Steer, Roger. *J. Hudson Taylor: A Man in Christ.* Wheaton, Illinois: Harold Shaw Publishers, 1990.

Stockwell, Foster. *Westerners in China: A History of Exploration and Trade, Ancient Times through the Present.* Jefferson, North Carolina: McFarland, 2002.

Students of TE. Interview notes by author. China. March, 2005.

Sugirtharajah, R. S., ed. *Asian Faces of Jesus.* Maryknoll, New York: Orbis Books, 1995.

Sullivan, Lawrence R. *Historical Dictionary of the People's Republic of China: 1949–1997.* Lanham, Maryland: Scarecrow Press, Inc., 1997.

Suman, Michael D. *The Church in China: One Lord Two Systems.* Kothanur, Bangalore: SAIACS Press, 2006.

Sung, John. *Forty John Sung Revival Sermons.* 2 vols. Translated by Timothy Tow. Singapore: Christian Life Book Centre, 1978–83.

Tang, Yi-Jie. *Chinese Culture: Confucianism, Buddhism, Daoism, Christianity and Chinese Culture.* Washington D. C.: Library of Congress Cataloging, 1991.

Taylor, Dr. and Mrs. Howard. *Hudson Taylor in Early Years: The Growth of a Soul.* 2 vols. Reprint, with introduction by D. E. Hoste. Originally published in London: China Inland Mission, 1911. Littleton, CO: OMF International, 1997.

Thompson, Laurence G. *Chinese Religion*, 5th ed. California: Wadsworth Publishing Company, 1996.

Thomas, Winburn, and Rajah B. Manikam. *The Church in Southeast Asia.* New York: Friendship Press, 1956.

Thornton, Arland, and Hui-Sheng Lin. *Social Change & the Family in Taiwan.* Chicago, Illinois: The University of Chicago Press, 1994.

Tien, Ju-kang. *Peaks of Faith: Protestant Mission in Revolutionary China.* Leiden: E. J. Brill, 1993.

Tong, John. "Patterns of Conversion within the Chinese Catholic Christian Community." *Word & World* XVII no.2 (1997): 196–202.

Tow, Timothy, trans. *Forty John Sung Revival Sermons*, Vol 1 & 2. Singapore: Christian Life Book Centre, 1978.

_____. *John Sung My Teacher.* Singapore: Christian Life Publishers, 1985.

Townsend, William J. *Robert Morrison: The Pioneer of Chinese Missions.* Reprint. Originally published in New York: Fleming H. Revell, 1888. Salem, Ohio: Allegheny Publications, 2004.

Trmura, Eileen H., Menton, Linda K., Lush, Noren W., and Francis K. C. Tsui. *China: Understanding Its Past.* Honolulu, Hawaii: University of Hawaii Press, 1998.

Tucker, Ruth. *From Jerusalem to Irian Jaya: A Biographical History of Christian Missions*, revised. ed. Grand Rapids, Michigan: Zondervan, 2004.

Tung, Siu Kwan. "More about the Jesus Family." *Bridge* 60 (Aug. 1993):11–15.

_____. "The Waves of the 'Local Church'." *Bridge* 56 (Nov.–Dec. 1992):2–23.

_____. "The Waves of the 'Local Church'." *Bridge* 57 (Jan.–Feb. 1993):2–23.

Twitchett, Denis, and John K. Fairbank, eds. *The Cambridge History of China.* 15 vols. Cambridge, New York, Melbourne: Cambridge University Press, 1991.

Van Houten, Richard, ed. *Wise as Serpents, Harmless as Doves: Christians in China Tell Their Story.* Pasadena, California: CCRC and Wm Carey Library, 1982.

Varg, Paul A. *Missionaries, Chinese and Diplomats: The American Protestant Missionary Movement in Chin, 1890–1052.* Princeton, New Jersey: Princeton University Press, 1958.

Varghese, Simon K. "The Church as the Household of God: A Biblical and Sociocultural Study." D. Miss. Dissertation. Wilmore, Kentucky: Asbury Theological Seminary, 2004.

Virginia, Lee and Suh. *Asian Christian Spirituality: Reclaiming Traditions.* Maryknoll, New York: Orbis Books, 1992.

Visser't Hooft, William Adolph. *The Renewal of the Church.* Philadelphia, New Jersey: The Westminster Press, 1956.

Waley, Authur, trans. *The Analects of Confucius.* New York, New York: Vintage Books, 1989.

Wallace, Anthony F. C. "Revitalization Movements," *American Anthropologist* 58 (April 1956): 254–81.

Wang, Gungwu. *The Chineseness of China.* New York, New York: Oxford University Press, 1991.

Wang, Jiali. "The House Church Movement: A Participant's Assessment." *Word & World*, XVII no.2 (1997): 175–82.

Wang, Richard T. *Area Bibliography of China.* Scarecrow Press, Inc., Lanham, Maryland: Scarecrow Press, Inc., 1997.

Wei, Francis C. M. *The Spirit of Chinese Culture.* New York, New York: Charles Scribner's Sons, 1947.

Wesley, Luke. *The Church in China: Persecuted, Pentecostal, and Powerful.* Baguio City, Philippines: AJPS Books, 2004.

Whitehead, Raymond L., ed. *No Longer Strangers: Selected Writings of Bishop K. H. Ting.* Maryknoll, New York: Orbis Books, 1989.

Whyte, Bob. *Unfinished Encounter: China and Christianity.* London: Collins, 1986.

Wickeri, Philip L. *Reconstructing Christianity in China: K. H. Ting and the Chinese Church.* Maryknoll, New York: Orbis Books, 2007.

_____. *Seeking the Common Ground.* Maryknoll, New York: Orbis Books, 1988.

Wilfred, Felix. *Sunset in the East? Asian Challenges and Christian Involvement.* Madras, India: University of Madras, 1991.

Wilson, Ron. *Changing China: Opening Windows to the West.* Wheaton, Illinois: OMF IHQ, Ltd., 1997.

Wong, Chi-tong. "Introducing the Jesus Family." *Bridge* 54 (1992): 7–14.

Wong Ming-Dao. *Day by Day.* Crowborough, East Sussex: Highland Books, 1989.

Wu, Yao Ting. "The First Eight Months of the Three-Self Reform Movement." In *Documents of the Three-Self Movement: Source Materials for the Study of the Protestant Church in Communist China*, edited by Wallace C. Merwin & Francis P. Jones, 34–40. New York, New York: Far Eastern Office, National Council of the Churches of Christ in the U.S.A., 1951.

Xin, Yalin. "The Future of Christianity in China: An Internal Reflection." *The Asbury Journal* 64 no.1 (2009): 79–82.

_____. "Inner Dynamics of the Chinese House Church Movement: The Case of the Word of Life Community." *Mission Studies* 25 no.2 (2008): 157–84.

Xu, Peter. Taped interview by author. Los Angeles, California. December, 2004.

Yang, C. K. *Chinese Communist Society: The Family and the Village*. Cambridge, Massachusetts: The M.I.T Press, 1959.

_____. *Religion in Chinese Society*. Illinois: Waveland Press, Inc., 1991.

Yao, Kevin Xiyi. *The Fundamentalist Movement among Protestant Missionaries in China, 1920–1937*. Lanham, Maryland: University Press of America, Inc., 2003.

Yuan, Zhiming. *Repentance of the Divine Land: God and China for Five Thousand Years*. Hong Kong: Hanguang Inc., 1996.

Zhang, Xinxin, and Sang Ye. *Chinese Lives: An Oral History of Contemporary China*, edited by W.J.E.Jenner and Delia Davin. New York, New York: Pantheon Books, 1987.

_____. *Chinese Profiles*. Beijing, China: Chinese Literature Press, 1987.

Bibliography (Chinese Language)
中文参考书目

王明道 (Wang, Mingdao)。时代的信息 (Messages for Our Time)。香港：宣道书局印行，1964。

陈终道。(Chen, Zhongdao) 我的舅父倪柝声 (My Uncle, Watchman Nee)。Petaluma, California: Chinese Christian Mission, 1985.

汤清 (Tang, Ching)。中国基督教百年史 (The First Hundred Years of Protestant Mission in China). 香港：道声出版社，1987。

赵天恩 (Chao, Jonathan)。〈大陆教会蒙神赐福的秘诀（一）〉 (The Secrets of the Church in China Being Blessed by God)。《中国与教会》63 期 (1988 年 1–2 月）。

_____.〈大陆教会蒙神赐福的秘诀（二）〉 (The Secrets of Mainland China's Church Being Blessed by God) 。《中国与教会》63 期（1988 年 5–6 月）。

_____. 赤地之穗－来自中国大陆的见证 (Testimonies from Mainland China) 。台北，台湾：中国福音会出版社，1992。

_____. 灵火淬炼－中国大陆教会复兴的秘诀 (Purified by Fire—The Secrets of House Church Revivals in Mainland China)。台北，台湾：中国福音会出版社，1993。

_____. 扶我前行－中国福音化异象 (Lead Me to Go Forward—The Vision of the Evangelization of China)。台北，台湾：中国福音会出版社，1993。

_____. 洞烛先机－中共宗教政策及三自会论评 (Prophetic Penetration—Critique of Chinese Communist Religious Policy and the TSPM)。台北，台湾：中国福音会出版社，1993。

_____.〈今日中国教会－公开登记教会及家庭教会〉 (The Church in China Today—Openly Registered Churches and the House Churches). 《中国与福 音》20 期（1997 年 9–10 月）。

_____.〈从当前的中共宗教政策及法制看徐永泽事件〉(Looking at the Incidence Revolving around Xu Yongze from the perspective of the Contemporary Religious Policy and Legal System of the Chinese Communist Party)。《中国与 福音》21、22 期（1997 年 11 月–1998 年 2 月）。

_____.〈总结〉(Conclusion)。《中国与福音》21、22 期（1997 年 11 月–1998 年 2 月）。

_____.〈中国家庭教会宣言〉(Declaration of the House Churches in China)。《中国与福音》28 期（1999 年 1–2 月）。

_____.〈迎向二十一世纪中国宣教的挑战〉(The Challenge of Mission in China in the 21st Century)。《中国与福音》32 期（1999 年 9–10 月）。

_____.〈当今中国教会面临的压力〉(The Pressure on the Church in China Today)。《中国与福音》34 期（2000 年 1–2 月）。

_____.〈二十世纪神在中国教会的作为－摧毁与重建〉(God's Work in China in the 20th Century—To Demolish and Rebuild)。《中国与福音》35 期（2000 年 3–4 月）。

_____.「基督教在当代中国的本色化过程：历史与神学的反省」(The Process of Indigenization of Christianity in China: A Historical and Theological Reflection)。陈渔，张乐宣编。《薪尽火传－赵天恩牧师纪念文集 (The Undying Fire of the Burning Branches—A Posthumous Essay Collection of Dr. Jonathan Chao)。台北，台湾：中福出版有限公司，2005。

_____.「从中国文化背景看救恩」(Salvation from the Perspective of Chinese Culture)。陈渔，张乐宣编。《薪尽火传－赵天恩牧师纪念文集 (The Undying Fire of the Burning Branches—A Posthumous Essay Collection of Dr. Jonathan Chao)。台北，台湾：中福出版有限公司，2005。

_____.「逼迫、苦难与教会增长」(Opposition and Suffering in Relation to Church Growth)。陈渔，张乐宣编。《薪尽火传－赵天恩牧师纪念文集 (The Undying Fire of the Burning Branches—A Posthumous Essay Collection of Dr. Jonathan Chao)。台北，台湾：中福出版有限公司，2005。

_____.「大陆基督教发展概况 1996–2001」(The Development of Christianity in Mainland China from 1996–2001)。陈渔，张乐宣编。《薪尽火传－赵天恩牧师纪念文集 (The Undying Fire of the Burning Branches—A Posthumous Essay Collection of Dr. Jonathan Chao)。台北，台湾：中福出版有限公司，2005。

_____.「基督教与中国精神文明的重建」(Christianity and the Reconstruction of Chinese Spiritual Civilization)。陈渔，张乐宣编。《薪尽火传－赵天恩牧师纪念文集 (The Undying Fire of the Burning

Branches—A Posthumous Essay Collection of Dr. Jonathan Chao)。
台北，台湾：中福出版有限公司，2005。

_____. 「二十世纪中国教会十大运动」(Ten Important Movements in the Chinese Church during the 20th Century)。陈渔，张乐宣编。《薪尽火传－赵天恩牧师纪念文集 (The Undying Fire of the Burning Branches—A Posthumous Essay Collection of Dr. Jonathan Chao)。台北，台湾：中福出版有限公司，2005。

赵天恩，庄婉芳。(Chao, Jonathan) 当代中国基督教发展史，1949–1997 (A History of Christianity in Socialist China, 1949–1997). 台北，台湾：中国福音会出版社，1997。

陈渔，张乐宣编。(Chen, Yu, and Zhang Lexuan, eds) 薪尽火传－赵天恩牧师纪念文集 (The Undying Fire of the Burning Branches—A Posthumous Essay Collection of Dr. Jonathan Chao)。台北，台湾：中福出版有限公司，2005。

丹云 (Dan, Yun)。荆棘中的百合花－大陆教会血泪交织的见证 (Lilies of the Fields Testimonies from the Church in China)。台北，台湾：基督教橄榄文化事基金会出版部，1990。

云 (Yun)。天上人见证－神爱中国 (The Heavenly Man—God Loves China)。China Care International Ltd., 2000.

林荣洪。(Lin Hongrong) 王明道与中国教会 (Wang Mingdao and the Chinese Church)。香港：中国神学研究院，1982。

_____. 属灵神学－倪柝声思想的研究 (The Spiritual Theology of Watchman Nee)。香港：中国神学研究院，1985。

梁家麟。(Leung, Kalun)〈宋尚节的重生教导〉(John Sung's Teaching on Rebirth)。《建道学刊》4 期（1995）。

_____.〈中共建国前后吴耀宗的教会改造思想〉(Wu Yao-zong's Perspective on Church Reconstruction before and after the Founding of the People's Republic of China)。《建道学刊》6 期（1995 年七月）。

_____.〈奋兴布道家对华人教会的塑造〉(The Influence of Revivalists on the Chinese Churches)。《建道学刊》41 期 (1999 年)。

_____. 改革开放以来的中国农村教会 (The Rural Churches of Mainland China Since 1978)。香港：建道神学院，1999。

_____.〈还原主义与中国基督教本色化－二十世纪上半叶的华人自由派神学〉(Reductionism and Indigenization in China—Chinese Liberal Theology in the 1st Half of the 20th Century)。《建道学刊》19 期（2001）。

_____. 超前与堕后－本土释经与神学研究 (Far Ahead and Lagging Behind: Studies in Contextual Hermeneutics and Theology)。香港：建道神学院 2003。

＿＿＿＿．〈有关家庭教会独立登记问题的探究〉(An Investigation on the Issues around the Registration of the House Churches)。《建道学刊》24 期（2005 年）。

邢福增。(Xing, Fuzong)〈从社会阶层看当代中国基督教的发展〉(A Look at the Development of the Contemporary Chinese Christianity from the Perspective of Social Class)。《建道学刊》15 期（2001 年）

何光沪。(He, Guanghu)〈中国现代化的矛盾与教会应取的态度〉(The Controversies of the Modernization in China and the Proper Attitude that the Church Should Adopt)。《建道学刊》12 期（1999 年）

远志明。(Yuan, Zhiming)〈基督教信仰与中国文化的未来〉(The Future of Christian Faith in Relation to Chinese Culture)。《中国与教会》99 期（1994 年 1–2 月）。

＿＿＿＿．〈福音在当代中国的传播（上）〉(The Spread of the Gospel in Contemporary China)。《中国与福音》2 期（1994 年 9–10 月）。

＿＿＿＿．〈福音在当代中国的传播（下）〉(The Spread of the Gospel in Contemporary China)。《中国与福音》3 期（1994 年 11–1 月）。

＿＿＿＿．神州忏悔录－上帝与五千年中国 (*Repentance of the Divine Land: God and China for Five Thousand Years*). 香港：汉光（2000）有限公司，2000。

黄剑波 (Huang, Jianbo)。〈城市化进程中的中国基督教〉(Christianity in China in time of urbanization)。《基督教与中国文化研究中心通讯》38 期 (2005 年 10 月)。

薛励德。〈全球化－教会的挑战〉(Globalization—Challenge to the Church)。《鼎》第 22 卷 总第 126 期（2002 年秋季）。

弥维礼。〈中国基督徒－社会转变的催化剂〉(Christians in China—Catalyst of Social Change)。《鼎》第 22 卷 总第 126 期（2002 年秋季）。

中国基督教三自爱国运动委员会。(TSPM) 回忆吴耀宗先生 (In Memory of Mr. Wu Yaozong)。上海，中国：中国基督教三自爱国运动委员会，中国基督教协会，1982。

＿＿＿＿．基督教三自爱国运动四十周年征文选 (Selected Essays for the 40th Anniversary of the Christian Three-Self Patriotic Movement)。上海，中国：中国基督教三自爱国运动委员会，1990。

沈德溶。(Shen, Derong) 吴耀宗小传 (A Brief Biography of Wu Yaozong)。上海，中国：中国基督教三自爱国运动委员会，中国基督教协会，1989。

＿＿＿＿．在三自工作五十年 (Working in the TSPM for Fifty Years)。上海：中国基督教三自爱国运动委员会，中国基督教协会，2000。

区应毓。(Qu, Yingshu) 苦难与希望－生死苦难与终极归宿论 (Suffering and Hope)。温伟耀，陈荣毅编。基督教与中国文化丛书（八）。Scarborough, Ontario: 加拿大福音证主协会，1998。

林慈信。(Lin, Cixin) 先驱与过客－再说基督教新文化运动 (Forerunners and Passers-by—Revisiting the Christian New Cultural Movement)。温伟耀，陈荣毅编。基督教与中国文化丛书（四）。Scarborough, Ontario: 加拿大福音证主协会，1996。

吴宗文。(Wu, Zongwen) 迷信与信仰－中国宗教文化的困惑及出路 (Superstition versus Faith)。温伟耀，陈荣毅编。基督教与中国文化丛书（六）。Scarborough, Ontario: 加拿大福音证主协会，1997。

天路客。(Tian, Luke) 〈中国教会的复兴〉(The Revival of the Chinese Church) 《传》一九九六年三、四月。

_____.〈今日大陆教会的难处与路向〉(The Difficulties and Signposts of the church in Mainland China Today)。《传》一九九七年三、四月。

朱昌凌。(Zhu, Changling) 〈人手能制造复兴吗？〉(Can Human Hands Produce Revivals?)。《传》一九九六年三、四月。

念华。(Nian, Hua) 〈家庭教会近貌〉(House Churches Today)。《传》一九九五年三、四月。

_____.〈苦难中的家庭教会〉(The Suffering House Churches)。《传》一九九六年五、六月。

家声。(Jia, Sheng) 〈患难中的家庭教会〉(The Suffering House Churches)。《传》一九九六年十一、十二月。

慕义。(Mu, Yi) 〈当前中国教会形势的分析〉(An Analysis of the Church in China Today)。《中国与福音》32 期（1999 年 9–10 月）。

华申。(Hua, Shen) 〈中国家庭教会宣言－教会正邪之辩〉(Declaration of the House Churches in China—An Appeal on the Distinction between Orthodoxy and Cult)。《中国与福音》25 期（1998 年 7–8 月）。

申先锋。(Shen, Xianfeng) 〈我们真的是邪教吗？〉(Are We Really Cult?)。《中国与福音》25 期（1998 年 7–8 月）。

钟晚。(Zhong, Wan) 〈受苦太值得了－一位大陆肢体的见证〉(It Is So Worthwhile to Endure Suffering)。《传》一九九五年三、四月。

中国教会研究中心编辑部。(CCSC) 〈野地神学院跟踪报道之一〉(Report of the Seminaries of the Fields, Part One)。《中国与教会》(1986 年 9–10 月) (CCSC 1986 I)

_____.〈野地神学院跟踪报道之二〉(Report of the Seminaries of the Fields, Part Two)。《中国与教会》(1986 年 11–12 月) (CCSC 1986 II)

_____.〈欲晤葛培理大陆教会重要传导人被捕〉(Well-known Mainland Chinese Evangelist Arrested for Intended Meeting with Billy Graham)。《中国与教会》64 期（1988 年 3–4 月）。

_____.〈福音使者的秘诀（一）〉(The Secrets of the Messengers of the Gospel, Part I)。《中国与教会》81 期（1991 年 1–2 月）。

_____.〈福音使者的秘诀（二）〉(The Secrets of the Messengers of the Gospel, Part II).《中国与教会》82 期（1991 年 3–4 月）。

_____．〈福音使者的秘诀（三）〉(The Secrets of the Messengers of the Gospel, Part III).《中国与教会》83 期（1991 年 5–6 月）。

张家恩。(Zhang, Jiaen)〈参加农村家庭聚会有感〉(Reflection on Participating the House Church Meetings)。《中国与教会》一九八五年八月。

何牧华。(He, Muhua)〈国内家庭教会的培训模式〉(Models of Training in Mainland China's House Churches).《中国与教会》一九八五年十一月。

_____．〈过去十年神在家庭教会中的作为〉(The Work of God among the House Churches in China in the Past Ten Years).《中国与教会》68 期（1988 年 11–12 月）。

信徒眼。(Xin, Luyan)〈参加「生命会」之体验〉(Experiencing the 'Life Meeting').《中国与教会》93 期（1993 年 1–2 月）。

郝慕仁。(Hao, Muren)〈对大陆重生派「生命会」的观察与分析〉(Observation and Analysis of the 'Life Meeting' among the Born Again Community in Mainland China).《中国与教会》92 期（1992 年 11–12 月）。

陈渔。(Chen, Yu)〈正统、异端与中共宗教政策〉(Orthodoxy, Cult and the Religious Policy of the Chinese Communist Government).《中国与福音》21、22 期（1997 年 11 月–1998 年 2 月）。

_____．〈1995－1998 年中共、三自与家庭教会动向〉(An Observation of the Chinese Communist Government, the TSPM and House Church from 1995–1998).《中国与福音》28 期（1999 年 1–2 月）。

司马长声。(Sima, Changsheng)〈清心一颗念合一—中国家庭教会合一运动发展史（一）〉(A Pure Heart for Unity—The Development of the Unity Movement among the House Churches in China, Part One).《中国与福音》28 期（1999 年 1–2 月）。

湖心。(Hu, Xin)〈某地教会发展史〉(A History of A Local Church).《中国与福音》31 期（1999 年 7–8 月）。

李锦纶。(Li, Jinlun)〈评析极端、异端、异教与邪教—从神学及教会历史的角度判断〉(An Anylasis on the Extremists, Cults, and False Religions from the Perspective of Theology and Church History).《中国与福音》21、22 期（1997 年 11 月–1998 年 2 月）。

王瑞珍。(Wang, Ruizhen)〈重生派的救恩论〉(The Soteriology of the Born-Again Community in China).《中国与福音》21、22 期（1997 年 11 月–1998 年 2 月）。

周功和。(Zhou, Gonghe)〈重生派是否异端？〉(Is the Born-Again Community in China Cult?).《中国与福音》21、22 期（1997 年 11 月–1998 年 2 月）。

陈辉明。(Chen, Huiming)〈重生派特点与争议的反思〉(A Reflection on the Characteristics and Controversies of the Born-Again Community in

China)。《中国与福音》21、22 期（1997 年 11 月–1998 年 2 月）。

艾桦。(Ai, Hua) 〈大陆教会发展现象之我见〉(Personal Understanding of Church Growth in Mainland China)。《中国与福音》21、22 期（1997 年 11 月–1998 年 2 月）。

金戈。(Jin, Ge) 〈中国宗教政策的宽与严〉(Religious Policies in China). 《中国与福音》21、22 期（1997 年 11 月－1998 年 2 月）。

毕明。(Bi, Ming) 〈宏观中国大陆的「基督教热」是否「发高烧」？〉("Christian Fever" in Mainland China)。《中国与教会》98 期（1993 年 11–12 月）。

生命之道工作室。(The WOL Editorial Office) 〈真理实践课程，上册：十架救恩〉(Truth Practical Curriculum, Part 1: Salvation through the Cross), 2003。

_____. 〈真理实践课程，下册〉(Truth Practical Curriculum, Part 2) 2003。

_____. 〈天国福音－奋兴会讲章选集〉(The Gospel of the Heavenly Kingdom) 1980s–1990s

_____. 〈生命讲章〉(Sermons of Life) 1980s–1990s.

_____. 〈婚姻与童身〉(Marriage and Celibacy) 1980s–1990s.

Index

Venn, Henry, 45

Wallace, Anthony, 35, 39, 56, 73, 110
Wang, Liland, 24-25
Wang, Mingdao, 25, 29, 46, 88, 139, 160
Wang, Ruizhen, 71, 75
Weeping Sect, 69. *See* the Word of Life
Wei, Paul, 24
Wesley, John, 27, 178
Wheaton Conference, 170
Wicheri, Philip L., 37, 45
Winter, Ralph, 40
Witness Lee, 106
WOL. *See* the Word of Life
women in the WOL, 104-05. *See also* Deborah Xu
Word of Life
     network, 126, 128, 136, 161;
     organization structure, 100, 138;
     structure, 96, 104, 147, 165, 170, 180, 182;
     theology, 86, 152, 162, 181
Wu, Y. T., 29

Xiao Min, 124
Xie, Moses, 46
Xin, Yalin, 42, 183
Xinjiang Autonomous Zone, 108
Xu, Deborah, 82, 91, 97, 110
Xu, Peter, 32, 42, 67, 70, 77-114, 135-36, 149-50
Xu, Yongze. *See* Xu, Peter

Yao, Xiyi, 45
Yun, Brother, 85, 87-88, 90, 107-08, 111-13, 132, 150

Zhang, Barnabas, 24
Zhang, Lingshen, 24
Zhen li hui. See Truth meeting
Zhou, Gonghe, 71, 75

CPSIA information can be obtained at www.ICGtesting.com
Printed in the USA
LVOW061333010412

275607LV00003B/4/P